AMERICAN ACCOUNTING ASSOCIATION

MONOGRAPH NO. 6

AMERICAN ACCOUNTING ASSOCIATION

Established in 1935 as the continuation of the American Association of University Instructors in Accounting, the American Accounting Association has the following objectives:

1. To encourage and sponsor research in accounting and to publish or aid in the publication of the results of research.
2. To develop accounting principles and standards and to seek their endorsement or adoption by business enterprises, public and private accountants, and governmental bodies.
3. To promote studies of accounting as an agency of control of business enterprise and economic affairs in general.
4. To improve methods of instruction and to demonstrate the social benefits of a more widespread knowledge of accounting.

Membership in the Association, although primarily academic, includes public and private accountants, social scientists, and other persons interested in the scientific development of accounting principles.

The proceeds of the sales of monographs, less cost of publication and any royalty for authors, will be added to the publication fund of the Association out of which the research projects of the Association are financed.

In all monographs published by the Association the views expressed are those of the authors, and publication does not imply agreement on the part of the Association or its Executive Committee.

AMERICAN ACCOUNTING ASSOCIATION
5717 Bessie Drive
Sarasota, Florida 34233

THE PHILOSOPHY OF AUDITING

by

R. K. MAUTZ, Ph.D., C.P.A.
University of Illinois

and

HUSSEIN A. SHARAF, Ph.D.
Lecturer, Faculty of Commerce
University of Cairo

AMERICAN ACCOUNTING ASSOCIATION

Second Printing, 1964
Third Printing, 1967
Fourth Printing, 1968
Fifth Printing, 1970
Sixth Printing, 1972
Seventh Printing, 1973
Eighth Printing, 1974
Ninth Printing, 1976
Tenth Printing, 1980
Eleventh Printing, 1982
Twelfth Printing, 1985
Thirteenth Printing, 1987
Fourteenth Printing, 1989
Fifteenth Printing, 1991
Sixteenth Printing, 1992
Seventeenth Printing, 1993
Eighteenth Printing, 1997

PRINTED IN THE UNITED STATES OF AMERICA
ISBN 0-86539-002-9

This volume is affectionately dedicated to Professor A. C. LITTLETON whose inspiration and influence extend through his students and their students far beyond his modest expectations.

PREFACE

We trust the title of this book will not be misunderstood. It was chosen because it describes the center of interest of this study, not because we feel the study adequately presents a complete and finished philosophy. So far as *the* philosohy of auditing is concerned, we recognize that our efforts here are both incomplete and inconclusive.

The research leading to this monograph developed out of our interest in the nature of audit evidence. At commencement of the project we had little expectation that it would lead us as far afield as subsequently occurred. As the work progressed, however, we found it necessary to develop postulates as a basis for proposing a concept of evidence. This naturally led us into consideration of other concepts suggested both by the postulates and our experience in auditing practice and research.

It will be apparent to the reader that our concern has been primarily with independent rather than internal auditing although we feel that much of the work, particularly that concerned with the theory of evidence, has pertinence to the work of internal auditors as well.

Much of the research on which this monograph is based was made possible by a grant of funds from the Graduate Research Board of the University of Illinois for which we wish to express our gratitude. Without this support it is unlikely this work could ever have approached its present scope or depth.

We are also indebted to a number of friends and associates who read the manuscript in full or in part and offered helpful suggestions. The contributions of Professor Samuel R. Hepworth, Director of Research of the American Accounting Association, and Mrs. Rosannah Steinhoff of the Bureau of Business Research, the University of Michigan, merit special recognition. To all these and others whose ideas and suggestions have contributed much, we express our appreciation. For errors and other shortcomings, we accept full responsibility.

We have enjoyed this project thoroughly. At times it has been a very real burden but it has never been dull; on the contrary, there have been experiences which we can only describe as intellectually exciting. We offer the results of our work as a full attempt to develop a theory of auditing and as a possible pattern for research in auditing and accounting. We hope it will have usefulness in both these areas.

R. K Mautz

April, 1961 Hussein A. Sharaf

TABLE OF CONTENTS

CHAPTER 1

TOWARD AN AUDITING PHILOSOPHY

This is an attempt to outline the theory of auditing. To some this may appear an unlikely if not an impossible task; to others it may at best seem futile. Many think of auditing as a completely practical, as opposed to theoretical, subject. To them, auditing is a series of practices and procedures, methods and techniques, a way of doing with little need for the explanations, descriptions, reconciliations, and arguments so frequently lumped together as "theory."

It is our contention that there is a theory of auditing, that there exist a number of basic assumptions and a body of integrated ideas, the understanding of which will be direct assistance in the development and practice of the art of auditing. Further, it is our belief, which we will attempt to support in the following pages, that an understanding of auditing theory can lead us to reasonable solutions of some of the most vexing problems facing auditors today.

Present Status of Auditing Theory. Currently, there is very little available in the professional literature that can be described as auditing theory. Certainly there is little in auditing literature to compare with the wealth of material one finds on accounting theory. On reflection, one sees something incongruous in the existence of a professional group drawing its status primarily from the practice of auditing, but having no perceptible body of theory to support that practice. Considerable attention is given to accounting theory — indeed there are certain works which may appropriately be described as "classics" — but there has been little concern with auditing theory. It is this paradox which has encouraged us to investigate the possibility of an integrated body of auditing theory.

To forestall the argument that discussions of auditing theory are lacking because there is no such theory, let us hasten to point out that this lack is easily explained in the historical development of auditing. We do not contemplate a lengthy digression on the history of auditing, but a few illustrations can be cited which indicate that auditing developed as a procedure of detailed checking, in which theory seemed neither necessary nor desirable, and that only recently has it outgrown that stage. Auditing came into existence as the offspring of law and custom with prescribed forms and procedures.

...They (the rolls) correspond, as required by the rule derived from the Exchequer, leaf by leaf, page to page, almost line to line. The "probatum," the mark of audit, has been affixed to the sum of every page, and to the sum of every leaf on its second page, and in some cases, where the sum has been apparently corrected by a second audit, a second mark is affixed to the finally stated sum...[1]

Thus the early auditor was encouraged only to investigate correspondence of the matter under investigation with a model or standard. This does not differ a great deal from the situation in Germany today.

The legal requirements instead of indicating a minimum standard of disclosure, have come to be accepted as "the" standard for the presentation of published statements.[2]

There is little in the task of checking conformity with a given standard or requirement that leads one to question the nature of the auditor's fundamental purposes, limitations, and activity. As recently as 1942, a committee of English experts, in discussing the future of auditing in Britain, wrote, somewhat intemperately:

Attempts to persuade the accountancy profession to take a wider view of their public responsibilities have so far met with little success ... there is little or no evidence during the last twenty or twenty-five years to show that the professional accountant, qua professional accountant, has produced a single idea of value to industry or the State. He has merely ticked and cast and trusted in God.[3]

This was written almost ten years after Carr-Saunders, in a study of the various professions in England, had criticized the professional groups rather severely for a lack of attention to theoretical study and research.

It is difficult to avoid the inference that the want of proper facilities for theoretical training is in part responsible for the scanty interest displayed by accountants in the study of their craft. One of the advocates of educational reform from whom we have already quoted would extend his proposals to cover a wider field. "There is a real need," he urges, "in accountancy, for sustained academic study and research....

---

[1] Richard Brown, *A History of Accounting and Accountants* (Edinburgh: T. C. and E. C. Jack, 1905), p. 75.

[2] Hellfried Peter Holzer, *Corporate Financial Statements in Germany Contrasted with American Practice*, M.S. Thesis (University of Illinois, Urbana, 1956), p. 2.

[3] "The Future of Auditing," Anonymous, *The Accountant*, Volume 106, January 17, 1942, p. 31.

But so far as I am aware, the Institute and Society have not directly concerned themselves with academic study of accountancy or research work."[4]

In the United States, auditing has not been subjected to the type of influence which the Companies Act could scarcely do otherwise than exert in England. As American practice developed an differentiated itself more and more from its British counterpart, an interest in matters of a theoretical nature appeared. For many years practicing auditors have emphasized the reasons for the use of various procedures as well as the steps in the procedures themselves, the "why" as well as the "how" as it is so often described. And this is indeed a beginning for a discussion of auditing theory. More than this is needed, however, and more has been forthcoming. In recent years, bits and pieces of auditing theory have appeared in the professional literature. The differentiation of techniques, procedures, and principles, the recognition of standards, the attention given to the nature and classification of "evidential matter," and the relationship of evidential matter to audit techniques may be cited as illustrations.

Unsolved Problems in Auditing. At the present time, auditing is plagued with a number of perplexing problems involving a wide variety of subjects. For example, are the customary tests and samples on which the auditor relies sufficient to justify his opinion? Here, it must be recognized, he is dealing in probabilities. In the past we have considered the judgment of an experienced practitioner adequate; the new interest in the application of statistical sampling methods to auditing requires that we examine this assumption that experience per se sufficiently qualifies one to judge the adequacy of tests and samples. Perhaps we must understand the laws of inference and probability theory as well. A question exists as to whether there is a minimum audit program required in every case and, if so, what it includes? How far in the direction of advocacy in tax work and in giving operating and financial advice through management services can an independent auditor go without weakening his independence?

---

[4] A. M. Carr-Saunders and P. A. Wilson, *The Professions* (Oxford, England: Oxford University Press, 1933), pp. 225-226.

But not only is the appropriate extent of the auditor's services a matter of some doubt, the extent of his responsibility in the performance of even his historical function is far from settled. Some contend that an independent auditor has a responsibility to disclose to his client and possibly to others any weaknesses in internal control which he discovers during his examination; some dispute this. The auditor's responsibility for the discovery of irregularities of various kinds has been the subject of several papers published within the last few years. This problem leads to the question of whether management inefficiencies and faulty judgments should be disclosed, a version of the "policy audit" with overtones of disclosure.

How far auditors are responsible for disclosing the limitations of traditional types of financial reports during a period of substantial changes in general price levels is a question that has not yet received an adequate answer. Even the general purpose of an auditor's verification tests is not agreed upon. Should it be to determine how far the system of internal control can be trusted to produce reliable data, or is it to assure the auditor that the amounts reported in the financial statements are reasonable and reliable in themselves?

This is an imposing list of problems and unsettled areas, and with little effort even more could be added. It is not our purpose to suggest that auditing has more than its share of unsolved problems. Similar perplexities encumber every field of knowledge, and auditing is neither better off nor worse off than many other professions. Nevertheless, there is cause for concern. First, the existence of so many fundamental questions implies the absence of accepted principles which might serve as guides for their solution. Second, the attitude of some practitioners toward solving certain of these problems is unfortunate indeed. Too many practicing auditors seem to say, "It doesn't matter to me which way we decide these questions, just so we get a firm decision and know where we stand." Of course it matters how such questions are handled. It matters immediately because some suggested solutions add to the burdens, responsibilities, or prestige of the auditor while others detract. But more important, it matters in the long run. Problems must be solved in such a way that the answers are compatible or at least reconcilable. Inconsistencies have no place in auditing in the long run; they may be unavoidable at the moment, but if we are to have a profession worthy of the name we must work to eliminate them. Thus solutions which cannot be rationalized with one another lead only to additional problems.

Without sheer luck, the only way in which problems such as these can be satisfactorily and permanently solved is by appeal to certain basic ideas which constitute the philosophy of the particular study. It is our firm belief that the bits of theory now in the literature can be integrated and brought together as parts of a comprehensive system. Once this system is outlined and elucidated it will provide a framework within which these and similar problems can be attacked in a rational and consistent manner. Once such a theory is stated, if only in an elementary manner, its usefulness to practitioners and the profession will become apparent.

This is not to say that we propose to solve all the problems cited here in this brief volume. This is proposed as an introductory work only. Here is undertaken no more than an investigation into the possibility and nature of such a theory. Progress always comes slowly, and we will be content if we can do no more than point the direction

Purpose of Theory. One reason, then, for a serious and substantial investigation into the possibility and nature of auditing theory is the hope that it will provide us with solutions, or at least clues to the solutions, of problems which we now find difficult. This is a satisfactory reason in itself, but there is another that is even more important. If auditing is a learned profession, those who practice it should have some curiosity about it. It may be too much to expect every practicing auditor, busy as he is with the problems of daily practice, to spend a great deal of time philosophizing about what he is doing and why it is socially desirable. But as a profession, its members must have sufficient intellectual curiosity to roll back the frontiers of knowledge to some extent. There should be an eagerness to uncover the basic "laws" that govern its organization and activities. As an organized body of knowledge there must be some rhyme and reason to its system; there must be primary and secondary levels of knowledge; there must be relationships and interrelationships; there must be a reconciliation and rapport with other fields of knowledge. Our own curiosity about our work should lead us to look into these things. Robinson, in discussing the nature of science, expresses it beautifully.

> While it is generally admitted that the capstone of the edifice of science is its modifications of the conditions of human life, so as to add to the enrichment of human civilization and "to illumine man's little day," nevertheless the real motive which spurs on the true-hearted scientists is not practical but a burning curiosity to find out the truth. There is nothing as irritating to a true scientist as obscure and opinionated thinking. He longs to see everything as it actually is.[5]

One of the great thinkers of our times has expressed a similar thought:

> What, then, impels us to devise theory after theory? Why do we devise theories at all? The answer to the latter question is simple: Because we enjoy "comprehension." ... There is another more subtle motive. ... This is the striving toward unification and simplification of the premises of the theory as a whole....[6]

For years auditing has been so busy getting itself established and accepted that it has had little time for such introspection. But as it becomes more and more mature, this excuse becomes less and less valid. There is indeed something incongruous about a profession with no visible support in the form of a comprehensive and integrated structure of theory. We need a philosophy of auditing.

Philosophy and Auditing. Here some valid questions may be raised by those skeptical of such an effort as this. First, is auditing of such a nature that it can have or ought to have a philosophy? Second, what do we mean by a philosophy of auditing? Third, are auditors qualified to erect their own philosophical structure, or is this something which only trained philosophers are competent to do? Dare we invade a field so foreign to our daily activities; and

---

[5] Daniel Sommer Robinson, *The Principles of Reasoning* (New York: Appleton-Century-Crofts Inc., Third Edition, 1947), p. 220

[6] Albert Einstein, "On the Generalized Theory of Gravitation," *Scientific American*, Volume 182, No. 4 (April, 1950), p. 13.

even if we dare, have we any real hope for success? Answers to these questions require at least a brief examination of the nature of philosophy, the nature of auditing, and the possibility of applying the methods, aims, and purpose of philosophy to auditing.

Before this is attempted, however, it should be pointed out that other areas of specialization have developed their own philosophies. As other disciplines attained a degree of maturity, they too began to question their purpose and nature and to look for philosophical guidance. Science, history, education, law, and others have developed special philosophies that are well recognized as acceptable contributions not only to the subject in question but to the sum of philosophical understanding.

Almost without exception these specialized philosophies have been developed primarily by experts within the fields themselves. As will become apparent in our study of concepts of auditing in the latter part of this monograph, a broad knowledge of the special area of interest is essential if one is to explore it as intensively as required. Science has had particular success in the development of its philosophy, a large portion of such success being attributable to men like Poincaré about; whom Bertrand Russell writes:

> Poincaré's philosophical writings ... are not those of a professional philosopher: they are the untrammeled reflections of a broad and cultivated mind upon the procedure and postulates of scientific discovery. The writing of professional philosophers on such subjects has too often the deadness of merely external description; Poincaré's writing, on the contrary ... has the freshness of actual experience, of vivid, intimate contact with what he is describing. There results a certain richness and resonance in his words: the sound emitted is not hollow, but comes from a great mass of which only the polished surface appears.[7]

Of course auditing has not reached the advanced stage which many of the sciences have attained. Yet it has reached a stage of maturity at which it will do well to pause for a bit of introspection and to take stock of its presuppositions, aims, and methods. It is our hope that some of the "broad and cultivated minds" now active in our own circles will be encouraged by this work to consider aspects of auditing that have not yet been given sufficient attention.

---

[7] Bertrand Russell, preface to Henri Poincaré's *Science and Method* (New York: Charles Scribner's Sons), pp. 5-6.

Phenix gives us further encouragement here.[8] He points out three classes or grades of philosophers. First there are the "philosophic greats" who have made major contributions to philosophy; second are the professional philosophers who have mastered the field and who generally write and teach on this subject; third, there are many intelligent and inquiring individuals who are concerned with their problems, their goals, their relationships with others, and who seek through reflection and study to find solutions to these matters. Brennan refers to this last group:

> Professional philosophers sometimes wince when they hear businessmen talk about "the philosophy of advertising" or the "philosophy of the suburban home owner." Yet even this popular usage of the term "philosophy" shows concern with basic presuppositions or first principles. The common phrase "philosophy of life" refers to some set of primary beliefs according to which a man guides his conduct. A "philosophy of history" proceeds from those basic assumptions upon which a particular historian's interpretation of history depends. A "philosophy of science" sets forth principles more basic and comprehensive than the conclusions of the individual sciences.[9]

Auditors, then, need not be reluctant to philosophize about auditing. Indeed it is better that auditors turn to philosophy in attempting to work out the fundamental theory of auditing than that philosophers turn to auditing. But here a note of caution is needed. There is more to the task than merely expressing feelings or subjective opinions about auditing. A great many people have been doing this for many years without any significant degree of success in developing auditing theory. Philosophical research, if it is to be carried out competently and to have some fair degree of successful accomplishment, must be conducted within the rules of procedure of that type of research. Professional philosophers have a unique function in this respect. It is not their assignment to work out the philosophical problems of every field of knowledge. Rather their responsibility is to teach artists, scientists, auditors, and others how to develop their own philosophies. Professional philosophers teach us how to play the

---

[8] Philip H. Phenix, *Philosophy of Education* (New York: Henry Holt and Company, 1958), p. 8.

[9] Joseph Gerard Brennan, *The Meaning of Philosophy* (New York: Harper and Brothers, 1953), pp. 1-2.

game in our own backyard. They teach us what methods are available to us, what the rules are, and when we are out of bounds. Then they leave us to play our own game, to work out the philosophy of auditing for ourselves.

In doing this, we must have full regard for rules and boundaries. We must point out that development of a philosophy of auditing is a far more serious matter than an individual's search for a personal "philosophy of life." In the final analysis, a philosophy of auditing must stand the scrutiny of experts. On the one hand, it must recognize the particular nature of auditing, its objective, method, and economic function. On the other hand, it must realize that philosophy has both a critical and a constructive function. The critical and constructive activities are so closely related that some philosophers contend that they engage the mind simultaneously.

The Philosophical Approach. Although philosophers themselves disagree somewhat as to the purpose and methods of philosophy, some basic ideas are generally accepted, and these will guide us in this study. They are:

1. Philosophy gets back to first principles, to the rationale behind the actions and thoughts which tend to be taken for granted.
2. Philosophy is concerned with the systematic organization of knowledge in such a way that it becomes at once more useful and less likely to be self-contradictory.
3. Philosophy provides a basis whereby social relationships may be molded and understood.

For our purposes, therefore, such definitions of philosophy as: "the body of principles underlying a given branch of learning" and "a system for guidance in practical affairs" are directly useful. Yet they are much too brief to give us a real understanding of philosophy's scope and nature.

For the essence of philosophy, we turn to the following quotation from the *Dictionary of Philosophy:*

> Philosophy: (Greek: *Philein*, to love; *Sophia*, wisdom). The most general science. Phythagoras is said to have called himself a lover of wisdom. But philosophy has been both the seeking of wisdom and the wisdom sought.

> Originally, the rational explanation of anything; the general principles under which all facts could be explained; in this sense, indistinguishable from science.
>
> Later, the science of first principles of being; the presupposition of ultimate reality.
>
> Now, popularly, private wisdom or consolation; technically, the science of sciences, the criticism and systematization or organization of all knowledge, drawn from empirical science, rational learning, common experience, or whatever.[10]

As a beginning, then, philosophy is an attitude toward knowledge, not just an accumulation of knowledge. Philosophy is the love of wisdom, the search for wisdom. But how can the love of wisdom be applied to such a subject as auditing? Recently, the philosophical approach has been characterized as consisting of four parts: (1) comprehension, (2) perspective, (3) insight, and (4) vision. Brief attention to each of these may be helpful.[11]

Comprehension implies the understanding of the whole rather than individual parts alone. Because he is concerned with understanding human life in the broadest sense, the philosopher "employs concepts of great generality such as 'matter,' 'mind,' 'form,' 'entity,' 'process,' which are comprehensive in that they apply to the whole range of human experience. He also tries to discover relationships between seemingly diverse aspects of the world, and through these connections to comprehend the world as a meaningful whole."[12]

If we apply this idea to auditing, we must look for ideas relatively as general in our own discipline. This directs us to a consideration of such general concepts as evidence, due care, disclosure, and independence. The study of such broadly applicable concepts leads to the development of a comprehensive and coherent body of knowledge based on an interpretation of auditing as a socially useful discipline. This is much more realistic than the view now held by many that auditing is merely a set of rules concerned with the best method of completing a given engagement.

---

[10] Dagobert D. Runes, Editor, *Dictionary of Philosophy* (New York: Philosophical Library, No date), p. 235.

[11] Philip H. Phenix, *loc. cit.*, pp. 6-8.

[12] *Ibid.*, p. 6.

Perspective, as a component of the philosophical approach, calls for the breadth of outlook necessary to grasp the true and full significance of things. Thus the philosopher "would endeavor to consider any proposition in broad perspective — and not merely from the view of a special pleader — so that he can make well-grounded judgments about it."[13]

If we apply this idea to the development of a philosophy of auditing, we see the need to brush aside special pleas and transcend private concerns and vested interests. Each issue must be considered in the light of its aggregate importance and ramifications rather than from one or more limited points of view. Immediate consequences count for very little if they conflict with more significant and far-reaching effects.

Insight, the third element of the philosophical approach, emphasizes the depth of the proposed inquiry. "The search for philosophic insight is another way of saying that the philosopher seeks to uncover the basic assumptions which underlie our views of life and the world."[14] Basic assumptions are not only the foundation from which we reason, but like many other foundations they tend to be hidden and their importance is therefore unrecognized. No special subject can make real progress until its basic assumptions, their nature, weaknesses, and implications are uncovered and examined. In this respect, it must be admitted that auditing has fallen behind certain other disciplines, although it is not alone in this respect. As auditing has increased in importance, the work of the auditor has come to touch upon some of the more important aspects of contemporary society, as we shall see in developing some of its concepts in later chapters. Yet its underlying assumptions have not been brought forth for scrutiny and evaluation. So long as these remain implicit only, arguments and discussions will continue with little hope of constructive conclusions. Disclosure and acceptance of these postulates as the basis for a theory of auditing is essential if we are to avoid bias and eliminate unsound reasoning in this area of knowledge. Until this is done, the trivial may pass for significant and judgment will be susceptible to influences which are no more than superficially important.

---

[13] *Ibid.*, p. 7.

[14] *Ibid.*, p. 7.

Vision, as the term is used in describing the philosophical approach, "... does not mean unbridled speculation or irrational mysticism. It means that the philosopher has a view that lifts him from purely immediate and common concerns to the wider possibilities of the world ideally and imaginatively conceived."[15]

In special philosophies, particularly those concerned with current and future activities rather than with the history of thought only, vision is an essential quality for the study of the problems relevant to the subject. This quality, however, is not granted equally to all. Those really detached from the exigencies of daily problems and long devoted to developing their area of knowledge are most likely to be able to see and express, ahead of their times, the consequences of alternative solutions to given issues. Others can cultivate it, however, as they strive for and acquire a detached and yet serious concern for their subject. This capacity to penetrate to the reality of a question and its implications for the future is most essential in defining the prospects and establishing the goals of a young and growing discipline like auditing.

Thus far we have seen that to think philosophically about a subject is to adopt a synoptic view through which the subject can be comprehended in its totality and in relation to the world at large, to consider every issue in the light of aggregate interrelationships, to penetrate beyond casually accepted beliefs to the implicit premises of its reasoning, and to look far ahead in visualizing its prospects and goals. If this is the nature of the study to be undertaken, what is the method to be followed?

The Method of Philosophy. Each field of inquiry has its own peculiar method of inquiry, and philosophy is no exception. Thus the method is the same whether the subject is a special or a general philosophy.

One of the principal aspects of this method is aptly described in the following:

> The philosophical way of treating questions ... can be contrasted sharply with other common ways of handling an issue, such as fighting about it, voting upon it, or compromising concerning it. None of these other methods compels its users to *understand* the problem

---

[15] *Ibid.*, p. 9.

> in hand. So that the philosopher's solution, which almost always takes more time in the beginning, and looks less promising than the others, generally has the great advantage of being more lasting, because less superficial, in the end. Philosophizing about a thing implies an unusually stubborn attempt to understand it as thoroughly as possible, so as to give it the most thoughtful treatment of which we are capable.[16]

Complementary to this emphasis on thorough understanding is the procedure of developing "questions" which by their nature encourage study and understanding. This principle is epitomized in the following statement:

> Any meaning that philosophy has for individuals or for society must take into consideration what Byron once termed the "eternal spirit of the chainless mind": Man has eternally questioned "Why?" ...
>
> Perhaps there has never been a more penetrating insight into the real task of philosophy than this statement: "Philosophers see questions where the rest of us see facts."[17]

Of the traditional approaches recognized in the study of philosophy we find the analytic and valuational methods to be the more fruitful in developing auditing theory and we will integrate and use these two. Auditing is concerned with social responsibility and ethical conduct as well as with the collection and evaluation of evidence, so each of these methods has a place in this work.

On the authority of a contemporary writer, these approaches are described as follows:

> The Analytic Approach: Many come to philosophy because they feel it important to subject to analysis and critical reflection notions which are taken for granted by most of us. Such persons are attracted by the rigor and precision in thinking; they admire exactness in procedure. The analytical philosopher asks "How do you know?" for he is interested in problems concerning the range, methods, and limits of human knowledge. He asks, "What do you mean?" for he is convinced that many problems of philosophy will be solved if inquiry is made into the meaning of the terms of the argument. Today the analytic philosopher uses the highly developed technique of modern logic to help him in his analysis of philosophical problems....

---

[16] Harold A. Larrabee, *What Philosophy Is* (New York: Macy-Masius. The Vanguard Press, 1928), p. 61, author's emphasis.

[17] William J. MacLead, *Contagious Ideas and Dynamic Events* (Privately Published, Baldwin-Wallace College, Berea, Ohio, 1959), pp. 278, 280.

> The Valuation Approach: There are, among others, two types of values, moral and esthetic.... Many come to philosophy seeking answers to the question "What is the good life for man?" Such a philosopher whose dominant interest is *moral* presents us with a "philosophy of life," a doctrine concerning the nature of man, desirable goals for human life, principles by which we may guide our conduct....[18]

By its very nature, auditing lends itself to the analytic approach in certain of its aspects and to the moral-valuation approach in others. For example, audit judgment rests upon the quality of belief acquired through the collection or creation of evidence. This warrants the study of the theories of knowledge and proof as developed in philosophy. When the facts asserted in financial statements are argumentative, belief is justified only so far as one can reason from established evidence. The more rigorous the reasoning, the more accurate the conclusions and the more reliable the judgment.

In a very real sense, the auditing function is accomplished under an "honor system" that brings ethical conduct to the fore. Without readily applied standards of measurement or rules of conduct for an examination, the primary assurance of satisfactory performance inevitably becomes the auditor's sense of professional responsibility. His standard of values, therefore, becomes controlling. Thus, in auditing, we have two kinds of problems requiring two different methods of study: problems of fact and problems of value. These are given additional attention in the following chapter but are mentioned here to suggest the necessity of an integrated analytic and valuational approach in this study.

The applicability of the valuational approach points out that philosophy is not analytical only. It has important social implications as well, and these are of particular significance in a professional field such as auditing.

> Philosophy is not merely, or even primarily, a conceptual process, as many people in our culture are included to believe. It is a social process as well, and a very important one it is. The verbal tradition that we call philosophy equips each growing child within its embrace with a uniform set of beliefs, of ideas and ideals. It thus makes

[18] Brennan, *op. cit.*, pp. 5-6.

> for uniformity of behavior, which is essential to coherent social organization and the effective conduct of group life. A philosophy not only provides people with information needed for action; it stimulates them to action; inspires them, and defines the goals for which they shall strive. A philosophy is therefore an important means of social integration. It is, so to speak, the peculiarly connective tissue of human society....[19]

The applicability of this description to auditing may be seen even more clearly if we are permitted to paraphrase the last four sentences in this fashion:

> Philosophy thus makes for uniformity of professional performance, which is essential to coherent professional organization and the effective conduct of the profession. A philosophy not only provides professional men with information needed for action; it stimulates them to satisfactory professional performance, inspires them, and defines the goals for which they strive. A philosophy is therefore an important means of professional integration. It is, so to speak, the peculiarly connective tissue of a profession.

It is in this last function of philosophy that we find the clues to some of the problems that face auditing as a profession. If a philosophy, an underlying structure of reason and purpose, can be developed, it should provide a basis for determining professional action. And if difficult problems still remain insoluble, at least to that extent the underlying philosophy remains inadequately developed

Having considered the nature of a philosophical investigation, let us now turn to the nature of auditing. Does auditing lend itself to this type of study? What is its nature and what will be gained by such an inquiry? It appears from the preceding discussion that a considerable amount of good can come from a thorough and penetrating study of auditing. The existence of numerous unsolved problems indicates the need. Little more justification seems necessary. Yet it is desirable to give attention to the nature of auditing at this point so that we may have some agreement respecting the essence of our subject. The foundation of a philosophy of auditing necessarily starts with the nature of auditing itself. What type of activity is it? How may it be described?

---

[19] Leslie A. White, *The Evolution of Culture* (New York: McGraw-Hill Book Co., 1959), p. 264.

What is its relationship to other fields of knowledge? From what other disciplines does it borrow ideas?

Auditing as a Discipline. Many of us tend to think of auditing as a subdivision of accounting, possibly because that is how it was introduced to us when we first studied it and because every auditor we know is also an accountant. As a matter of fact, however, it is quite incorrect to consider auditing to be a subdivision of accounting. Auditing is concerned with accounting, which explains why auditors are accountants first, but it is not a part of accounting. If we search more deeply into those things which auditors do, into the nature of the audit process, we find that auditing has its roots elsewhere. The relationship of auditing to accounting is close, yet their natures are very different; they are business associates, not parent and child. Accounting includes the collection, classification, summarization, and communication of financial data; it involves the measurement and communication of business events and conditions as they affect and represent a given enterprise or other entity. The task of accounting is to reduce a tremendous mass of detailed information to manageable and understandable proportions. Auditing does none of these things. Auditing must consider business events and conditions too, but it does not have the task of measuring or communicating them. Its task is to review the measurements and communications of accounting for propriety. Auditing is analytical, not constructive; it is critical, investigative, concerned with the basis for accounting measurements and assertions. Auditing emphasizes proof, the support for financial statements and data. Thus auditing has its principal roots, not in accounting which it reviews, but in logic on which it leans heavily for ideas and methods.

An apt analogy is difficult to find, but to some extent at least the relationship of accounting and auditing may be likened to that of an author and an editor. An author starts with certain raw materials: ideas, impressions, experiences, perhaps the results of his research; these he begins to develop into an article, a book or a play. He has a goal in mind: to communicate to his readers certain entertaining, elevating, or edifying ideas, and he strives by every device at his command to produce a work that will attain this goal. Plot, characterization, vocabulary, and style are his tools. When he feels he has fulfilled his purpose, his finished product goes to an editor. Now the editor's goal is much the same as that of the writer, but his function, method of approach, and tools are entirely different. His job is not to construct, it is to examine and judge. He does not draw together ideas, characters, scenes; he compares the author's ideas, characters, and scenes with what he knows of real life. Are they believable? His function is one of criticism; his tools are analytical and critical ability, literary standards, ethics, and taste. He attempts to be objective, but there is of necessity a strong element of subjectivity in his work.

Writing and editing complement one another. Neither is a subdivision of the other; both are parts of some larger area, that of literary endeavor which lies within the fine arts. So it is with accounting and auditing; they are also complementary. Although concerned with the same general subject matter, their functions, tools, and approach are substantially different. Thus we cannot expect to find the fundamental ideas of auditing by an examination of accounting theory and practice. We must go deeper than this; we must inquire into the nature of the auditing function and discover where this leads us.

Auditing is concerned with verification,[20] the examination of financial data for the purpose of judging the faithfulness with which they portray events and conditions. Financial data are mainly assertions of intangible facts. Their verification requires application of the techniques and methods of proof. Proof is a part of the field of logic which has been described by some as the "science of proof." Logic is concerned with how we establish facts, conclusions, and inferences as valid or invalid. As such, logic is basic not only to auditing but to law, which inevitably borrows its ideas and theories of proof from logic. In fact, any discipline which relies heavily on evidence is based on logic.

---

[20] The term "verification" is here used in its accepted dictionary meaning "verify — to check or test the accuracy or exactness of." The profession has some reluctance to use this term (see *Generally Accepted Auditing Standards*, p. 8), but we find it entirely appropriate. The general subject of proof is discussed more fully in Chapter 5.

Insofar as the use of evidence is concerned, law and auditing are thus applications of logic to certain real situations; they are applied logic just as engineering may be said to be applied mathematics. But engineering is more than just mathematics, it requires the synthesis of mathematics with concepts and methods drawn from sciences such as physics, chemistry, and mechanics. Similarly, auditing has its primary roots in logic, on which it draws heavily, but it reaches into other fields as well, such as mathematics, the behavioral sciences, communications, and ethics for portions of its theory. And although auditing does borrow a good deal from other fields, this does not mean that it has no independent identity.

Recently, there has been growing recognition of the interrelationship among different fields of knowledge.[21] As will be seen later, auditing has borrowed, and will probably continue to borrow, from other fields what it needs to elaborate its method and fulfill its function. However, there must be careful selection of those ideas and procedures which can be of assistance. Generally speaking, successful adoption of this kind requires an understanding of the subject's own problems as much as an understanding of the nature of the borrowed tools. Rarely are ideas and methods in other fields such that they can be accepted without some modification. Two examples will illustrate: Auditing is concerned with evidence. Therefore in perfecting its theory of evidence, it is logical that it should resort to the study of the theory of knowledge, the ways of obtaining belief. But it is equally important to note that the theory of knowledge deals with evidence and belief in general; it is not limited to the specific frame of reference of auditing inquiry. Hence, the theory of knowledge becomes helpful to auditing only if it is suitably modified and adapted to the problems of auditing.

Auditing is also concerned with sampling and should naturally resort to a study of the theory of statistics. But, in order to successfully adopt sampling techniques in audit verification, se-

---

[21] See for instance, Wm. Oliver Martin, *The Order and Organization of Knowledge* (Ann Arbor: University of Michigan Press, 1957) and Oliver L. Reiser, *The Integration of Human Knowledge* (Boston: Extending Horizon Books-Porter Sargent Publisher, 1958). This will be further discussed in Chapter 10.

rious attention must be given to the nature of business data and the characteristics which differentiate them from the data of other fields of inquiry. Unless this principle is kept under continuous study in theory and observed in practice, more harm than benefit may result.

In addition to this discriminative selection, auditing has to formulate unique concepts which cannot be borrowed elsewhere because they are peculiar to the nature and function of auditing. Independence is an illustration. Both borrowed and formulated ideas are integrated into a coherent body of thought. This together with its peculiar function, method, and precepts give to auditing its status as an independent discipline. Basic to this discipline is a set of particular assumptions which, in combination with the foregoing components, provide its characteristic features. The selection, modification, and integration of borrowed ideas, plus the development of additional necessary concepts and methodology, give auditing an independent status.

After lengthy and serious consideration, we can come to no other conclusion than that auditing is a specialized field of knowledge, that it warrants and needs the type of study attempted in the remaining chapters of this monograph, and that the development of a sound philosophy of auditing is a challenge worthy of the best minds the profession has to offer. Auditing deals with abstract ideas; it has its foundations in the most basic types of learning; it has a rational structure of postulates, concepts, techniques, and precepts; adequately understood, it is a rigorous intellectual study worthy to be called a "discipline" in the current sense of that term. Thus auditing provides opportunities for and even demands strenuous intellectual effort. It is by such effort that its underlying theory may be discovered, developed, comprehended, and used for the improvement of the profession.

Auditing is also an "applied" discipline, and because an applied discipline draws its "principles" or basic theory from many other fields, some of them pure and some of them also applied, there is always the possibility that it will lose sight of its connection with and dependence on the more basic or abstract fields of learning. Thus it may neglect its theory and give a disproportionate part of its attention to applications and to immediate day-today problems. This is always unfortunate because the strength of any discipline lies in its foundations. Auditing can scarcely be accused of neglecting its theory, however, because it is still so young as perhaps never to have become really aware of its relationship to the fundamental disciplines.

Yet the danger is present nonetheless. We have a strong tendency in auditing to adopt a pragmatic approach. Whatever works well is adopted and strongly advocated; what has not yet been found applicable has little appeal. To some extent this is a natural tendency, yet we must keep it in bounds. We must continually test our practices and procedures, not only in actual practice, but against the theory which underlies auditing. And we should continually search theory for possible approaches to both new and old problems. If we forget the theoretical foundation of auditing and let it dwindle to a mere collection of rote procedures and practices reminiscent of its early history, it will not only lose stature in the eyes of the world but will forfeit the best method of solving its most perplexing problems.

CHAPTER 2

THE METHODOLOGY OF AUDITING

In the preceding chapter we proposed that development of a philosophy of auditing requires a study of its nature and problems in the light of first principles. This calls for an examination of its method, presuppositions, and concepts. In this chapter we well be concerned with the study of "method" in auditing. As used here, this term may be subdivided into attitude and methodological procedure. That is, we are interested in the attitude of those who practice in the field as well as with their method of attack, the intellectual approach they use in the performance of their work.

If one carefully observes the methods followed in different disciplines, he will discover that each has developed an attitude and procedure peculiar to itself. Some of these approaches have important characteristics in common, but there are also significant differences. As each discipline develops into maturity, it continually experiments and modifies its procedures and attitude until it finally devises a method appropriate to its particular needs and essential to its activities. The method of inquiry thus becomes as much an integral part of the discipline as does the subject matter itself.

Any method has a limited ability to be transferred to another field. Its success in one discipline is no guarantee at all that it will be successful elsewhere. In some cases there are similarities among fields that permit an established method to be largely taken over, but even so there must be modification and adaptation to the new subject. Methodology grows with the field of inquiry, and, in its growth and degree of refinement, represents to some extent the stages of intellectual development in the subject itself.

Reflection on different methods in relation to the disciplines they serve indicates that the method of inquiry is largely governed by the type of problem which the inquirer faces, the nature of the judgment he makes, and the character of the data examined. Thus the method of history cannot be identical with the method of law because the problems, judgments, and data tend to be quite different, and the method of physical science must differ from both. Each must use its own distinct line of attack.

In this respect, like other special fields, auditing has a method consisting of an attitude and a procedure, and these are peculiar to it and to its problems, judgments, and data. Proceeding on this idea we will examine the method of auditing in the light of the nature of the problems it faces and seeks to resolve. Our purpose is to obtain a better understanding of the nature of auditing by analyzing the way in which it functions. In doing this we will find it impossible to restrict ourselves to description only and will find ourselves dealing also with certain formative aspects of the auditing method. This will be most apparent if we compare the auditing method with the scientific method which is used as a standard because of its advanced development, success, and prestige.

The Scientific Attitude. Physical scientists have been more successful than workers in any other field in increasing the amount of verifiable knowledge available to mankind. It is not our purpose here to examine all the reasons for this remarkable success, but certainly a goodly portion of it is due to their development of a method of attack, a way of thinking that has been eminently useful. Without claiming perfection for the methods followed by scientists, students of methodology have studied their procedures in an attempt to distill the essence of the scientific method for use in other areas of research and problem solving. Although there is some lack of unanimity among those who have sought to analyze the scientific method, there are sufficient similarities in their conclusions to give us an adequate insight into what one of them has described as "...the most trustworthy method for testing the truth of propositions."

The scientific method is at once an attitude of mind and a procedure for reasoning. It is difficult to judge which is the more important, but it is unlikely that either could have attained its present success without the other.

The scientific attitude consists first of all of a searching and abiding curiosity. Within his specific area of inquiry, the scientist is a philosopher at heart. He continually asks the question: "Why?" As he looks about in his field of interest he finds innumerable questions which lead him into research and investigation to discover why things are — or if they really are — what they seem to be. Apparent similarities or dissimilarities arouse his interest; he must find out why they exist and what their significance is. Events, actions, and interactions whet his curiosity, and he must discover why they occur and what their implications and effects are.

At the root of this curiosity is a desire for knowledge — reliable knowledge. Thus the scientist is never content with quick or superficial answers. He wants to get to the very bottom of things and therefore is continually skeptical of the evidence and the answers he obtains. His continual "Why?" is matched with another question, "Is it really so?" He cannot rest content until he has tested his explanations and solutions and convinced himself that the evidence at his command provides a conclusive foundation.

While it is true that each scientist should and does have a certain amount of faith in the work of his colleagues, he is typically endowed with such an eternal and searching curiosity that he must prove things for himself. Hence there is much replication in science. Testing the conclusions reached by previous research rather than resting on the authority of such conclusions is one of the features of scientific inquiry. Science continually repeats, reviews, and revises its discoveries, and this, in part, accounts for its progress and prestige.

Wishful thinking, prejudices, unsupported assertions, these have no standing whatever in scientific work. Only that knowledge which is supported with unquestioned evidence can be accepted as valid. Therefore the true scientist strives to strip himself of mental bias, cautiously and alertly watches for any sign of errors inherent in the data he uses or in the method he follows, and in submitting his conclusions candidly qualifies them with the limitations of confidence he feels they merit.

But the scientist is not satisfied with reliable solutions to a series of individual and detached questions. He has a more inclusive goal in view; that is to discover and reveal the basic order or pattern in that which he studies. As he solves any single problem, he tries to relate it to others, to examine the consistency of its solution with pertinent facts already established, thus fitting the conclusions obtainable from a diverse variety of problems into a coherent and integrated scheme of knowledge. In this way he continually seeks fundamental laws or principles that will explain still other as yet unsolved problems. Back of his curiosity and skepticism is an abiding faith that there is an order which, if it can be discovered, will hold the key to additional knowledge.

In these few paragraphs we have attempted to cover the characteristics of the scientific attitude. These may be summarized as a driving curiosity, reasonable skepticism, desire for conclusiveness with a willingness to revise as necessary, conscious avoidance of mental bias, alertness to error, awareness of limitations, and a tendency toward systematic generalization. With these in mind, it may be useful to turn to the more technical aspects of the methodological procedure of scientific reasoning.

In this connection we hear much about the "scientific method," but recently it has been pointed out that there is no one scientific method as such.[1] The method varies with the nature of the problem, the kind of science to which it belongs, and the state of development and analysis attained by the field. There is considerable difference, for instance, between the problems of fact with which natural sciences are primarily concerned and the problems of value with which social sciences must contend. To use the illustration given by Northrup in emphasizing this difference in method, we can contrast their problems as follows.[2] A natural scientist may face the question: "What is the character of the solar system?" but never a question like "What ought to be the character of this system?" On the other hand, the social scientist may face both the questions: "What is the character of a given social institution?" and "What ought to be the character of such institutions?" It seems apparent that the method of obtaining evidence to support a conclusion to the first type of question must be considerably different from the method followed in attempting to answer the second.

Method also differs according to the stage of development attained by the science in question. As a given science develops it

---

[1] F. S. C. Northrop, *The Logic of the Sciences and the Humanities* (New York: The Macmillan Company, 1947), Chapters 1, 2, particularly pp. 17-19.

[2] *Ibid.*, p. 255.

passes from the phase of "natural history," in which it is concerned only with systematic observation, description, and classification, to the stage of "postulationally prescribed theory" in which it relies heavily on deductive formulation of concepts.

The Attitude of Auditing. If we turn now from science to auditing, it seems clear that auditing, as a special field of inquiry, has developed a method of investigation of its own. The auditing method has not been developed overnight or transplanted in total from some other field; it has grown and developed over the years to meet the needs of auditing. It may have some similarities with the methods of other fields, but this justifies neither a charge of plagiarism nor a contention on the part of auditing that its system of inquiry is equal to that found in other and perhaps more developed fields. Plainly and simply it is a method found useful and suitable for the needs of auditing. We would like to think that it is still evolving, and that as new problems appear it will be further modified and improved. That it is a distinct and identifiable method peculiarly appropriate to the problems of auditing seems apparent. We will examine first the attitude involved in this method; the procedural aspects will receive attention later in this chapter.

It is not our intention here to deal with the historical development of this method but rather to follow an analytical approach in explaining its composition and nature. In our view, the auditing attitude includes the following components:

1. Restriction of interest and inquiry primarily to matters on which judgment is requested.
2. Adoption of a position of impartiality in formulating and expressing judgments.
3. Basing judgment formation and expression on such evidence as is reasonably available.

In considering these components of the auditing attitude, it may be helpful to look briefly at the types of problems which auditors face in the performance of their duties. Like social scientists, auditors have both problems of fact and problems of value on which they must make judgments. The amount of cash, the number of shares of outstanding stock, the amount of accounts payable are very much like the questions of fact dealt with in certain other disciplines. But the auditor also has such problems of value as consideration of the desirable extent of disclosure in a given case, determination of whether an unusual item of gain should affect net income for the year or be carried to retained earnings, and the desirability of combining or showing separately in the financial statements items which have both similarities and differences. In addition, auditing has problems of value at the profession as well as the practitioner level. Not only does each audit raise such problems for the individual practitioner, but the profession as a whole must deal with such value problems as the extent of its responsibility for the detection of irregularities, the point at which disclosure becomes detrimental rather than beneficial, and the requirements of independence in the performance of managerial services.

The contrast between the auditing attitude and the scientific attitude with respect to the extent of interest is apparent. In the typical examination, the auditor has presented to him the financial statements he is to examine or at least the general ledger trial balance from which they are to be prepared. His examination seldom goes beyond matters directly related to items in the statements, although he must also give some consideration to any disclosures which he feels should be made and are not. The scientist, on the other hand, is almost completely unrestricted in the scope of his inquiries. They seldom commence with a specific assignment; and, even it they do, he does not feel himself confined to it. Any given inquiry may ultimately lead him far afield as he pursues questions which arise in its solution.

Impartiality, or independence as it is commonly described, is a feature of audit work that is probably not peculiar to auditing, although auditors have more occasion than others to emphasize this quality. It is likely that every sincere inquirer tries to maintain an attitude of detachment from the problem he is solving. None of them desire to be influenced to the extent that their judgment may be affected. Perhaps the increased emphasis results from the fact that in auditing there are a number of economic interests in the financial data examined, some of which tend to be in opposition to one another. The auditor's position is such that he could easily be influenced by one or another of those interests. Such an influence, if effective, would necessarily make his examination less useful to all other interests. He must stress impartiality because of the nature of the data with which he is concerned and the nature of the problems and judgments pertinent to his work.

Like researchers in many other fields, the auditor is interested in evidence and obtains it, evaluates it, and studies it before he forms a judgment. The difference between an auditor and a scientist in this respect is that the auditor must use such information as is available. He is required to come to a judgment in order to be of service, and he must reach that judgment at reasonable cost and within a reasonable time. He is in no position to extend his inquiry until he obtains evidence that convinces him absolutely on every issue before him. Certainly there are matters on which he is able to obtain conclusive evidence and be thoroughly satisfied. There are other matters on which he must accept something not so conclusive. But he must still formulate judgments. Another difference is that the auditor does not continually revise past judgments. Once a judgment is made and expressed, so far as the specific engagement is concerned, that particular problem is finally and completely solved. The auditor is not engaged in adding to the sum total of human knowledge but only in offering, in a specific situation and at a specific time, an opinion about the reliability of knowledge already available. He does, of course, continually review his own past judgments, inquiries, and applications of his methodology, so that he can do better in the future; but this does not alter the fact that on each engagement he formally and permanently records a final judgment, the best judgment he can make at that time and under the existing conditions.

Thus there are significant differences between the attitude of auditing and that of science. We fill find that there are equally significant differences also in the methodological procedure followed in each field. As we look at these differences, whether of attitude or procedure, we should keep in mind the well-deserved prestige of scientific methods and consider the extent to which they suggest the possibility of improvement in the auditing method.

Methodological Approach in Science. With the previously described attitude to guide the scientific mind, it has developed a systematic procedure of thinking which may be described in the following eight steps:[3]

1. Consideration of the preliminary data which suggest the problem.
2. Formulation of the problem.
3. Observation of facts relevant to the problem.
4. Use of previous knowledge.
5. Formulation of the hypothesis.
6. Deduction of the implications of the hypothesis.
7. Testing of the hypothesis.
8. Conclusion: The hypothesis is confirmed or disconfirmed.

First of all, something must come to the attention of the thinker to suggest a problem. No matter how curious one is, there must be some stimulus to set the mind to thinking. This stimulus may appear in any one of a considerable variety of forms. A natural or social phenomenon, a casual question, a previously unnoticed reaction or response to an occurrence, an event somewhat out of the ordinary, the failure or the success of an experiment, to mention only a few, may set the scientist to thinking, may encourage him to see a question that had not previously come to his attention. Once the stimulus attracts his attention to the possibility of inquiry and investigation, he naturally formulates a problem. This is commonly in the form of a question: how to account for the phenomenon, response, or event. Here is one of the points where the scientist excels. He has a carefully developed skill in formulating problems. He has deliberately trained his mind to react to such stimuli. Instead of wishing that unanswered questions and unexplained events would go away, he welcomes them as additional opportunities to find a clue to the ultimate order of things. He has trained himself to look for problems, and once having found one he has further trained himself to state it as clearly and concisely as possible. A fuzzy or foggy notion of something questionable is of little help. A sharp, clear statement of the essential problem is a long step on the way to ultimate solution.

[3] Lionel Ruby, *Logic* (New York: J. B. Lippincott Company, 1950), p. 349.

After formulating the problem as precisely as he can, the scientific thinker does not hasten to a quick and easy answer. First he gathers all the relevant facts he can find, looking especially for those facts that may lead him to a useful hypothesis. Here again, training is helpful, for careful and discriminating observation is an art in itself. Then with the problem in mind and such facts as are available before him, the thinker calls upon his store of knowledge and experience to make what he can of the situation. The greater the store of usable knowledge and experience, the more likely one is to find a clue to the present problem. Likewise, the greater one's ability to see similarities between this and previously solved problems, to get at the very essence of the situation, to recognize relationships and to note significant differences, the more likely one is to arrive at a realistic hypothesis.

A hypothesis is in the nature of a tentative solution to the problem at hand. It is the most reasonable explanation the thinker can find to account for the data that first stimulated him to recognize the problem. In developing it, he may have discarded one or more other possibilities, some of which he will return to if his attempts to test his hypothesis indicate that it is unsatisfactory. But at this point, he has settled on a "probably best" hypothesis after careful consideration of the problem, the facts surrounding the problem, and his own accumulated knowledge and experience.

Having arrived at a hypothesis which he believes is tenable, the scientific thinker's skepticism forbids him from accepting it outright. He must test it before acceptance. This he does first by deducing the implications of his hypothesis. It is not enough that the hypothesis accounts for the original data and the surrounding facts in a realistic fashion. Just what does the hypothesis imply? Are its implications reasonable? Are they compatible with the available facts or are there suggestions in them that cast doubt on the validity of the hypothesis itself? Does it lead to implications incompatible with other knowledge or experience? Thus by intellectual attack, the thinker attempts to destroy the hypothesis he has just created, for if it cannot stand the test of this attack, it well may be too weak to warrant further investigation.

If the implications of this hypothesis are not such as to render it less tenable, the scientist then attempts to test it more rigorously by securing additional evidence. Evidence may be obtained by observation, by experiment, or by any other method of obtaining knowledge recognized as satisfactory in the field of iniquity. He is looking not only for evidence that will support the hypothesis; he is searching for any evidence pertinent to it — that is, that either refutes or supports it. His attitude of skepticism demands not only that he find no evidence strong enough to destroy his tentative solution, but that he find positive evidence to support it. Of course the success of his efforts to obtain sufficient pertinent evidence will vary with the problem. In many cases additional evidence is difficult to find and a hypothesis may stand for years as a hypothesis until ways of testing it can be developed. In other instances, it may be relatively easy to put the matter to a test which proves conclusively that the hypothesis is or is not valid.

Having gathered evidence respecting the hypothesis, the scientific thinker examines the evidence for and against the hypothesis and reaches a conclusion. He may conclude that the hypothesis is valid, invalid, or requires further testing. At the same time he keeps his mind open to the possibility of additional problems for which his work with the problem at issue may have provided the stimulus.

An additional note about the scientific method seems desirable before we compare it with the methods used in auditing. From this brief discussion it may be apparent and yet worth emphasizing that scientific thinking, with rare exceptions, is purposeful. The scientist works to add to the sum of established knowledge; he wants to roll back the frontier. He does this by forming judgments, following a fairly definite pattern. But lest we gain the impression that judgments so formed are incontrovertible, we must point out that the scientist's judgments, like those of anyone else, rely heavily on the basic assumptions of the field in which the judgment is made. Philosophers point out that there is no field without basic assumptions or postulates. We are not always as aware of their existence as we should be but they are there nonetheless, and the validity of the judgments we form depends importantly on those postulates.

To illustrate, most of us remember the elementary course in classical economics in which the instructor started with an assumption of perfect competition and with that as a base led his students to conclusions about the effect on prices of various changes in supply and demand. The validity of the conclusions about the influence which changes in demand and supply exert on prices rested on the basic assumption. As students, many of us were impatient with such an assumption because we were convinced that perfect competition could not exist. Yet if we were patient, we found that later relaxing of the assumption made it possible to approach real conditions much more closely and to continue reasoning with some fair degree of reliability.

Even science must rely on assumptions. For example it is really an assumption that the experiment which was performed yesterday and the day before with identical results will produce essentially the same results today if performed again. Why must that which worked yesterday work today? Even if it has worked five hundred times, do we know beyond a doubt that it will work the five hundred and first? The scientist thus assumes an order in the universe, the existence of unfailing laws, and the continuance of things as they have been. Without this assumption, much of his scientific knowledge would be meaningless.

In answer to his own question: "What is the basic assumption underlying science?" Robinson answers:

> It is that nature itself is an ordered system. The whole universe is an ordered and systematic whole, not a chaos of isolated facts. The laws of nature express actual necessary relations between natural entities or facts. They are actual bonds which hold the facts together into systems. The scientist discovers the actual integrations constituting the nature of things. This is the basic inductive assumption underlying every scientific inquiry.[4]

Because knowledge in any field relies heavily on its underlying assumptions or postulates, the following chapter undertakes a study of such assumptions in auditing.

Methodological Procedure in Auditing. Now let us turn to auditing and compare its procedure of inquiry with the typical scientific method described previously. First it must be noted that auditing deals both with problems of fact akin to those of the natural sciences and with problems of value akin to those of the social sciences. Thus it must have two procedures, one for

---

[4] Robinson, *op. cit.*, p. 217.

dealing with each kind of problem. At this point let us turn our attention to the methodology followed in dealing with problems of fact.

The auditing methodology for dealing with problems or issues of fact may be outlined in these steps:

1. Recognition (acceptance) of the composite problem (the audit assignment).
2. Observation of facts relevant to the problem.
3. Subdivision of the composite problem into individual problems.
4. Determination of available evidence pertinent to each individual problem.
5. Selection of applicable audit techniques and development of appropriate procedures.
6. Performance of procedures to obtain evidence.
7. Evaluation of evidence
   a. With respect to pertinence and validity.
   b. For indications of any additional problems.
   c. With respect to adequacy for judgment formation.
8. Formulation of judgment
   a. On individual propositions.
   b. On the composite problem.

It is apparent that there are substantial differences between this methodological procedure and that designated as the procedure of scientific thinking. Yet there are some interesting similarities that make comparison of the two methods instructive.

In the first place, the auditor does not seek for stimulation or have the original data brought to his attention in quite the same way as the scientist. Requests for his opinion on the fairness of financial statements come to him in the ordinary course of his occupation. These requests present him with the motivation for initiating an inquiry. This is not to say that he never has the problem of recognizing original data as a stimulus for inquiry without a specific invitation, because he most certainly does. Throughout an examination the auditor must be alert to any signs which indicate something amiss, whether it be an obvious error or merely the suggestion of the unusual. Thus, for example, the fact that sales in December of the current year are well below sales for December of the preceding year should suggest a problem. How can he account for that difference? To the untrained mind this may be a mere fact to accept. Indeed, it may be so uninteresting that it makes no impression at all. But to the competent auditor, these comparative figures suggest a problem which demands a satisfactory answer.

Having accepted the composite problem of a request for his opinion on financial statements, he next observes or otherwise acquires any pertinent facts available. This requires him to review the internal control, educate himself in industry problems, consult last year's work papers for unusual conditions or personnel changes, discuss the current situation with the management, read the local papers, and generally attempt to gather any information that helps him to size up the situation or evaluate the general problem more carefully.

This accomplished, he proceeds to divide the composite problem into a host of individual problems, each of which is related to the major issue. As has been pointed out elsewhere,[5] financial statements consist of a large number of individual assertions, each of which becomes a problem or proposition to be tested by the auditor. In effect, these individual propositions become hypotheses. Based on the information he has accumulated the auditor takes a tentative position on each assertion. In many cases the most tenable position is that they are a fair presentation. All facts readily available may point to this: a sound system of internal control, including an effective internal audit department, a reputable management with more to lose than to gain by any lack of integrity, a competent accounting department staff, and financial data that are in no way unusual. On the other hand, weak internal control, untested management, an unfortunate local situation in one department or facet of the company's activities, or any one of a number of other symptoms may suggest that some propositions in the financial statements are not acceptable. In any case, as the auditor subdivides the composite problem into its constituent parts, he tends to take a position on each.

---

[5] See Chapter 5, p. 96

With his "hypotheses" developed, the auditor sets out to put them to the test. This he does by selecting the audit techniques that apply to the given proposition and then determining the procedures by which the techniques will actually be applied. In doing this he is guided to a considerable extent by the position he has taken on the propositions themselves. If he feels they are questionable, he is likely to apply more rigorous procedures, select the timing of application more carefully, and extend their application to longer periods or more transactions; if he feels they are satisfactory, he may fall back on a "minimum program." In either case, he does not proceed beyond the state of tentative acceptance or doubt without obtaining evidence directly pertinent to the specific proposition.

Performance of the audit tests supplies the evidence. As evidence is collected the auditor continually evaluates it as to its validity and pertinence and keeps alert to the possibility of additional problems requiring additional evidence. Once the evidence is all in, he then evaluates it in respect to the financial statement propositions. Is it sufficient to permit him to come to a reasoned judgment? If it is not, he must obtain more evidence or refrain from judgment. If it is sufficient, he then arrives at a judgment on each of the individual propositions. With these judgments in hand, he proceeds to consider them all together and to arrive at a judgment on the composite problem of the reliability of the financial statements themselves. This last step is an important one, of course, and must be understood. In many processes of judgment, the preliminary judgments form something of a chain. A failure of any one of these negates the final conclusion. This is not so with an audit judgment. The final audit judgment is not so much like a chain as like a bundle of sticks. If one of them is weak or broken, it weakens the strength of the entire bundle, but it does not necessarily mean the bundle has no strength. Thus the auditor weighs the negative judgments he has made on individual propositions against the positive judgments, considering the relative importance of each one. This leads him to a final all-inclusive judgment.

In this brief description of the methodological procedure of auditing we have stressed the similarities to the scientific method more than the differences. But these are perhaps equally important and require attention too. Some of them are related to the difference in attitude pointed out previously in this chapter but their importance is such that repetition is justified.

Differences Between Scientific Methods and The Auditing Method. The first of these follows from the difference in the two fields with respect to the quality of evidence required. The auditor must frequently be content with something less than the best possible evidence pertinent to a given problem, whereas the scientist can be satisfied only if he is confident that he has conclusive evidence. This difference, as suggested earlier, is explained by differences in the two fields. But in fairness to auditing, it should be pointed out that another factor is also involved. In the long run, scientists insist upon the best possible evidence; in the short tun they may well be satisfied with something less. Thus a scientist faced with a specific problem may solve it to the best of his ability with the time and resources at his disposal, just as an auditor does. However, the scientist, unless he were content that he had obtained final proof, would offer his judgment as tentative only until time and technological resources permitted him to continue his research and obtain the evidence he felt he needed. An auditor always works in the short run. His conclusions are more often tentative then not. It is a rare audit engagement in which there is no limit on either time, staff, or charges. Auditors must live with the hard facts of economics in the conduct of their investigations. This is a part of the environment of auditing that has an important effect on the ultimate validity of audit judgments.

This circumstance adds another judgment to those which the auditor must make. He must decide whether the evidence available to him within the limitations of his engagement is such that he can reach a valid conclusion. If, for example, he were permitted to obtain no evidence at all, there is no question but that he would have to refuse to make a judgment on the fairness of the presentation and could not give a professional opinion no matter what hypothesis he had formed. On a more restricted scale, if he is unable to test receivables by direct correspondence with the debtors, he finds it necessary to refrain from judging the fairness of their presentation unless he can obtain other evidence which he feels is adequate to test his hypothesis about their fairness. If this other evidence were nothing more than an unsupported statement of the validity of receivables made by officials of the company under examination, on the one hand, or a chance remark by an employee implying impropriety, on the other, he could not accept it as satisfactory. If, however, he is able to identify a substantial number of specific remittances with credits to accounts receivable, he may well conclude that this evidence is at least as strong as that obtained by the confirmation procedure.

To a lesser extent this same kind of judgment must be made time and again throughout an audit. Rarely does an auditor apply all possible procedures to any given problem. In most case he satisfies himself with something less than the best *possible* evidence. In this he resembles the applied scientist working in the short run rather than the pure scientist. It should be recognized that there is a danger in this acceptance of evidence less than the best, however necessary it may be. Once one dulls the edge of his skepticism and decides that something less than the best is satisfactory for his purposes, he must constantly be alert to any tendency to do this more and more readily. High standards slip rapidly and seriously if one is careless. To guard against any deleterious tendencies, the auditor, like the applied scientist, must first recognize exactly what he is doing when he accepts less than the best evidence available; second, he must examine the reasons which lead him to do this, whether they be economy, time, or whatever, to make sure they are valid; and third he must be cautious in accepting the conclusions which are reached on the basis of this kind of evidence

A second and more significant difference between the work of an auditor and what has been described as the scientific method has to do with the possibility of controlled experiments. In science, the testing of hypotheses is frequently, but not always, performed through laboratory experiments under which some conditions can be controlled so that the effect of a given factor or factors can be more clearly noted. The advantage of this is not only that the results of the test become more clear; it is also that the same test can be repeated by others, if desired, so that the results of the test can be verified. Because the conditions under which the experiment was performed were controlled, they can be duplicated with sufficient exactitude that, if performed the same way, there is a high degree of probability that they will produce the same results again and again.

This is definitely not true of an audit. Only under the most unusual conditions would an audit be performed twice, and even if it were, the results would not be equivalent to running a laboratory experiment twice. The timing of audit work is of the essence. One cannot test the same inventories with equal effectiveness at two different times. But more than this, so many intangibles work together to influence the judgment of the auditor, and quite properly so, that only by putting oneself in his position *at the time he made his decisions* can one really evaluate the propriety of his judgments. To some extent this explains the difficulty involved in determining whether any given audit was performed in accordance with generally accepted auditing standards. If the malfeasance were extreme, it can readily be judged, of course. But when it is a borderline case, the difficulty of reconstituting the precise conditions and evidence under which and by which the original judgment was reached effectively prevents realistic testing of the decision. This is explained, in the vernacular, as the use of hindsight. Judgments which appeared completely valid at the time they were made sometimes appear far less sound and reasonable when viewed, not so much "in the cold light of morning," as with the benefit of knowledge of changed conditions and additional data.

A third difference between applications of the methodologies of science and auditing is found in the fact that in auditing the basic assumptions or postulates on which the validity of reasoning rests are not at all well stated. This was brought out rather forcefully in the unfortunate Atlas Plywood case in which a question was raised by a prominent periodical with respect to the assumptions of auditing.

> Realizing that two or three executives strategically placed in key positions inside the company can achieve almost anything through the manipulation of facts, what assumptions does the auditor proceed upon in his relationship with management? Are these implicit, only known to the auditor, or well recognized and properly tested?[6]

---

[6] "The Mess at Atlas Plywood," Anonymous, *Fortune Magazine*, January, 1958, p. 118.

In all honesty we must admit that such assumptions are not well recognized, even by auditors, and in this the profession works at a real disadvantage. The importance of assumptions in all fields of intellectual endeavor has already been mentioned. General opinion to the contrary, the necessity for basic assumptions is not a confession of weakness at all. But failure to clearly state and recognize the assumptions underlying one's reasoning *is* a weakness. To a considerable extent, the difficulty encountered by auditing in solving some of its major problems is engendered directly by a failure to state its basic assumptions.

Probability in Science and Auditing. Not clear from the discussion of scientific method in this chapter is another important similarity between applications of the scientific method and the methodology of auditing. This is the degree of reliance on the theory of probability. There is little knowledge in this world that is absolute. To the extent that there exists any room for reasonable doubt at all, the conclusion is a matter of probability only. Thus an untested hypothesis has a lower order of probability than a hypothesis that has been tested, but both are still probabilities — the more severe the test, the greater the weight of accumulated evidence, the higher the degree of probability. Probability can approach certainty, but never quite reach it whether the question be one in science or in auditing.

Science has long used statistical methods and techniques as a useful method of attacking problems which otherwise would be beyond its means.

> The whole process of science actually consists, in part, in this drawing of inferences from the evidence available in a sample, and hence this aspect of probability theory has critical consequences for scientific method.[7]

In recent years, developments in statistical techniques and in their application have so improved the scientist's ability to draw accurate inferences that objections to their use, providing the application is in accordance with accepted principles of statistical inference, are seldom accepted as valid.

---

[7] C. West Churchman, and Russell L. Ackoff, *Methods of Inquiry: An Introduction to Philosophy and Scientific Method* (Saint Louis: Educational Publishers, Inc., First Edition, 1950), p. 370.

> One often hears objections to sampling because of sampling errors. Such objections can be sustained only if, after consideration of the other inaccuracies, the elimination of reduction of the sampling errors seems to be a wise investment. Sampling errors have the favorable characteristics of being controllable through the design of the sample. ... It is now possible to lay out sample designs in many types of surveys whereby one can state in advance the width of a band that will contain 99 per cent or any other per cent of the sampling errors. Sampling errors, even for the small samples, are often the least of the errors present. ... At present, sampling errors are the only errors that are in satisfactory condition, so far as theoretical and experimental knowledge is concerned.[8]

Auditing is like other applications of scientific thinking in its reliance on probability theory. The traditional influence of probability theory in auditing is best exemplified by the use of the term "opinion" in describing the auditor's final over-all judgment with respect to the financial statements examined. It appears also in his employment of tests and samples, a necessary and accepted practice. It seems fair to say that auditing does not rely on tests and samples to any undue extent, certainly no more than do various other fields. But it must be admitted that as yet auditing has not found ways of improving its use of probability theory through statistical applications to the same extent that other fields have. Thus this remains one of the areas in auditing in which additional experiment is necessary.

Let us now consider the procedure used by auditing in the solution of problems not concerned with facts alone. Although the steps in such a procedure are not as apparent, such a procedure does exist and, we think, is generally followed.

Methodological Procedure for Value Judgments. Like a social science, auditing has a variety of problems involving value judgment. These, it will be recalled, appear at two levels. In an examination the practicing auditor faces a number of these problems. The profession, in attempting to define its goals and responsibilities to society, also has value judgment problems.

We will first give our attention to those facing the practitioner on the job. Here again auditing has developed a distinct method

---

[8] William Edwards Deming, *Some Theory of Sampling* (New York: John Wiley & Sons, Inc., 1950), p. 47.

but it is entirely different, as might be expected, from that applied in solving factual problems. It may be described under the following headings:

1. Recognition of the problem.
2. Statement of the problem.
3. Formulation of possible solutions.
4. Evaluation of possible solutions.
    a. By drawing upon past experience with similar problems.
    b. By considering consequences of possible alternatives.
    c. By considering compatibility of possible alternatives with objectives of the profession.
5. Formulation of judgment.

Recognition and statement of the problem require no special attention at this point. Like other auditing problems, they are either apparent in the composite problem presented to the auditor or are suggested to the competent practitioner during the course of his examination.

Once such a problem comes to attention and has been satisfactorily stated, the first step in its solution is to think of all possible acceptable solutions. This is done on the basis of memory and invention. In some cases the auditor will have had identical or similar experiences previously, and solutions proposed at that time will quickly come to mind. In other cases his knowledge of the field and the work of others will suggest possibilities. Sometimes, however, the problem will be such that the auditor has had no experience of a similar nature whatever, nor has he read of similar cases. Under these conditions he has no alternative but to use his knowledge to invent possible solutions. In this he may be aided by the members of the client's accounting department staff who perhaps have already considered several possibilities.

With a number of apparently reasonable solutions before him, he begins a systematic evaluation of each one. First his own experience will tell him what was done in any similar cases with which he is familiar and whether the solution appeared to be accepted by others and worked out satisfactorily. Here he is guided to a considerable extent by custom, both as he knows it personally and as it appears in professional literature. This process of reviewing his experience will permit him, perhaps, to eliminate some of the solutions previously considered acceptable. Next he must consider the probable consequences of the remaining alternatives. If each of them were selected and applied, what is likely to result? Would it be good or bad? In this step, professional experience and knowledge are again critical. This process may permit him to eliminate other possibilities as leading to undesirable results. Finally, he considers the compatibility of the surviving possibilities with the purposes and aims of the profession itself. Do they measure up to the purposes of the profession or are they in some way in conflict with these purposes?

From this brief explanation of the procedure to be followed before making a judgment on a value problem, it should be apparent that broad experience, a perceptive memory, controlled imagination, and a sound understanding of the functions and responsibility of the profession are invaluable aids to the exercise of sound judgment. Conceivably, valid judgments on problems of fact could be arrived at by a practitioner who was little more than a skilled technician. But to arrive at consistently valid judgments on problems of value requires considerably more than technical skill. The successful practitioner here must have not only an acquaintance with but a real understanding of the history of his profession. It is not enough to know a minimum number of facts regarding its genesis and development. He must understand the forces that have played upon it and its reaction to them. For example, periods of business speculation, economic inflation and deflation, and other critical times have tested auditing in different ways. How well has it responded? How well is it responding to the needs of today? To comprehend his subject as fully as he must for real success, a serious effort is required to keep abreast of professional literature, particularly the writings of those who have made significant contributions. But even more is demanded. The successful practitioner must find some time for reflective thinking and for the development of insight and vision. He must have the ability to think in abstract terms so that his mind turns readily to the invention of new treatments and alternatives. Finally, he must have the professional courage not only to critically examine and perhaps discard the proposals of others but to submit his own inventions to the same kind of detached and searching evaluation.

It seems to us that if a man has the ability to deal satisfactorily with value problems in his daily practice, he also has the skill and courage to deal with them at the professional level. Certainly the procedure must be essentially the same. Historical analysis, examination of the logical consequences of alternatives, and careful consideration of compatibility with professional ideals constitute the bases for making valid judgments of this nature at whatever level.

It should be noted, however, that not only are judgments influenced by professional goals and ideals, but these professional ideals may be influenced by important judgments. If a substantial number of auditors were to make judgments which are incompatible with professional ideals, then it would be apparent that either the judgments were in error or a revision of the ideals was in order. Professional ideals are an evolving sort of goal; they tend to develop in response to the social needs of the times. These ideals should be jealously guarded and continuously improved. This requires the exercise of proper judgment by individual members as well as by the profession at large.

Chapter 3

The Postulates of Auditing

The preceding chapter has pointed out the importance of postulates in all fields and the fact that they are not clearly stated, or perhaps even recognized as existing, in auditing. The purpose of this chapter is to inquire further into the nature of postulates generally, to submit a statement of what we conceive the postulates of auditing to be, and to inquire briefly into the meaning of the suggested postulates. Subsequent chapters will investigate the implications of these postulates in some detail.

The Nature of Postulates. From the writings of logicians and philosophers, we can determine five general characteristics of postulates which are helpful to our understanding of them and their function. Postulates are:

1. Essential to development of any intellectual discipline.
2. Assumptions that do not lend themselves to direct verification.
3. A basis for inference.
4. A foundation for erection of any theoretical structure.
5. Susceptible to challenge in the light of later advancement of knowledge.

"Every demonstrative science," says Aristotle, "most start from indemonstrable principles, otherwise, the steps of demonstration would be endless."[1] In this brief sentence we find the reason for postulates. We cannot start reasoning or thinking without a starting point. We can "prove" nothing to the man who will accept nothing as a basis for discussion. This is true whether we are trying to satisfy ourselves or someone else. Postulates necessarily occupy the cornerstone position in any edifice of theory. It is not that they are such obvious truths that we do not doubt them, although this may be the case. It is more important that we just must have them, true or not, for without them we can establish nothing further.

---

[1] The Thirteen Books of Euclid's Elements, Translated by Sir Thomas L. Heath, Vol. I, Second Edition, New York, Dover Publications, Inc., 1956, p. 119.

Postulates are assumptions that do not lend themselves to direct verification. The propositions deduced from the postulates of a given system, however, can be directly verified and such verification bears evidence of the truth of the postulates themselves.

The first difficulty of directly verifying postulates is that they are at bedrock. Since they are the fundamentals in our structure of theory, there is nothing beneath them on which they rest and by which they can be demonstrated. Second, if they were directly verifiable they could be made to serve as hypotheses, and evidence could be marshalled to support or invalidate them. However, with the resources at our disposal we must accept these *a priori*, and we find that to do so is entirely satisfactory for our purposes.

This does not mean that postulates have no foundation in fact or truth. Some logicians have contended that postulates must be apparent truths; that is, they should be the kind of proposition we can accept without question. The difficulty with this point of view is that what so often appears unquestionably valid at one point in time can be demonstrated to be quite invalid at another. Churchman points out two additional requirements of a set of postulates that help us to see their reliability and usefulness in a theoretical structure.[2] First, they must be consistent with one another; we cannot have postulates that are in conflict, for we can build no sound structure upon contradictions. This requirement by itself insures that they will contain some measure of truth. Second, he contends that they must be sufficient to support or prove all the terms and theorems of the system for which they are the foundation. Although this last requirement says nothing about truth value in itself, it inherently demands truth. A structure built upon sand cannot endure. Theories founded upon inappropriate postulates will soon be discovered to be inconsistent, both with one another and with the facts of the real world. Thus the reasonableness of the theorems supported by the postulates becomes the ultimate test of the postulates themselves. As we find them satisfactory for the purpose for which they were

---

[2] C. West Churchman, *Elements of Logic and Formal Science*, New York: J. B. Lippincott & Co., 1940, pp. 10-11.

intended, we gain confidence in the postulates. If the structure is strong, its foundation must be sound.

This idea is expressed in the following quotation:

> Beside the common notions there are a few things which I must assume without proof, but which differ from the common notions in that they are not self-evident. The learner may or may not be disposed to agree to them, but he must accept them at the outset on the superior authority of his teacher, and must be left to convince himself of their truth in the course of the investigation which follows.[3]

Thus the success with which the postulates, at first accepted as tentative, undemonstrable propositions, satisfy the needs of the field of study for which they are proposed is the best test of their usefulness.

In this fact we find the clue to the next two important features of postulates. They provide the basis for making inferences which are valid and useful to the extent that the postulates themselves satisfy the needs of the particular discipline. Once we accept the postulates we can draw propositions from them. They provide a basis for thinking about problems and for arriving at solutions. We now have a starting point.

If we can reason deductively from these postulates, we can also trace all our conclusions back to them and test such conclusions, partly at least, on the basis of their compatibility with the basic assumptions. Thus postulates provide the framework for developing and testing theory. If the postulates are consistent and sufficient and if the inferences drawn from them follow the rules of logic and reason, the results should be consistent and satisfactory. Conclusions which cannot be traced back to the basic assumptions or are incompatible with them have no standing.

Finally, it must be emphasized, the postulates, once accepted as useful and valid, may at a later date be challenged and even demonstrated to be invalid. As noted earlier, postulates cannot be directly verified. Neither can they be proved untrue, or they would have no usefulness. That means that when a postulate can be proved untrue, it has lost its value as a postulate and must be discarded. Scientists and logicians alike are emphatic

[3]The Thirteen Books of Euclid's Elements, *op. cit.*, p. 124.

in their contention that we must continually review our postulates to see if, in the light of new evidence, they have become invalid. This suggests the importance of explicitly stating the postulates on which our conclusions are based. Hidden assumptions cannot be scrutinized or tested; their validity cannot be challenged. Unless we recognize clearly the nature and significance of the assumptions on which our theory rests and from time to time examine them carefully, we cannot have any real assurance that our theories and the conclusions to which we have been guided by that theory are sound. This is particularly true in applied fields such as accounting and auditing. Thus Paton writes of accounting:

> Impressed by the neatly ruled lines and the array of equal footings exhibited by the typical system of accounts and financial statements, the layman is likely to conclude that accounting deals with certainties, with data capable of exact and precise statement; that accounts are either accurate or inaccurate; that the principles and procedures of double entry, if applied without clerical error, will always lead to correct conclusions. Indeed, the accountant at times may be found slipping, somewhat unconsciously, into the same misapprehension.... It is believed that accountants are sometimes in danger of forgetting their own premises and, therefore, the limitations of their work. If the accountant sees clearly the foundation upon which he is standing, with all its implications, he is less likely to fall into the mire of improper applications and erroneous general conclusions....[4]

Paton goes on to say:

> The accountant should be thoroughly aware of his assumptions, however, else he is likely to forget the inherent limitations attaching to his exhibits and conclusions.[5]

Various efforts have been made to state the basic assumptions or postulates of accounting,[6] although to this date there

---

[4] W. A. Paton, *Accounting Theory* (New York: The Ronald Press Company, 1922), pp. 471-472.

[5] *Ibid.*, p. 499.

[6] See for instance: 1. W. A. Paton, & A. C. Littleton, *An Introduction to Corporate Accounting Standards* (The American Accounting Association: 1940), Chapter 2, 2. Thomas A. Sanders, *Contemporary Accounting* (New York: The American Institute of Accountants, 1940), Chapter 1, 3. Committee on Accounting Concepts and Standards, 1957 Revision "Underlying Concepts," *The Accounting Review*, October, 1957, pp. 536-537.

has been no general acceptance of any single such statement, but little effort has been made to list the basic assumptions of auditing. Before attempting to do this, it may be helpful to illustrate the characteristics of postulates noted in these paragraphs by means of a simple example.

A basic assumption of accounting, although not one included in every list of such assumptions, is the following: Financial transactions and conditions can be meaningfully stated in terms of monetary quantities. This is one of the starting points of any work with accounting, whether it be theoretical or practical. Without such an assumption there would be no entries, no debit and credit analysis as we know it, no records, no accounts. Release this assumption and accounting as we know it would be unsupportable. This is one of those propositions that the novice probably never thinks to question because he does not recognize its existence. If he did question it, his teacher would have some difficulty in establishing its validity except by pointing out that work based upon this assumption has proved useful and satisfactory.

That such an assumption is a basis for deductions is evident from the fact that financial statements, cost control procedures, income tax payments, and many other practices are based on it. We could not for a minute justify the payment of federal income taxes under our present laws if we did not feel that the monetary quantities stated in the accounts and tax returns presented with some meaning the transactions and conditions they purport to present.

It seems equally clear that this is but one of a series of interrelated assumptions. Certainly it is insufficient by itself to support the entire structure of accounting theory and practice with which we are familiar. Finally, we must face the possibility of the invalidity of this assumption. At times in the history of other countries, rapid and catastrophic changes in the value of the monetary unit have made accounting data largely useless for the purposes for which we commonly use them today. There are many who feel that the degree of inflation experienced in this country over the last twenty years has seriously decreased the usefulness of financial statements and reports. They feel it is time to scrutinize this postulate carefully.

Thus this postulate is an indirectly verifiable assumption, essential to the development of accounting. It provides a basis for drawing inferences with respect to accumulating and presenting financial data; and, if joined with similar postulates to make a "system," it would provide a basis for developing a theory of accounting. Finally it may later be found invalid; if so it would lose its status as a postulate.

The Postulates of Auditing. Although considerable attention has been given to stating the postulates of accounting and we are assured that more will be given in the very near future,[7] we find little on the postulates of auditing. It seems clear that such postulates do exist, otherwise we could not reason or come to conclusions in auditing. It is also obvious that we will be well advised to set forth our postulates so clearly and unequivocally that they are visible and available to all. We should want them scrutinized and examined critically; we should want their validity tested. Surely we want no hidden assumptions in auditing. Only by parading the postulates of auditing for all to see and criticize have we any assurance that they are appropriate and valid for our purposes as auditors. Those who found the Atlas Plywood Case an opportunity for raising some rather embarrassing questions about auditing in general would not have been in such a strong position if we had a clear, well-supported statement of our postulates from which to examine the conclusions reached by the auditors whose work aroused comment.

It might well be asked, how does one go about establishing a system of postulates for auditing? The postulates which we offer here were devised after careful study of the nature and activities of auditing. They were then carefully explored to determine their implications, completeness, and consistency, as will be apparent in the remaining chapters of this work. Some of those originally considered to be acceptable assumptions were found to conflict with others. Some were found to be unnecessary because a more

---

[7] The study of the "Basic Postulates and Broad Principles of Accounting" is one of the research projects announced by the Accounting Research Division of the American Institute of Certified Public Accountants. See "Official Releases—Announcement of Research Projects," *The Journal of Accountancy*, April, 1960, p. 73.

complete understanding of others indicated that they were sufficient to cover the field. Finally, as bit by bit we built up the framework of theory that follows, we found the need for additions as well as deletions. The postulates we offer now are those we arrived at through our own best judgment after considerable thought and experiment. At this time, we feel that they are *the* postulates of auditing, that they provide the foundations we need to develop a logical, integrated theory of auditing. Nevertheless, we must regard them as tentative. They may be found invalid and others may seem necessary. Of one conclusion we do feel certain. Some similar statement of postulates is essential if auditing is to have stature as an intellectual discipline, if it is to solve its problems, and if it is to weather the attacks of critics both within and without the profession.

TENTATIVE POSTULATES OF AUDITING

1. Financial statements and financial data are verifiable.
2. There is no necessary conflict of interest between the auditor and the management of the enterprise under audit.
3. The financial statements and other information submitted for verification are free from collusive and other unusual irregularities.
4. The existence of a satisfactory system of internal control eliminates the *probability* of irregularities.
5. Consistent application of generally accepted principles of accounting results in the fair presentation of financial position and the results of operations.
6. In the absence of clear evidence to the contrary, what has held true in the past for the enterprise under examination will hold true in the future.
7. When examining financial data for the purpose of expressing an independent opinion thereon, the auditor acts exclusively in the capacity of an auditor.
8. The professional status of the independent auditor imposes commensurate professional obligations.

On first reading, there is very little in these propositions of an unusual or provocative nature. Nevertheless, some readers may have difficulty in accepting one or more as fundamental assumptions in auditing. At this point all we can do is ask that they be accepted provisionally with whatever reservations the reader finds appropriate. We shall use them as the basis for deductions with respect to auditing theory and to integrate the entire body of theory which we feel is implicit in the practice of auditing. To the extent that these postulates are not valid, the resulting theory becomes suspect; to the extent the theory is unreasonable, either the postulates or the reasoning by which the theory was developed must be viewed with distrust.

First, however, it is desirable to give some little attention to an explanation of each postulate as some justification for their selection.

Financial Data Are Verifiable. The importance of this assumption is at once apparent. Unless financial data are verifiable, auditing has no reason for existence. If we release this assumption, we do away with the very subject of auditing.

To some, the term "verifiable" has unfortunate implications. Essential to the existence of auditing as this postulate obviously is, there are some who will take exception to it. They feel that verification implies proof beyond all doubt. Here again we fall back on philosophy and probability theory. There are very few absolute facts in this life and even fewer in the field of business data with which auditors are concerned. At this early point, however, it is not necessary to satisfy those who view the term with suspicion. Whatever word is selected to carry the connotation of "auditable," there must be something that auditors do to give them a basis for expressing an opinion on the reliability of the financial statements they examine. Later sections will develop the meaning of the term "verifiable" as we have used it here. Provisional acceptance of this term as well as others appearing in the postulates is all that is expected now.

In philosophy, verifiability is of the essence of logical statements. A proposition is neither meaningful nor useful until we have an idea of its verifiability. "In order to know what a statement means, we must know how to verify it; we must know what operations we would have to go through in order to determine its truth or falsity."[8] In much the same way, the propositions in financial statements and reports cannot be accepted as having real meaning until steps have been taken to indicate their verifiability. In the business world, this act of verification is the task of auditors, both internal and external. This philosophical truth about the necessity of verification is so well accepted that the business world has adopted a general practice of submitting such propositions to a verification process before they are given any serious consideration for many purposes. This verification takes many forms; sometimes it is the continuous examination of procedures and data performed by an internal auditing staff, sometimes the annual examination of an independent auditor, sometimes the investigation of an Internal Revenue Agent. Whatever the form the importance and fact of verification are well accepted.

Verification is the vehicle that carries one to a position of confidence about any given proposition. Such confidence may be positive or negative; that is, there may be assurance supplied by the verification procedure that the proposition is right or wrong, but the confidence cannot be blind. There must be evidence to support it, sufficient reason, sufficient "competent evidential matter." Otherwise the fancied assurance is nothing more than folly.

Thus the postulate that "financial statements and financial data are verifiable" is the basis upon which we develop our theory of evidence and proof. This will lead us into a study of the ways of attaining knowledge or truth, the subject with which logic is concerned. But is will require that we pay heed to factors other than the basic theory of proof found in logic. We must also look into the application of these methods of proof, or ways of knowing, to the subject matter of auditing. In familiar terms, this is audit program planning. To develop a foundation for program planning we must turn our attention to the techniques of auditing, their nature and limitations, and investigate their relationship to the ways of knowing accepted by logicians.

This in turn directs our attention to the responsibilities which an auditor can appropriately accept for the "truthfulness" of the data he has examined, the meaning of his "opinion." Also closely

---

[8] John Hospers, *An Introduction to Philosophical Analysis* (Englewood Cliffs, N.J.: Prentice Hall, Inc., 1957), p. 195.

related to the subject of verification and the proof of financial statement propositions is probability theory and the subject of statistical sampling.

Thus, based on this single postulate, we find (1) the theory of evidence, (2) the procedure of verification, (3) the application of probability theory in auditing, and (4) some establishment of the bounds of the auditor's responsibilities.

No Necessary Conflict of Interest Between Auditor and Management. The general reasonableness of this postulate seems apparent. Management is concerned with the progress and prosperity of the enterprise it directs; auditors perform a service which is intended to benefit the various interests in the enterprise by providing some degree of assurance as to the reliability of the financial data essential to various important decisions. Surely these are compatible purposes. Indeed, management is one of the interests that should benefit by the availability of verified rather than unverified information about the enterprise. Hence there is a substantial mutuality of interest and it is reasonable to assume that there is no conflict between auditor and management.

Yet there could well be conflict in the short run. Under certain conditions a given management might feel that deceiving the auditor would be to the immediate benefit of the enterprise, or perhaps at least to the management itself. Perhaps the enterprise desperately needs credit, or the management has a bonus arrangement contingent on the amount of income. Perhaps there are reasons why management would feel that its own immediate interests were opposed to the auditor's goal of determining and revealing the fairness of the financial statement data which basically are the representations of the management.

An auditor must be aware of these possibilities. Although there usually exists so substantial a mutuality of interest that a conflict between management and independent auditor seems unlikely this mutuality of interest may fail in specific instances. The independent auditor must be fully aware of such contingencies.

To pursue this further, let us consider the result of releasing this particular assumption. What happens to auditing if we assume that management and auditors are necessarily in conflict? Ignoring, for the moment, that from a practical standpoint an audit without the co-operation of management becomes virtually an impossibility, we can only conclude that an audit based on the assumption that management and auditor were in conflict would require an extremely extensive and detailed examination. No management responses to questions or representations could be given any credence whatever. It is doubtful whether the statements of employees, who must be considered to be under management control, could be accepted as in any way useful. Certainly the records and documents under management control would be regarded as completely unreliable. We are left with a situation in which the auditor must first attempt to ferret out the transactions that took place, then prepare a set of records and accounts, and finally make his examination. But by the time he had performed the first two steps he would be disqualified as an auditor.

Thus the essential nature of this postulate becomes apparent. We must assume, regardless of the rare cases in which management's immediate interests might be opposed, that generally there is no conflict between the auditor and the management of the enterprise under examination. At the same time we must face the fact of occasional direct conflict. Hence we postulate no *necessary* conflict as the assumption on which we can most reasonably develop auditing theory.

Based on this assumption we may deduce corollary propositions, for example, that management acts rationally in acquiring assets, in directing the affairs of the enterprise, and in making commitments. Unless there is evidence to the contrary we assume that management is honest and not involved in fraudulent activities. To those who point out that these assumptions do not always apply we must inquire as to the results if such assumptions are entirely released. Can we proceed under the assumption that there necessarily *is* a conflict of interests between management and independent auditor? If auditing is to be economically and operationally feasible, such assumptions as these are essential.

Of course this does not mean we never view the assertions of management with any degree of suspicion. We assume only no *necessary* conflict, not the impossibility of conflict. The experienced auditor, although he accepts the assumptions in the preceding paragraph and plans his work accordingly, never closes his mind to the possibility that in any given instance they may be false. He remains alert to an indication that in the present engagement management has acted irrationally or with intent to defraud. Here is one of the most difficult areas of auditor responsibility. Without a clear statement of the basic assumptions on which an audit is performed, satisfactory definition of the auditor's responsibility is most unlikely. More attention is given to this subject in a later chapter.

Involved in the management-auditor relationship implied in this postulate is the question of allegiance. To whom does the auditor owe his primary allegiance? Is it to the management of the enterprise under examination, its shareholders, readers of the financial statements to which his opinion will be attached, or does he perhaps have responsibilities to society at large to perform a protective function required by the type of economy which he serves? Several areas for inquiry and investigation appear to be related to this postulate.

Freedom from Collusive and Otherwise Unusual Irregularities. Release of the assumption that financial statements are free of unusual irregularities places the auditor in a position at least as difficult as we found him when we released the postulate discussed in the preceding section. If we assume that the data under examination do include irregularities resulting from extensive collusion and of the most unusual nature, we must design an audit program far beyond anything now considered necessary. In fact, there is some question whether any type of examination could be designed that would give even a reasonable assurance that all such irregularities would be discovered.

Let us anticipate the later discussion of the auditor's responsibility for the discovery of irregularities by pointing out that this assumption in itself does not relieve him of all accountability for the discovery of unusual or collusive irregularities. If, for example, an irregularity brought about through collusion was so apparent that the auditor should discover it without difficulty through the application of ordinary tests designed to discover non-collusive irregularities, he should not be excused if his examination is so deficient as not to disclose it. The degree of care required of auditors must be further explored before this and similar questions can be settled; thus, this postulate leads us directly to the discussion of a concept of due audit care. For now, it is enough to point out that the auditor's responsibility for the discovery of irregularities is based largely on this postulate although it must be modified to some extent by others as well.

Internal Control Eliminates the Probability of Irregularities. Almost every treatment of the subject of auditing points out that the extent of an audit program depends on the extent of the internal control in the given situation. This well-accepted idea is based on the assumption stated here, that the existence of a good system of internal control eliminates the *probability* of irregularities. It should be noted that the term "probability" rather than "possibility" is used. It is doubtful that the possibility of irregularities can ever be eliminated, although of course it can be reduced. Likewise, the term "eliminated" is used because that is exactly what the assumption means. But note it is the probability of irregularities that is eliminated, not irregularities themselves. Irregularities are still possible under good internal control, but they are no longer probable. On the other hand, if the internal control is not satisfactory, then errors and irregularities must be considered something more than merely possible.

If we release this assumption we are faced with a situation in which errors and irregularities are always probable, an impossible situation in which to perform any reasonable audit service. Such a condition would require either complete disclaimer for the discovery of irregularities or an extremely detailed and tedious examination, and even with the latter some disclaimer of responsibility would still be required.

Recognition of this postulate helps to emphasize the importance of internal control to the auditor and also the nature of his interest in it. On the basis provided by this postulate, we must deduce the extent of the auditor's interest in internal control, the nature of his review thereof, the influence which internal control has on his examination, and the responsibility he should take for the improvement of the internal control system, for disclosing weaknesses in it, and for the discovery of irregularities permitted by the system in effect. This introduction of internal control, which is basic to the auditor's performance of his function, gives this postulate independent status.

Generally Accepted Principles of Accounting and Fair Presentation. To judge the fairness of financial statement presentations, auditors must have some standard. This is provided by generally accepted accounting principles. As pointed out in Chapter 1, auditing and accounting are separate although related fields. Auditing borrows from accounting the latter's generally accepted principles and uses them as a standard for judging the propriety of the financial data submitted for examination. Just as auditing borrows from statistics certain ideas about sampling, it goes to accounting for its ideas about the presentation of financial data in reports and statements.

Release of this assumption would leave auditing no standard for judging the fairness with which financial position and the results of operations are presented in financial statements. With no generally accepted guide, auditors' opinions would become so personal as to be of little value to anyone.

We must recognize, of course, that many auditors also act as accountants, and that as accountants they may have had a hand in developing the generally accepted principles of accounting they now use as a guide in auditing. Nevertheless, there is a clear line between auditing and accounting activities; acting as an auditor, one uses a ready-made standard. He does not create one of his own. From this postulate we can deduce the function of the auditor with respect to the development and application of generally accepted auditing principles. Just as the scientist must recognize the nature of the things he works with and their limitations, the auditor must similarly understand the characteristics of generally accepted accounting principles. Another closely related question has to do with the auditor's responsibility when these principles are deficient or even absent.

Perhaps none of the suggested postulates are accepted in practice with greater reservations than this one. Because we do not yet have a satisfactory statement of generally accepted accounting principles, because there are sharp differences of opinion about the desirability of certain of the practices we now choose to call "principles," and because of dissimilarities between industries, as well as for other reasons, auditors, as auditors, do not accept the principles they have developed as accountants nearly so fully as they might. This will give us further concern in our discussion of a concept of fair presentation in Chapter 7. Although the postulate is now accepted only with substantial reservations we feel it should be included in the scheme, first, because it already has real force; second, it can be expected to have greater strength as research into the principles area continues; and, third, because release of this assumption would deprive independent auditors of any standard of fairness whatever.

That Which Held True in the Past Will Hold in the Future. Unless the auditor can assume that what has held true in the past will hold true in the future for the enterprise under examination, barring any clear indications to the contrary, he has no basis for accepting or rejecting such assertions as the valuation of receivables and inventories, the economic usefulness of fixed assets, or the adequacy of internal control. This is the continuity or going concern concept of accounting, of course, but it contributes something more. It provides a guide to the auditor in the performance of all his verification work and is thus a protection against economic and business changes unforeseeable at the time of the verification.

If he finds a management that consistently tends to overstate certain assets and perhaps understate others, he is obligated to take this into account in performing his examination. If management has acted rationally in the past in acquiring plant assets or in its advertising expenditures, he can safely assume that it will do so in the future. If fixed assets were purchased to facilitate a certain type of activity which has been conducted according to plan, the auditor, in the absence of contrary evidence, can expect the activity to continue and the assets to be so used. Again, if in the past internal control has been found deficient and certain assets have been susceptible to conversion to the personal gain of employees, the auditor must be on guard against this same type of irregularity in succeeding engagements.

Thus, like any other of the postulates, its release makes auditing improbable, if not impossible. Acceptance of this postulate places important limits on the extent of an auditor's responsibilities and provides a basis for deducing the extent of his obligation to forecast the future and to have his work judged on the basis of hindsight.

An Auditor Acts Exclusively as an Auditor. Although an independent accountant may serve his clients in a considerable variety of ways, once he has commenced an audit examination, he must act exclusively in the role of an auditor while performing the examination. This is somewhat similar to the position of a lawyer who is available to clients for a number of different services. Once he accepts a retainer to represent a given client, however, he has accepted certain responsibilities that prevent him from acting as freely as he otherwise might. He cannot, for example, represent simultaneously two clients with conflicting interests. He has an obligation to represent his client as effectively and energetically as possible and to permit no conflicting interest to interfere.

An auditor has a similar type of responsibility. Although textbooks take pains to point out the variety of ways in which an independent accountant can serve his client while performing an audit, these services must be regarded as of secondary importance; if they interfere in any way with the appropriate discharge of the accountant's duties as an auditor, they must be considered to be downright harmful.

The major point at issue with respect to this postulate is the auditor's independence. Independence is of the essence in auditing. It follows from this postulate that anything that tends to infringe upon independence must be viewed with serious concern. Important as independence is, however, there is even more involved in this assumption. The auditor, like any professional man, has a responsibility to the society that recognizes and encourages his professional status as well as to the clients he serves directly. It behooves us, therefore, to give some attention to this responsibility. What is the social function of the auditor? What responsibilities flow from it?

Professional Status Imposes Commensurate Obligations. Auditors have long claimed professional status and with increasing public recognition of this status, they have accepted more and more professional obligations. To a considerable extent, the auditing standards currently recognized by the profession reflect the profession's acceptance of such responsibilities. Thus it appears there will be little objection to the eighth and last of our proposed postulates.

Although it may cause little objection, like the other postulates it has not been clearly stated or subjected to scrutiny. As a postulate it occupies an important place in our scheme. Together with Number 7, which requires exclusive attention to auditing during an examination, it provides the basis on which we determine the auditor's responsibility to society, to his client, and to fellow auditors. On this postulate rests the professional concept of due care, the requirement of service before personal interest, and the standard of professional efficiency. It is hoped that the importance of this postulate in the theory of auditing will become apparent as we investigate its implications in later chapters.

The Postulates as a Group. Even this brief introduction to the eight postulates proposed here indicates rather clearly that they are not self-sufficient nor mutually exclusive. On the contrary, some important inter-relationships are readily apparent. Almost every one, for example, has a direct bearing on the auditor's responsibilities, although some are more restricted in this respect than are others. This characteristic of interrelatedness has implications for the organization of the rest of this study. We cannot, for example, study the implications of these postulates one by one because we would inevitably be drawn away from one into others which are concerned with the same subject. Thus we find it most useful to attack the problem area by area (theory of evidence, extent of appropriate services, responsibility for detection of irregularities, nature of due care, and independence) referring back to whichever postulate supports the point at issue.

It seems equally clear at this time that none of the proposed postulates are in conflict with one another; at least there are no apparent contradictions. Caution is required, however, in reaching such a conclusion so early in the investigation. It may be that further analysis and study of the implications of these postulates will lead us to conclusions that do appear to be in conflict. Throughout the study we must continually be alert to this possibility. If a real conflict is discovered, it immediately casts doubt on the validity of the postulates themselves.

Requirements of Postulates. With these tentative postulates of auditing in mind, we should examine further the nature and characteristics of postulates generally. A useful approach is to consider the requirements of a postulate. Here we are indebted to Susanne K. Langer for a concise and lucid statement of the essentials.

> All we ask of a postulate is, (1) that it shall belong to the system, i.e., be expressible entirely in the language of the system; (2) that it shall imply further propositions of the system; (3) that it shall not contradict any other accepted postulate, or any proposition implied by such another postulate; and (4) it shall not itself be implied by other accepted postulates, jointly or singly taken.
>
> The first of these characteristics is known as *coherence*. Every proposition in the system must cohere, in conceptual structure, with the rest.
>
> The second is *contributiveness*. If a postulate has no implications, it contributes nothing beyond the explicit fact which it states. This is, of course, perfectly permissible, but a system which contains such assumptions is not entirely deductive, and where no deduction is intended we do not class propositions as "postulates," to be distinguished from "theorems." The word "postulate" is ordinarily applied to *premises for deduction*. Contributiveness, therefore, is an important criterion of a good postulate; in fact, if we have two propositions one of which is to be taken for granted, the greater contributiveness of one as against the other may be the deciding factor in a choice between them.
>
> The third requirement is the most important; that is *consistency*. Two propositions which contradict each other, i.e., which cannot both be true, can never be admitted to the same system. Anything that is inconsistent is logically impossible. Incoherence is a grave fault, but often we can ignore the elements which are *meaningless* and still trace systematic connections under a mass of irrelevant concepts; non-contributiveness, or barrenness, is a serious blemish and spoils the deductive character of a system, but does not ruin its validity; but inconsistency is a fatal condition. Where this fault is tolerated there is simply no logic at all.
>
> The fourth criterion is termed *independence*. If a proposition is deductible from one of the postulates already given, then it is a theorem, a necessary fact, not another assumption. The fact that we "assume" rather than "prove" it to ourselves is a purely psychological circumstance which has no bearing on the logical status of a proposition; if it *might* be proved it is a theorem, and to regard it as

> a postulate is simply an error. Fortunately this error is not serious, since deductions made from a theorem are exactly as good as those made from a postulate; if we regard a theorem as a postulate and think ourselves to have one more arbitrary assumption than in fact we have, then we merely do not know how nice our system is.[9]

If the postulates proposed in this chapter are tested against these requirements, they will be found to meet these established tests. Of course this may not be apparent at first reading, but if one follows through the remaining chapters he will find that they are coherent, contributive, consistent, and independent. Part of the reader's obligation to himself, of course, is to seek satisfaction on this point.

A final word with respect to the usefulness of these postulates seems in order. We have already tried to emphasize their usefulness to auditors, both in developing and integrated body of theory and in meeting practical professional problems. Their usefulness to those who use the services of auditors and who are charged with evaluating their work appears equally evident. Establishment and general acceptance by the profession of a series of basic assumptions, together with the inferences logically drawn from these assumptions, should go a long way toward dispelling some of the misconceptions generally held about auditing, auditors, and their responsibilities.

---

[9] Susanne K. Langer, *An Introduction to Symbolic Logic*, Second Edition (Revised) (New York: Dover Publications, Inc., 1953), pp. 185-186.

Chapter 4

Concepts in Auditing Theory

In any complete structure of theory, concepts must occupy a key position. Whether the task is to organize an area of knowledge in which considerable progress has already been made or to develop a new field from scant beginnings, concepts are of great importance. In the organization of a fully developed field they provide the framework for the remainder of the structure. Concepts generally appear gradually, evolving from crude descriptions into full-fledged generalizations. Their initial appearance marks the commencement of intellectual awareness in the given field; refinement and rigorous re-examination of established concepts indicates a considerable degree of intellectual maturity. Since a study of some of the more important individual concepts of auditing makes up most of the remainder of this monograph, it is important that we give some attention to the nature of concepts, their usefulness, development, and variety, and to our reasons for emphasizing them.

Nature of Concepts. The Encyclopaedia Britannica gives two definitions of the term "concept":

> Concept...in philosophy, a term applied to a general idea derived from and *considered apart from* the particulars observed by the senses.... By the comparison, for instance, of a number of boats, the mind abstracts a certain common quality or qualities in virtue of which the mind forms the general idea of "boat." Thus the connotation of the term "boat," being the sum of essential qualities in respect of which all boats are regarded as alike, *whatever their individual peculiarities may be*, is described as a "concept." The mental process by which a concept is affirmed is called "conception," a term which is often loosely used in a concrete sense for "concept" itself.... Strictly, however, "conception" is contrasted with "perception," and implies the mental reconstruction and combination of sense-given data....
>
> ...When one carries one's thoughts back to a series of events, one constructs mentally a whole made up of parts which take definite shape and character by their mutual interrelations. This process is called *conceptual synthesis*, the possibility of

> which is the *sine qua non* for the exchange by speech and writing. It should be noted that this very common psychological interpretation of "conception" differs from the metaphysical or general philosophical definition given above, in so far as it includes mental presentations in which the universal is not specifically distinguished from the particulars.[1]

Concepts are thus abstracted forms derived from observation and experience, generalized ideas which help us to see similarities and differences and to understand better the subject matter in question. Without concepts, the field of study remains but a mass of unrelated observations. It is in the process of drawing generalizations out of a mass of observations or perceptions that conceptual thinking makes a contribution to the organization of any field of knowledge.

Science has been particularly successful in its use of concepts to simplify and generalize within its various fields of interest. The following statement is indicative:

> Scientists proceed by abstracting more and more fundamental forms (often seeing similarities among the abstracted forms, or concepts, themselves, and thus gathering several concepts into one); and by finding more and more things that fall under certain concepts, i.e., that inhibit certain general forms.[2]

As an illustration of a concept in science, we may take "oscillation."

> Consider for instance how many motions follow the general pattern called "oscillation." The swing of a pendulum, the swaying of a skyscraper, the vibration of a violin string over which the bow is passing, the chatter of our teeth on a cold day—all these are examples of the type-form called "oscillation." Now, if we were to define this type-form, we would omit all reference to skyscrapers and fiddle-strings and teeth, and describe it, probably, as "rhythmic motion to and fro," or in some such terms that would connote only the sort of motion we are talking about and *not* the sort of thing that moves.... The motions [of the above mentioned objects] are certainly not alike in appearance, origin, or purpose. But their motions have the common property of going rhythmically to and fro. This property is

---

[1] *Encyclopaedia Britannica*, Chicago, London, Toronto: Encyclopaedia Britannica, Inc., 1954, Vol. 6, p. 196.

[2] Langer, *op. cit.*, pp. 36-37.

> the *logical form* of their motions, and so we may call all these motions diverse instances of the same form.[3]

Thus the concept, oscillation, is drawn from, or generalized on the basis of, a number of observations which do not seem particularly related until some alert mind sees the similarity in the several different motions observed.

Concepts provide a basis for advancement in the field of knowledge by facilitating communication about it and its problems; without agreement upon concepts communication is impossible.

> It is impossible for me to make a sensation pass from my consciousness to another; ...all intellectual communication between men is an exchange of concepts. The concept is essentially impersonal representation; it is through it that human intelligences communicate.[4]

Discussions of oscillation, truth, virtue, or independence are impossible among men unless concepts of these are first established and given some degree of acceptance. This does not mean that universal acceptance of a concept in total is necessary, merely that there be agreement on essentials. However, development of universally acceptable concepts is the ideal.

In addition to permitting communication and discussion on an intellectual level, concepts also provide the core around which the accumulating knowledge in a new area can be organized.

> In fact, a few powerful concepts can systematize, or perhaps revolutionize, a whole field of observation, experiment, and hypothesis, called a "science."[5]

It is in this sense that concepts form the framework around which the structure of theory is organized and on which it depends for progress and improvement. Writers on auditing and accounting, as in other fields, frequently express themselves in favor of the systematization of these fields of knowl-

---

[3] *Ibid.*, pp. 35-36.

[4] Earle Edward Eubank, *The Concepts of Sociology* (New York: D. C. Heath and Company, 1932), p. 29.

[5] Langer, *op. cit.*, p. 35.

edge. Various attempts at statements of principles and standards are indications of the desire for such systematization. Such a laudable desire is not likely to be fulfilled, however, until we determine first what we mean by organization and second whether accounting and auditing are sufficiently well developed to permit the degree of organization we wish.

Some of the older fields of knowledge have developed their theory far more completely and thus find it possible to attain a greater degree of systematization than do youthful disciplines still concerned with basic ideas. Until its implicit assumptions are identified and subjected to study and at least its most basic concepts developed, no field can hope for much systematization of its knowledge. As a maturing discipline, auditing should strive for organization and ordering of its knowledge, and there is much that can be done to make progress in this direction. The essence of systematized knowledge lies in the formation of concepts and the organization of knowledge around them. Auditing is in the process of refining certain basic concepts; to the extent that these can be formulated with some degree of specificity and then obtain acceptance, an important step toward the ultimate organization of its theory will have been made.

Some consideration of the way in which concepts emerge in a new and growing subject will at once help us to understand their nature and purpose more fully and to comprehend the significance of the conceptual approach followed in the remaining chapters.

The Development of Concepts. The complete development of a concept involves a number of stages. For our purposes, we may reduce them to four:

1. The observation of facts related to the given field of activity.
2. The formulation of generalizations based on the observed facts.
3. Interrelating of these generalizations to eliminate duplications, inconsistencies, and omissions.
4. Re-examination and scrutiny of generalizations for continuing usefulness.

Before commencing a discussion of the nature of the development in each of these stages, it may be desirable to emphasize the relationship that exists among perception, conception, and the use of language, because it is through the appropriate use of these that knowledge is acquired and organized. There is general agreement that perception and conception are interrelated mental actions, leading to the acquisition of knowledge. Perceptions are sensations, the result of becoming aware of objects or thoughts through use of the senses. By themselves, perceptions are isolated experiences having little intellectual value beyond the effect of their initial impact. They become far more useful when they are related, associated, interpreted, and used as a basis for drawing generalizations. Thus one may perceive a great many boats. Each one is interesting, but until the perceiver recognizes in this number of perceptions the existence of certain common characteristics, he has not recognized that they constitute a class and that they can be named, described, and referred to as such. Until then, each of them was an isolated individual object. Generalizations drawn from a number of observations are concepts. Thus one begins to form concepts almost as soon as one has perceptions. The more accurately and discriminatingly one can observe or otherwise obtain perceptions, the more likely he is to develop useful concepts. This intellectual process of generalizing is called conception and results in the formulation of concepts. Perception and conception together lead to knowledge.

> Our knowledge springs from two main sources in the mind, the first of which is the faculty or power of receiving representations (receptivity of impressions); the second is the power of cognizing by means of these representations (spontaneity in the production of conceptions).[6]

The growth of knowledge calls for a combination of the two processes. In technical terms, it is said that sensations have to be transmitted into ideation. Here is where language enters the picture. Beyond the crudest ideas, the mind cannot

---

[6] Immanuel Kant, *Critique of Pure Reason*, Translated by J. M. D. Meiklejohn (New York: Willey Book Co., Revised Edition, 1953), p. 44.

think without language; language is essential for ideation. Thus it follows that concepts are related to percepts on the one hand and to language on the other; they are based on perception, but without language to permit ideation or generalization, they never would advance beyond the stage of unorganized percepts. Recognition of the importance of language to the formulation of concepts leads to a more practical designation of the term "concept" and one that is particularly helpful for our purposes:

> The term *concept* thus involves combination of two things: on the *content* side it stands for a distinctive *idea:* on the *linguistic* side it stands for the distinctive term which is the *verbal symbol* for that idea.[7]

It is interesting that language benefits as much from the formation of concepts as it contributes. As suggested previously in this chapter, concepts make communication about certain things possible where communication would otherwise be impossible. "Conceptual thinking elevates language from a clumsy tool of limited utility to an instrument of infinite expressiveness."[8] This in turn adds to our ability to learn and gain knowledge as is indicated in the following excerpt:

> Concepts, therefore, are collective representations. That is what makes conceptual thought so valuable for us. If concepts were only general ideas, they would not enrich language a great deal, for...the general contains nothing more than the particular. But if before all else they are collective representations, they add to that which we can learn by our personal experience all that wisdom and science which the group has accumulated in the course of centuries.[9]

This adds the important thought that concepts are seldom, if ever, complete or closed. On the contrary they are open-ended in that the discovery of new aspects of the phenomena they describe may require either their expansion or their modification. A recent discussion of the development

---

[7] Earle Edward Eubank, *The Concepts of Sociology* (New York: D. C. Heath and Company, 1932), p. 28.

[8] *Ibid.*, p. 29.

[9] *Ibid.*, p. 29.

of concepts for the study and teaching of history describes this characteristic in these words:

> Most empirical concepts are open-ended or essentially incomplete because it is not possible to formulate a complete description of them. There are two reasons for this fact. First, no matter how many features one may state about an object or event, there is always something more that can be said about it. For example, new techniques of observation may be formulated which would enable us to observe some properties of an object or event not previously observed. Second, there is always a possibility that current terms will be used to refer to emergent sets of events.[10]

Although this comment deals with empirical concepts, it is also applicable to concepts generally. For example, in auditing we have a concept of independence. If the auditor's relations with his clients expand to include managerial services and even business counseling, modification of the concept of independence becomes necessary. As we experiment with and gain experience in the application of statistical sampling techniques, it will be essential to expand our concept of evidential matter to include these ideas. This illustrates again the part concepts play in providing a framework around which theory can be constructed. Once all the essential concepts of a discipline have been developed, additional concepts as well as principles, standards, and precepts will find their place in relation to those concepts.

In the first stage of development of any field, attention must be given to the observation of facts related to the given subject. The method of observation and collection of facts necessarily varies, but the basic process is the same. For example, the sociologist observes empirical facts about human associations by living in a community while he studies those features of community life in which he is most interested.

The student of auditing might observe auditors and note the procedures they follow in counting cash, confirming re-

---

[10] Ella C. Leppert, Roland F. Payette, Dana Kurfman, and Othanel B. Smith, *Developing Concepts—A Study in the Teaching of History*, Illinois: Illinois Curriculum Program, November, 1958.

ceivables, examining documents, and the like. Or he might observe the practices of the business community in presenting financial data in summaries and statements. At this stage, all the sociologist and the auditor have are perceptions, observations of what is done, nothing more. But these are essential, and in the beginning this is the only way to start gathering knowledge.

The second stage of development consists of drawing out of the observed data such generalizations as appear. The sociologist notes the tendency of human beings to live and work together and designates this tendency as "group," and their exchange of ideas as "communication." In the same fashion, the student of auditing, noting the various practices followed by auditors preparatory to making judgments, might designate the results obtained through such practices as "evidence" and the various attempts to exhibit the results of financial transactions in statements as "disclosure." Once terms are found to designate generalizations, the stage is set for creative study and analysis. The scattered observations can then be classified according to their sources, types, results, or on whatever other basis seems useful. They can be compared and contrasted with similar items in other fields. Their implications can be studied and they can be interrelated with one another and with the concepts of related fields. This intellectual type of activity is described by Professor Eubank:

> Just there is the fulcrum point of understanding.... When we use concepts as tools for analysis it becomes possible to break up the phenomena into their constituent parts and test them out by seeing whether the concepts which apply in one case properly fit in another. They become our logical yard-sticks for measuring, our logical scales for weighing, one fact against another.[11]

It should not be assumed that the formulation of generalizations is an easy task; some concepts may be anything but obvious and it may not be until the discipline has made considerable progress that all its major concepts appear. In

[11] Eubank, *op. cit.*, p. 34.

the early stages of development, a young discipline might resort to similes, figures of speech, and expressions borrowed from other fields to convey ideas. To some extent, this is what we are doing when we describe independence as "a mental attitude" or due care as the "gateway to all procedural standards." Lack of accepted concepts becomes evident in an accompanying lack of a well-developed technical language for communication among specialists in the field.

As we progress, however, concept becomes better and better developed. The third stage is one in which the concepts are well enough developed that they can be related to one another, thus forming a "frame of reference" for the given field. At this point the essence of a logical system begins to appear, or, as Eubank puts it: "a schematics whereby the several parts appear as segments of a united congruous whole." Where once there were only isolated facts, then individual concepts, there now appears a set of interrelated concepts, each one supporting the others and consistent with them. This is what makes up a comprehensive treatise on any given field of knowledge; it is the first important step in systematizing knowledge. A familiar illustration of this is the well-known work, *An Introduction to Corporate Accounting Standards*, by Paton and Littleton, in which the fundamentals of accounting knowledge are organized around a few, interlocked concepts (cost, revenue, income, surplus, and interpretation). An additional merit of such a work is the exposition of each part in relation to the integrated whole, in co-ordinating the hewn-out fragments into a pattern. Any part can be studied best and can be fully understood only in connection with the whole of which it is a part. Thus an arm or a hand makes some sense when studied by itself, but it makes a great deal more when it is viewed as an essential part of a human body. Although the following statement by Herbert Spencer was made in discussing the basis of philosophical belief, it aptly expresses the thought intended here:

> Every thought involves a whole system of thoughts; and ceases to exist if severed from its various correlatives. As we cannot

> isolate a single organ of a living body, and deal with it as though it had a life independent of the rest; so, from the organized structure of our cognitions, we cannot cut out one, and proceed as though it had survived the separation. The development of formless protoplasm into an embryo is a specialization of parts, the distinctness of which increases only as fast as their combination increases—each becomes a distinguishable organ only on condition that it is bound up with others, which have simultaneously become distinguishable organs; and similarly, from the unformed material of consciousness, a developed intelligence can arise only by a process which, in making thoughts defined also makes them mutually dependent—establishes among them certain vital connections the destruction of which causes instant death of the thoughts.[12]

The analogy is not perfect, of course. Concepts can be studied individually. But there is a serious danger in doing so. The possibility of developing inconsistencies with related concepts, of neglecting implications for the subject concept which exist in others, and of permitting serious overlap is every present.

The fourth and final stage in the formulation of concepts consists of the careful examination and scrutiny of concepts already at least roughly formulated. This adds philosophical analysis to the steps necessary to get the concept formulated. In this stage concepts already more or less finished are examined critically to see if they adequately serve their purpose and are then searched for implications that may lead to their extension. This is the intention of the present work, to study the concepts of auditing with a view toward determining their adequacy, strength, interrelationships, and implications. An analogous process is recognized and applied in science and is described in the following statement which distinguishes between the scientist as a scientist and as a philosopher:

> The scientist as scientist need not scrutinize all the conceptual tools he uses; but to the extent that he does, he is simply a "philosophical" scientist. When Einstein, for example, critically examined the Newtonian concepts of absolute space, ab-

---

[12] Herbert Spencer, *First Principles* (New York: Edited by the DeWitt Revolving Fund, Inc., 1958), pp. 141-142.

> solute time and absolute motion, his activity was essentially philosophical. But while it may be necessary for the scientist to reflect upon fundamental presuppositions every once and awhile and thus to become "philosophical," the distinction between philosophical analysis and scientific investigation remains clear cut.[13]

We feel that auditing has gone a long way toward formulating concepts. Some of these have been fairly well stated; others are at best but partially formed. Little effort has been made either to interrelate these concepts or to subject them to critical examination. Interrelation and critical examination of concepts are essential steps in the development of a systematic theory of auditing.

Types of Concepts. It has been stated in this chapter that concepts are found in all fields of knowledge. It should also be pointed out that there are different kinds of concepts. To help make this clear we may classify concepts as:

1. Philosophical (or nonspecific) and native (or specific).
2. Ideal and real

These two bases for classification are independent; the first is related to the discipline which developed the concept and to which it therefore belongs; the second is concerned with the nature of the concept, whether real or fictional.

Philosophical concepts are those which do not belong exclusively to any particular science or art. Examples are truth, probability, cause, proof, physical object, meaning, and necessity. Those who work with mathematics, an exact science; physics, an experimental science; astronomy, an observational science; or law, history, and auditing, will find themselves concerned at times with these particular abstractions in the course of developing the theoretical framework of their respective disciplines. Theorists and practitioners alike utilize these concepts. The practitioner of law or auditing must contemplate the essence of truth or proof or probability whenever he claims to be in search of the "truth" in a given case, endeavors to obtain "proof" of a given incident, or concludes that a certain inference has a given degree of

---

[13] Arthur Pap, *Elements of Analytic Philosophy* (New York: The Macmillan Co., 1949), p. 6.

"probability." Because practitioners and theorists in a variety of disciplines are concerned with the same concepts no one field can claim them exclusively. Such concepts underlie the development of all disciplines and thus "belong" to all. This places them in sort of a public domain of knowledge, general philosophy. Almost any basic treatise in any organized system of knowledge will have in its background some reliance on these philosophical concepts. The more insight the researcher in any special subject has in these philosophical concepts, the more promising will be his exploration of the concepts of his own field.

Native or specific concepts are those which originate in special branches of knowledge. Examples of native concepts are acceleration in mechanics, chemical neutralization in chemistry, conditioned reflex in psychology, cross-fertilization in botany, marginal cost in economics, and evidence in auditing. These concepts are peculiar to the discipline which originated them and therefore remain the concern of researchers in the special subjects. It should be observed, however, that many of the concepts which fall in this class are not the monopoly of any single field. Such concepts as evidence exist in law, history, and auditing, for example. This is more than just a coincidence of terms. Evidence, whether legal, historical, or audit, is related to proof which in turn is rooted in the theory of knowledge. In this respect there is no essential difference between evidence in law, history, or auditing. Yet each of these fields, although it relies on the basic nature of evidence generally, also uses evidence in a very special sense made necessary by the peculiarities of the field itself. Thus the concept of legal evidence differs from historical evidence and both of these from audit evidence. They have much in common; they also have important differences. The criteria of evidence will vary from field to field and it is these criteria which give the same concept its distinct color and connotation in each field, thus converting what may be essentially a philosophical concept into a native concept.

As such concepts have aspects of both a general philosophical concept nature and of a native concept nature it behooves the individual working with them to be aware of both sides of their nature, to recognize their basis in common knowledge and their distinguishing characteristics derived from the special field. A given discipline may concern itself with only a limited number of the total aspects of a given concept. Internal control, as an illustration, is a subdivision of the general concept of control and therefore includes at least some if not all the features of that general concept. It is also of interest in some special fields. Internal control is important to the student of management who might see it as a means of dominating and keeping informed on the several aspects of a company's activities, thus emphasizing the production of prompt information useful for stimulating and guiding corrective action; the systems specialist's concern with internal control might center primarily on its soundness of construction as a system, and therefore stress organization, communication, and data flow; finally, the auditor finds it significant also, but he is concerned with the protective aspects of the system and its potential for reducing and revealing irregularities of all kinds. Depending on the interest of the individual concerned, he must have some knowledge of the basic concept of control plus a familiarity with the special features of internal control pertinent to his work and problems.

Ideal concepts are not ideal in the sense that they approach perfection, but in the sense that they are not concerned with the realities of actual situations. They are fictions and are developed purposefully by a logical process which purifies and synthesizes their constituent elements to form an image which may not actually exist at all outside the minds of those concerned with the concept. Thus we have the economic man, the representative firm, prudent behavior, and perfect competition. Fictions though they may be, such concepts are useful in theoretical analysis and the development of knowledge. For example:

> The fiction of the economic man was highly useful for many purposes in examining and predicting the behavior of human beings in relation to the production and distribution of wealth. It is still highly useful. Without it we should know a great deal

> less than we do about the nature of human affairs and we should not be as well equipped to deal with many situations of life, large and small.[14]

Students sometimes object to such concepts on the grounds that because they are not representative of reality, they have little apparent usefulness. To the more sophisticated intellect however, their usefulness is apparent. They represent logical relationships among other concepts which do have a basis in reality and their use permits us to study the relationships among other concepts in a way not otherwise possible. We may conclude, then, that they are not fictitious in the sense of being invalid or inapplicable. They contribute to the theoretical advancement of their respective fields. Comparison of the realities of a given situation with the related ideal concept singles out the practical problems which have to be faced and solved. For example, comparison of a given individual's actions with a concept of prudent behavior indicates the extent of his conformity with or deviation from a desirable standard. Thus, in a court of law, this imaginative, or "as if," concept has not only theoretical value but also practical significance.

A real concept, on the other hand, is not a fiction but a general class of real things or events. The following is an example of a real concept:

> We observe that in Western civilization many economic tasks are carried out by organizations of people who have certain legal and other responsibilities for what the firm does, and who enjoy certain rights and rewards for their services. This general class of persons we can group together under the concept of *business executives*. A concept of this nature is sometimes referred to as a *real type*.[15]

In auditing, an applied subject, we are concerned primarily but not exclusively with real concepts. The real con-

---

[14] *Theory and Practice in Historical Study*, A Report of the Committee on Historiography, New York: Social Science Research Council, Bulletin 54, no date, p. 8.

[15] *The Social Sciences in Historical Study*, A Report by the Committee on Historiography, New York: Social Science Research Council, Bulletin 64, 1954, p. 92.

cept of independence, to illustrate, would be the concept on which practicing auditors now act. Its discovery would consist of describing present practice. But we are also concerned with what the concept of independence ought to be if auditing is to meet its social responsibilities and opportunities. Therefore we may wish to contrast the real concept with an ideal concept to see where the real concept should be modified both in theory and in practice. Without the use of ideal concepts as a standard against which to measure real concepts, we have little basis for a useful analysis of concepts as we actually find them.

The Conceptual Approach. We believe that a conceptual approach is more likely to lead to progress in the construction of a sound theory of auditing than any other. We take this position because auditing is at the stage where a rigorous examination of its concepts is needed and because we feel the most widely recognized alternative approach, a mathematical one, is not applicable. The mathematical approach is the ideal of all sciences and has been used with some success in fields such as economics. The development of mathematical models and their manipulation to reveal relationships and tendencies have been found very useful. We do not believe that this approach will have a similar usefulness in auditing.

Granted that language, logic, and mathematics are the basic tools for the development of human knowledge, it must be emphasized that not all disciplines use these tools in equal proportions. In some areas, theoretical development draws heavily upon language and logic and to only a minor extent upon mathematics. Such is the nature of auditing. Thus we feel the conceptual approach as described is more likely to succeed.

In this connection we are impressed by the contentions of Mr. Wroe Alderson in his recent work, *Marketing Behavior and Executive Action.* In discussing the relative extent to which progress in various disciplines depends on the use of formal logic and perfect syllogism and the possibility of using mathematical equations to state and study the relationship among the variables in these fields, Mr. Alderson points out that there are great differences among the fields of knowledge. At one extreme are the physical sciences, the variables of which can be readily stated as mathematical formulae; at the other extreme are the social sciences in which the multiplicity of variables and their limited measurability tend to hinder such a development.

> Many physical laws are stated as mathematical equations expressing the way in which one quantity varies with another.... Many working in other scientific fields regard the logical and mathematical precision of physics as the model they should attempt to follow. It is granted that this can only be achieved in the distant future, because of the great complexity of data which must be handled in such fields as the social sciences.[16]

Even in some of the sciences, the mathematical approach has serious limitations:

> Central to general biology is the theory of evolution, which is a set of propositions concerning genes, mutations, the struggle for survival, and other factors which are believed to affect the development of the species. Only a few aspects of the general theory can be expressed in mathematical form....[17]

One of the common misconceptions is that concepts which cannot be tested by collecting empirical evidence are not very useful for the development of theory. This view must be resisted, particularly in fields such as auditing, in which empirical evidence for testing concepts is difficult to obtain and not particularly useful in any case. As suggested previously, auditing is concerned not only with discovering what its concepts now are but also with what they ought to be. Thus we have more than a casual interest in ideal concepts. That concepts not subject to empirical testing may be useful in the development of theory is illustrated in the following rather unusual illustration:

> Psychoanalytic theory as developed by Freud consists of a series of daring and sweeping statements about the sources of

---

[16] Wroe Alderson, *Marketing Behavior and Executive Action: A Functional Approach to Marketing Theory* (Homewood, Illinois: Richard D. Irwin, Inc., 1957), p. 5.

[17] *Ibid.*, p. 5.

> human desire and the difficulties encountered on the way to emotional maturity. His famous model of personality structure utilizing the concepts of id, ego, and super ego were not fully worked out until Freud was in his seventies. The ramifications of libido and the death instinct, of repression and defense mechanism, of symbols and the interpretation of dreams were suggested by Freud's experience in the treatment of mental illness. Many of these concepts have yet to be subjected to the test of statistically valid research.[18]

This illustration points out that there are conceptual models as well as mathematical models and that conceptual models, even without empirical support, can be extremely effective in the development of theory. This fact is important to us because we find the development of mathematical models, except possibly the most simple type, to be inapplicable in auditing at this stage in its development.

One other matter requires attention at this point. This is the operational approach to concepts outlined by P. W. Bridgman in his outstanding book *The Logic of Modern Physics.* Bridgman stresses the idea that a concept consists primarily of a set of operations; in effect, we understand things in terms of what we do about them. If the concept relates to something physical, the operations are physical; if the concept is mental, the operations are mental. Without knowing the operations involved, we cannot understand the concept. He illustrates this in these words:

> The new attitude toward a concept is entirely different. We may illustrate by considering the concept of length: What do we mean by the length of an object? We evidently know what we mean by length if we can tell what the length of any and every object is, and for the physicist nothing more is required. To find the length of an object, we have to perform certain physical operations. The concept of length is therefore fixed when the operations by which length is measured are fixed: that is, the concept of length involves as much as and nothing more than the set of operations by which length is determined. In general, we mean by any concept nothing more than a set of operations; *the concept is synonymous with the corresponding set of operations.* If the concept is physical, as of length, the operations are actual physical operations, namely, those by

[18] *Ibid.*, p. 6.

> which length is measured; or if the concept is mental, as of mathematical continuity, the operations are mental operations, namely those by which we determine whether a given aggregate of magnitudes is continuous.[19]

Thus the first requirement of a concept, to Bridgman, is that it consist of or include a set of operations. The second requirement is that the operations be unique. A difference in operations indicates a difference in concepts.

> *In principle* the operations by which length is measured should be *uniquely* specified. If we have more than one set of operations, we have more than one concept, and strictly there should be a separate name to correspond to each different set of operations.[20]

Although writing primarily about physics, Bridgman does not confine himself to that subject. He feels that his ideas of concept formation apply to all fields of inquiry and that the reward for utilizing them would be a far-reaching reform in the habits of thinking about science or any other subject.

> It would doubtless conduce greatly to clarity of thought if the operational mode of thinking were adopted in all fields of inquiry as well as in the physical.[21]

Initially, Bridgman's thesis was aimed at sharpening the language of science and improving the rigor with which it attacked its problems. However, operationalism entailed an over-all methodological movement and became so closely related to the problem of theory construction that we can hardly find a modern treatise on scientific method or logic that fails to refer to operationalism and discuss it in more or less detail. Theorists in such fields as economics and sociology have become aware of the implications of this doctrine and have attempted, often with considerable success, to apply it in the development of theory in their respective fields.

There is general agreement that concepts must be clarified and in a rigorous fashion if progress in theory is to pro-

---

[19] P. W. Bridgman, *The Logic of Modern Physics* (New York: The Macmillan Co., 1958), p. 5.

[20] *Ibid.*, p. 10.

[21] *Ibid.*, p. 10.

ceed at a satisfactory pace. But operationalism, like empirical testing, is but one way of clarifying. Some see serious limitations to the operationalism approach and recommend against relying on it too strongly.

> One facet of the polemic...between the "fact-minded" and the "theory-oriented" sociologists has been a disagreement about the importance of the operational definition. The debate is a rather complex one, but its central point was whether a concept is most usefully and precisely defined by describing the operations which observe, measure, and record a given phenomenon. The "fact-minded" group has leaned toward the opinion that a concept like "mass" or "length" or "social cohesion" means a set of operations....
>
> Against this stand, the opposition group has contended that when we think of such a concept, we do not mean merely these operations. Rather they are simply the techniques we have to use in order to get at, or measure, something behind those operations—the phenomenon itself. Such procedures, then, are useful because we cannot directly observe or measure, say, "social cohesion." However, it is "social cohesion" that we really wish to discuss, not these operations.[22]

These writers contend that the best solution is to combine the precision of operationalism with the significance of traditional conceptual definitions and to use each where it best fits. This seems to be good advice. We feel that there are concepts in auditing which lend themselves to the operational approach with no great difficulty. We feel that there are some other concepts in which the operations concerned cannot be as readily or as precisely stated because of the infinite variety of possibilities. In every case, however, we believe that as operational a statement of the concept as possible is useful.

Primary Concepts in Auditing. The remainder of this volume is concerned with the development of a small number of what we conceive to be the primary concepts of auditing. These are: evidence, due audit care, fair presentation, independence, and ethical conduct. We do not claim completeness for this list. There may well be other significant

---

[22] William J. Goode, and Paul K. Hatt, *Methods in Social Research* (New York: McGraw-Hill Book Company, Inc., 1952), p. 53.

concepts which should be added. On the other hand, we are confident that each of these occupies an important position in the structure of auditing theory. We hope that others will be moved to add to this type of analysis until in time all the useful concepts of this discipline have been stated and subjected to philosophical examination.

Chapter 5

Evidence

The importance of evidence in any disciplined inquiry seems apparent from the discussion in the preceding chapter. If our beliefs are to be anything more than mere chance or emotional feelings, they must be based on evidence of some kind. The hypotheses which we develop, whether in our ordinary, daily activities or in some type of scientific endeavor, become strong enough to justify belief in them only if they are adequately supported by evidence. Evidence gives us a rational basis for forming judgments.

Auditing is like other disciplines in this respect. The auditor requires evidence in order that he may rationally judge the financial statement propositions submitted to him. To the extent that he makes judgments and forms his "opinion" on the basis of adequate evidence, he acts rationally by following a systematic or methodical procedure; to the extent that he fails to gather "sufficient competent evidential matter" and fails to evaluate it effectively, he acts irrationally and his judgments can have little standing.

The Nature of Evidence

General Types of Evidence. In very general terms, evidence may be said to fall within one or another of three broad classes: (1) natural evidence, (2) created evidence, and (3) rational argumentation.

Natural evidence exists all around us and is relied upon commonly in every mental activity we perform. A table is its own evidence for existence. We see inventory and we are convinced that it exists. As will be emphasized later, natural evidence is among the most convincing evidence available.

Created evidence is not naturally existent in the world about us; some effort is required to bring it forth. When a scientist performs an experiment he is creating evidence. Water is its own evidence that it exists in nature and one can learn a good deal about its apparent physical characteristics by observing it intelligently. More can be learned through laboratory experiments that analyze water into its components, subject it to pressures, flows, and confinements to discover its hydraulic characteristics, heat it, chill it, and submit it to other analytical procedures. In the one case, the evidence is naturally available; in the other, it must be made or developed by the scientist.

From this simple example it should be evident that observation of evidence, whether it be natural or created, is something of an art in itself. The skilled observer sees far more than the unskilled and what he sees has more meaning to him. As mentioned in an earlier chapter, a scientist—and here the term is used broadly—must be skilled in observation if he is to make the best use of the evidence available to him.

Some areas of inquiry lend themselves to the experimental method; in others it is very difficult to use at all. Until fairly recent times, for example, astronomers could do little more than observe the heavenly bodies and develop their theorems from what they saw. Without other means of obtaining evidence, many of these theorems necessarily remain untested. Telescopes and similar instruments are hardly more than tools to make observation possible where otherwise it might not be so, or perhaps to make it easier where it otherwise would be difficult. The controlled experiments of certain other sciences are not possible in astronomy. Chemistry, on the other hand, is readily adaptable to laboratory experiment. Many hypotheses can be tested for validity quickly and easily. Those who question the results of such experiments can for their own satisfaction repeat them under identical conditions. This adaptability to the scientific method enables one area to be developed more rapidly and with greater authority than another.

The third kind of evidence consists of rational argumentation. Much of what we believe does not result directly from observation of natural evidence or of experimental or otherwise created evidence. Ideas frequently follow logically from observed facts and seem true to us, yet at the same time mental effort is required to proceed from the simple observed fact to the conclusion our minds find appealing. In legal proceedings, for example, a skillful attorney may develop an extremely convincing "case" based on a number of established facts and a great deal of rationalization. The commonness of the expression "It seems logical" indicates the frequency with which we rely on this type of evidence.

These three broad classes of evidence are not equally compelling to the mind. It is very difficult for any of us to deny the existence of physical objects; barring, for the moment, the possibility of faulty vision, improper identification, and errors of this type, a table placed before us is accepted as a table. The evidence for its existence, the table itself, is very convincing. Our minds are compelled to believe. To the extent that created evidence is equally simple and clear, it may be equally compelling. If it requires a complex process of development, however, such as a lengthy sequence of chemical analyses, the mind untrained in the techniques involved may find it very hard indeed to accept. What we cannot comprehend, our minds tend to reject.

Much the same is true of rational argumentation. If it consists of but one or two simple steps of reasoning, we can understand it and may feel compelled to accept it. The long and involved rationalizations of higher mathematics, however, are too much for many of us, and if we accept the results at all, the decisive factor is not the strength of the arguments submitted as evidence but rather the testimony of the mathematician.

Evidence, Truth, and Knowledge. Evidence provides the means by which we can achieve that state of assurance described as "knowing" as opposed to merely "believing." It is thus the key to truth, which may be described as "conformity with reality." We strive to attain truth through the use of our senses, but these are not always reliable. Seeing is not always believing.

For example, a child sees a cloud and to him it is a tremendous mass of whipped cream; an uneducated adult, looking at the same cloud, might see a large solid mass floating in the air; the those comprehending even the rudiments of meteorology, however, it is an accumulation of water vapor. What we "see" may be influenced by our knowledge, our experience, and our desires. To a lesser extent, what is true of natural evidence may be true of created evidence. One may be so enthusiastic about a given line of research that he misinterprets data or sees favorable developments where less susceptible minds would find reason to doubt.

For the purposes of this study, truth may be divided into three general types. This classification will have direct usefulness when we later attempt to analyze the verification problems of the auditor. At this point it will help us to grasp the more general problems related to the nature and use of evidence. Truth, then, may be classified as: (1) material truths, (2) mathematical truths, and (3) other abstract truths.

Material truths are those which are impressed on our minds by natural evidence. Scotus describes the mind as having qualities which cause it to necessarily apprehend objects and events brought to the immediate attention of the senses.[1] Thus the mind cannot deny having seen an object placed before the open and normally functioning eye; it is obliged to assent to the existence of what is so forcefully brought to its attention. If we then have an object which exists naturally (that is, it is its own evidence of existence) and is such that it can be clearly and distinctly perceived, the mind necessarily apprehends it and assents to its existence. When this occurs, the mind can have a "certitude" of knowledge, it not only knows but it knows that it knows, and there is no room for doubt whatever.

Other logicians may question whether complete certitude is ever possible, but that is too fine an argument for our purposes. It is useful, however, to be aware of this concept of certitude so that we can compare it with the assurance one has about other types of truth.

Mathematical truths are those which result from acceptance of the basic postulates and assumptions of mathematics. We accept as true that two and two are four, without considering that this rests on certain assumptions about the nature of unity, the meanings of the terms involved, and the rules for the manipulation of numbers. Mathematics deals in abstractions and any number is an abstraction. Abstract truths of a mathematical type, providing they are simple enough for us to comprehend and common enough so that we do not suspect them simply because they are unfamiliar, are likely to be as compelling as material truths to our minds. We know with as much assurance that two and two make four as we know that the table before us exists.

In addition to material truths and mathematical truths, we have a host of other truths which, like mathematical truths, are abstract. These abstract truths offer a wide diversity and varying

---

[1] Peter C. Vier, *Evidence and Its Function According to John Duns Scotus* (New York: The Franciscan Institute, 1951), pp. 54-55.

degrees of complexity. We know for example that the earth revolves around the sun; that is, we accept this as true. But is the mind as confident of this proposition as it is of the existence of a table, or that two and two are four? By their very nature, nonmathematical, abstract truths are more difficult to comprehend and assent to. The existence of the Empire State Building is an abstract truth to the man who has never seen it. He has less certainty that it exists than he has about the house he currently lives in, because he does not have the same kind of evidence about the two phenomena. In apprehending nonmathematical, abstract truths, rational argumentation is required; the mind must infer the truth of the proposition from a combination of types of evidence. A friend may have seen the Empire State Building and may testify to its existence. The mind reasons that the friend is a truthful person, has no reason to mislead, is able to comprehend an object of this description, and therefore *may* be believed. Note that whereas the mind is compelled to believe what it apprehends directly, it is not compelled to accept what is less directly apprehended. It may be strongly persuaded, but it is not constrained.

Obviously, little progress could be made if any field of study which is restricted to material truths or even to material and mathematical truths. Until we pass beyond mere comprehension and description into the area of classifications, differences, similarities, and interrelationships, we have made but a start. Every discipline includes many abstract truths. It must be recognized that these are different from natural and mathematical truths and require different kinds of evidence if they are to be accepted. Certitude about abstract propositions is impossible, but they may be so highly probable that we approach certitude. On the other hand, if the evidence is not strong, the mind may be reluctant to accept the reasoning, and we may be only slightly more inclined to accept the proposition as true than to consider it false.

Probability. At this point it may be well to digress slightly and add a few words about the meaning of probability, a term generally used to indicate the relative certainty or uncertainty that a proposition is in accord with reality.

Wolf tells us that there are two kinds of certainty, subjective and objective.

> Certainty or uncertainty may originate in different ways. It may be the result of the moods and dispositions, hopes and fears, habits and prejudices of the individual who is judging. These are subjective, personal factors, which vary from individual to individual. Some people confidently expect a certain event merely because they wish it to happen, and they are sanguine by temperament. Others may be extremely uncertain about some event, either because they are not keen about it, or because they have a morbid habit of expecting the fates always to thwart their wishes.
>
> In contrast with such merely subjective causes of certainty or uncertainty, there are objective or logical grounds on which they may be based. They are the kind of grounds on which we usually appeal when we try to convert others to our views, and do not rely entirely on our powers of bullying or of coaxing. Such rational grounds do not vary from individual to individual, but are valid for all intelligent beings. Now, the kind of uncertainty with which probability is concerned is that based on rational grounds. It is not concerned with mere feelings or convictions arising we know not how, but with those varying degrees of assertiveness which are correlated with corresponding degrees of rational support which our judgments find in the available evidence.[2]

There seems to be agreement that probability is concerned only with the kind of knowledge we obtain by inference or reasoning.

> Part of our knowledge we obtain direct; and part by argument. The Theory of Probability is concerned with that part which we obtain by argument, and it treats of the different degrees in which the results so obtained are conclusive or inconclusive.
>
> In most branches of academic logic, such as the theory of the syllogism or the geometry of ideal space, all the arguments aim at demonstrative certainty. They claim to be *conclusive*. But many other arguments are rational and claim some weight without pretending to be certain. In Metaphysics, in Science, and in Conduct, must of the arguments, upon which we habitually base our rational beliefs, are admitted to be inconclusive in a greater or lesser degree. Thus for a philosophical treatment of these branches of knowledge, the study of probability is required.[3]

Most of us have had some experience with statistical measures of probability, and we may tend to think of probability only

---

[2] A. Wolf, *Essentials of Scientific Method* (New York: The Macmillan Company, 1925), pp. 134-135.

[3] John Maynard Keynes, *A Treatise on Probability* (London: Macmillan and Co., St. Martins Street, 1948), p. 3. Author's emphasis.

in this respect. But it is important that we see the possibility of "rational probability" as well, because it is with rational probability that we deal most commonly in auditing. Given two lines of argument starting with the same accepted facts and reaching opposed conclusions, one will have more appeal, will seem more reasonable, more rational than the other. The quality of rationality cannot be reduced to a mathematical formula, at least not at our present state of development, but certainly some reasoning is more probably correct than others.

The difference between two opposed lines of reasoning may result from a number of different factors such as contradictory interpretations of the basic facts, greater experience on the part of one reasoner, bias, or failure to reason logically. If the reasons for difference are apparent, the probability of one's being more correct than the other is clear. Where the faultiness of the weaker argument is not apparent, evidence must be adduced to determine which is the sounder and therefore the more rationally probable.

But it is not necessary to this concept of rational probability that we have two opposing lines of reasoning from the same evidence. Any given line of argument or of reasoning may be examined by and of itself. Anyone adequately trained in logical analysis can determine whether or not the conclusions follow from the evidence, that is whether the reasoning is valid. This is an exercise that auditors are expected to perform may times in the course of their examinations. They note the conclusions reached by others on the basis of given facts, and they test those conclusions by objectively reviewing the reasoning from the evidence to the conclusion. They will also, of course, judge the validity of the evidence since that too bears on the rationality of the conclusion.

Evidence in Different Disciplines. Different fields of knowledge use different methods of research, have different types of propositions to resolve, and rely upon different types of evidence. To explore the nature of audit evidence further, it will be helpful to compare and contrast it with evidence in some other fields. First, however, it may be well to indicate in a general way what we mean by the nature of evidence.

The nature of anything may be defined as (1) its essential character, (2) its distinguishing qualities, or (3) its constitution. As a generic term, evidence may be considered that which gives rise to proof, thereby contributing to the formation of rational belief. Belief, in turn, may be viewed as "the holding of an attitude toward a proposition." The character and constitution of evidence are affected considerably by the nature of the field in which it is used, that is, the purpose which the evidence is to serve. Among the characteristics which vary from field to field are the following:

1. The special purpose of the area of interest. Some scientific endeavor is directed at a better understanding of the physical world about us, some to a better understanding of the origin and development of man and his social behavior. Such different purposes have interesting and important influences on the kind of evidence which is available and useful in the process of attaining the truth.
2. The subject matter to which the evidence is pertinent. It seems clear that the evidence necessary to support an assertion of physical existence would differ from the evidence required to support an abstract proposition like a balance sheet classification. Recognition of the influence which this difference has on the foundation of judgments may not be quite so clear.
3. The method of collection or development. In some fields the judgment-maker is restricted to observing evidence brought to him; in other cases he may go seeking evidence; in still other cases he may develop his own evidence through experimentation or perhaps by rational argumentation.
4. Rules for the use of evidence. Mature and well-developed disciplines have rules or standards for the collection and evaluation of evidence. These may be so common as to be accepted without specific statement, or they may be given formal expression.
5. The influence of time on the judgment process. Time may or may not be an important factor in the collection and use of evidence. In some cases evidence must be obtained and judgment rendered within rather strict time limits; in other instances, such as in fundamental research in the physical sciences, time is not a factor in any way at all.

6. The degree of compulsion exerted on the mind of the judgment-maker by the evidence. As we have already seen, some evidence is very compelling, while other evidence exerts relatively little force on the mind that receives it.

The table on page 92 and 93 contrasts the evidence required in five important areas of research, including auditing. It presents some interesting facts to the careful reader, both with respect to differences in the type of evidence required in different fields and the nature of the judgment-formation problem in those fields.

In the pure or exact sciences, mathematics, and symbolic logic, evidence is directed at the establishment or support of abstract relationships among defined terms. Evidence to support these relationships is developed through deductions based on established postulates and other accepted propositions. The one judging the truthfulness of the propositions at issue must either develop the deductions supporting the proposition or must at least follow through their development so that he in effect gathers the evidence which he then judges. The rules of formal logic or of mathematical manipulation of terms govern the deductive process of creating evidence. Time is not an important factor in judging the evidence thus made available. To the extent that the deductive evidence is valid, it is absolutely compelling on the judgment-maker.

Scientists working on experimental or observational problems are concerned with natural and physical phenomena. They obtain evidence by experiment, frequently under strictly controlled conditions, and observation. Thus the scientist, the judgment-maker, may either play a passive role, merely observing that evidence which is available to him, or an active role by creating evidence through experimentation. The process of creating evidence is governed by standards of laboratory experiment so that conclusions may be tested by repeating the process. In addition, because few opportunities for exhaustive research are possible, the rules of statistical inference also apply. The only urgency derives from the normal human desire to accomplish results without undue loss of time. The compulsiveness of the evidence obtained varies from near absolute—and perhaps even absolute in the case of certain observations—to merely persuasive. In some cases its probability can be measured mathematically.

Law differs from the physical sciences in important respects. The evidence which it requires relates to occurrences at given times and places; in application, law is always concerned with the specific. In the process of litigation, evidence is presented to the judge by the opposing parties, thus the judgment-maker himself has no real part in its collection. Various legal presumptions and a host of special rules of permissibility govern the admission and use of evidence once it is made available. Time is normally an important factor, since the judge must render a decision within a reasonable time and because, with the passage of time, the possibilities of obtaining credible evidence diminish as eyewitnesses to the given event die or memories fade. Evidence presented in court would never be considered absolutely compulsive. Some small parts might be, such as the existence of a murder weapon, but such facts are normally combined with others conveying less certitude. Final judgments are thus made on less certain evidence.

History directs its attention to the interpretation and understanding of the past by studying the influence of events and developments on the organization and behavior of human groups. Its evidence consists of documents, relics, and the written recollections and impressions of people who knew or thought they knew something about the period or event under study. These scraps of evidence are not made or created by the historian; they already exist. His task is to discover them, draw them together for study, and then to submit them to critical examination. Thus the judgment-maker plays a positive role in the collection of evidence, but it is still a different kind of role from that of the mathematician or experimental scientist who actually creates evidence. Time is not of great significance to the historian, although it must be recognized that the longer the period between an event and the time it is studied, the more difficult it will be to discover and collect eyewitness and other reliable accounts of it. Thus time is of some concern but is not a critical factor. Indeed, a case can be made for requiring a reasonable period to elapse before historical interpretations are attempted, so the personal interest and bias

FIGURE I
COMPARATIVE CLASSIFICATION OF EVIDENCE IN FIVE FIELDS

Significant Characteristics	*Pure or Exact Science (Mathematics, Formal Logic)*	*Physical Science (Experimental or Observational)*	*Law*	*History*	*Auditing*
Special purpose of area to which evidence is pertinent	Statement of all significant relationships within closed system governed by accepted postulates	Development of generalizations governing natural universe	Maintenance of justice	Interpretation and understanding of the past	Protection of statement readers
Subject matter to which evidence is pertinent	Abstract relationships	Natural and/or physical phenomena	Occurrences at given times and places	The influence of events and developments on human organization and behavior	Financial statement propositions
Method of collection or development	Deduction from established postulates	Induction from experimentation and observation Deduction Combination of induction and deduction	Presentation by opposing parties Rational deduction and inference	Collection of existing materials and submission to critical examination	Submission by interested and disinterested parties Collected and developed by independent party Rationalization

FIGURE I (Continued)
COMPARATIVE CLASSIFICATION OF EVIDENCE IN FIVE FIELDS

Significant Characteristics	*Pure or Exact Science (Mathematics, Formal Logic)*	*Physical Science (Experimental or Observational)*	*Law*	*History*	*Auditing*
Role of judgment-maker in collection or development	Positive	Both positive and passive	Passive	Positive—yet different from mathematics and experimental scientist	Both positive and passive
Nature of rules governing the study of evidence	Rules of formal logic	Standards of laboratory experiment to permit replication Rules of statistical inference Rules of logic	Logical presumptions Rules of admissibility and relevance	Rules of external and internal criticism	Professional standards
Importance of time in judgment formation and evidence collection	None	None	A controlling factor	Little	A controlling factor
Compulsiveness of evidence in judgment formation	Absolute	Variable from near absolute to probable Often subject to mathematically measurable probability	Persuasive	Persuasive	Varies from absolute to persuasive

of the historian and those from whom information is gathered will have less influence. It is difficult to take a cool, dispassionate, historical view of a battle if one is in its very midst. The evidence available to a historian can seldom be more than persuasive. Rarely is he interested merely in whether a material object exists; his interest is in whether it existed at a given time and either reflects or may have caused certain influences. This he can seldom know with certitude.

Turning finally to auditing, we find additional differences in the nature of its problems and in the evidence on which it relies. Auditing is concerned with the protection of those who read financial statements; its purpose is to assure them that certain standards of accuracy, clarity, and completeness have been met. Its total subject matter is probably narrower than that of any of the fields mentioned in this chapter, but its specific problems are not necessarily narrower than the specific problems of any other. The subject matter to which audit evidence must be pertinent consists of the propositions in financial statements or other financial data. Some of this evidence is obtained by gift, as it were, some is sought out or created by the auditor, and some is reasoned from other evidence. Thus an auditor will have certain information made available to him by the company employees and officers, he will develop other data by sending out confirmations or by preparing reconciliations and analyses, and still other evidence will come from his own line of reasoning about similarities between the instant case and others of his experience. Thus the auditor, who is also the judgment-maker, finds himself primarily in a positive role in the development of evidence, although in some cases he receives certain kinds of evidence more or less passively.

Time is a controlling factor in most audit work; the auditor's judgment is normally required within a relatively short time after the occurrence of the transactions and other events reflected in the financial statements. Time is vital in another way as well, particularly if the internal control is not as strong as is desirable. If the auditor is to form a judgment on the existence of inventory, we expect him to see that inventory and to see it reasonably close to the balance sheet date. We have a feeling, again particularly in cases of weak internal control, that securities, notes receivable, and cash on hand should be counted, counted simultaneously, and counted close to the year-end; this is why "year-end work" must be done at or near the close of business on the last day of the year. Unlike the situation in the other fields considered, time is of the essence in the collection of audit evidence and the formation of audit judgments.

Audit evidence will influence the auditor in degrees which vary all the way from being compelling to being little more than persuasive. When he has seen and counted petty cash, he is constrained to accept its existence and amount. When he has verified arithmetical assertions on the financial statements by recomputation, his mind assents fully to the arithmetical accuracy of the stated figures. The collectibility of receivables is another matter; he may be persuaded that they are generally collectible but he can seldom be absolutely certain.

Because audit evidence is our principal interest in this chapter, we will examine it more intensively in the following section. At this point we are interested in establishing certain general notions about evidence in any field and in dispelling mistaken impressions. For example, the workings of our legal processes are so much more familiar to most of us than are the procedures and practices of scientists and historians, that we tend to draw conclusions about evidence and its usefulness and limitations solely from our notions, which may well be mistaken, of legal proceedings. Thus many of us feel that there is something improper in a situation in which one both gathers or creates evidence and then evaluates it. So there is, if the purpose is to arrive at a just and impartial decision between two rival claims. But in fields where justice is not involved, where competing claims are not for damages or punishment but merely to assert the relative truthfulness of propositions, it is common practice for the judgment-maker to develop or create his own evidence. If his interest is in discovering truth, he is entitled to take steps to seek it out.

Another erroneous impression may be that all evidence is alike in usefulness and applicability. As clearly indicated by the table on page 92 and 93, evidence varies considerably from field to field. As problems and pressures differ, evidence will differ. Thus, if auditing is to have a theory of evidence, it will have to look to itself for the development of that concept. It can borrow ideas from others and learn from their experience; but like law or history, it must develop a concept peculiar and pertinent to its own needs. What is legitimately accepted as truth in one field may not meet either the standards or the need of another field. This suggests that a first step toward the development of a theory of evidence for auditing is to examine the nature of the propositions to be judged and for which evidence is required. In other words, what is the peculiar nature of the judgment problem in auditing and what kind of evidence is required?

Propositions and Evidence in Auditing

Types of Propositions to be Judged in Auditing. Auditing is concerned with the verification or testing of financial statements and similar data. Such data consist of a series of assertions. A balance sheet asserts that the enterprise has cash, receivables, inventories, and so on. The statement further asserts that these items are appropriately disclosed and described and that their classification accords with an acceptable interpretation and application of generally accepted accounting principles. The total number of assertions included in a set of financial statements is considerable, but our interest here is in the essential nature of these propositions, not in their number. What different classes do they fall into; how can they best be studied? We are accustomed, of course, to dividing them into classes or groups by subject matter. We think of them as relating to a given asset such as inventories or receivables, or to liabilities, expenses, and the like. But this does not get at their nature and so is of little assistance in examining the kind of evidence required to test their validity.

For our purposes here, determining the problems of judgment and evidence involved, financial statement propositions can be classified as follows:

I. Assertions of existence or nonexistence

A. Of physical things

1. Present

2. Not present

B. Of nonphysical things

II. Assertions of past events

III. Assertions of quantitative conditions

A. Simple quantities

B. Amounts involving value judgments

IV. Assertions of qualitative conditions

A. Expressed

B. Implied

V. Mathematical assertions

A. Resulting from single calculations

B. Resulting from multiple calculations

The auditor is obviously concerned with the existence of certain physical assets such as cash on hand, securities, inventories, and tangible fixed assets. Most of these are normally on hand and subject to direct examination. Others, such as cash in bank, inventories stored in public or other distant warehouses, and marketable securities held for safekeeping by a financial institution, are not available for his inspection. Reverting for a moment to the basic types of truths noted earlier in this chapter, it seems clear that, other things being equal, an auditor can be more sure of the existence of those things available for his personal examination than of those not physically present. In logical parlance, he can have a certitude of knowledge. (Obviously, this certitude is limited to physical existence only and does not extend to such important matters as grade, quality, condition, or value. Even quantity may present a separate problem.)

The expression "other things being equal" is an important qualification. Many seasoned auditors would rather have a statement from a reputable financial institution attesting to the fact that it is holding securities for the company under examination than to have a statement by an inexperienced assistant that he had seen and counted the securities in the company's vault. The possibility that the assistant might not be a satisfactory observer is only one factor influencing the auditor in this respect; the other may be a feeling that a signed letter from the bank will give him better protection if his verification program is ever questioned in court. From the standpoint of the nature of evidence, neither of these is a valid position. If the asset can be examined physically, the strongest type of evidence, the asset itself, is available. Equally strong evidence is not available if the asset is not present for examination.

In addition to assertions respecting physical things, financial statements contain a number of assertions respecting the existence of nonphysical assets and liabilities. Accounts receivable, goodwill, patents and trademarks, accounts payable, and other liabilities are all alike in that they have no physical existence which the auditor can examine directly. There may be documents which represent them, but the asset or liability itself cannot be examined. With these, as with physical assets unavailable for examination, the auditor cannot obtain compelling evidence. He must be content with something less than certitude.

It is important to realize that a financial statement not only asserts the existence of those items listed in it, it also asserts the nonexistence of those items not so listed. If the liability section fails to include an amount for notes payable, the balance sheet thereby asserts that the company has no obligation represented by notes payable. If no marketable securities appear on the asset side, then we can accept the balance sheet as stating that the company owns no such securities. This type of negative proposition presents a different problem to the auditor. First, it is not as clearly stated or brought as forcefully to his mind as is the positive assertion of existence. Second, evidence to establish its validity or lack of validity is more difficult to acquire. If a company claims the existence of a given asset, the auditor can call for positive evidence—either the asset itself or some other evidence that it exists. If such evidence is made available, he can reach a conclusion promptly; if it is not available, then he can just as promptly reach a negative conclusion on the proposition. But on a negative assertion, such as that there are no unrecorded liabilities, there is no simple piece of positive evidence that will convince him of the truthfulness of the assertion. Certainly there are steps he can take, like the various procedures involved in the search for unrecorded liabilities. But even when these have been performed, he cannot be as sure that this assertion is true as he can be that cash exists in a given amount.

For example, how does one search for unrecorded assets? Over-depreciation, "conservative" maintenance and repair capitalization policies, current expensing of research and development costs, and LIFO inventory practices, for example, may lead to what can be described only as unrecorded assets. Granting that some effort could be made to uncover these, it seems apparent that real assurance of the nonexistence of even substantial unrecorded assets is unlikely.

Thus within the class of financial statement assertions dealing with the existence or nonexistence of things, the validity of some propositions can be determined in a way that is compelling in its influence on the mind of the auditor; compelling evidence for others can never be provided and the auditor can be nothing more than persuaded.

The many transactions whose effects are reported in the balance sheet or which themselves are reported in the income statement or statement of retained earnings are all, at the balance sheet date and at the date investigated by the auditor, past events. Here we see a considerable similarity to historical research. The historian is concerned with what have been called "ineradicable past events." To a considerable extent the auditor is also concerned with ineradicable past events.

When we turn to that class of financial statement proposition described as quantitative conditions we find a similar situation. Most financial statement items include amounts. The assertion is that the company possesses cash and in a certain amount, or that it has income and in a certain amount. These two illustrations are useful in pointing out the difference between the subdivisions of this major classification, assertions involving simple quantities and assertions about amounts involving value judgments.

The amount of cash asserted to be possessed and on hand is obtained by counting the various units of coin and currency; determination or verification of that amount is a simple process of counting. The same might be true of the number of shares of authorized stock or of shares reacquired and held in the treasury. These we refer to here as simple quantities. The amount of income for the period is quite another type of quantity. There are no units to be counted either to determine the appropriate amount or to verify it. As we well know, the net income figure is affected by a great many component amounts, many of which represent value judgments. The collectibility or uncollectibility of the accounts receivable must be estimated and a provision must be made for bad debts or those determined to be uncollectible (a value judgment) must be charged to expense. Any error in this particular judgment will carry forward into the net income figure as will errors in numerous other estimates and calculations.

If a financial statement assertion involves a simple amount, the auditor can test that proposition and be fairly certain that the amount is truthful. Like units can be simply enumerated by the auditor with results that are almost as compelling to his mind as would be the examination of physical assets. But where the amount, the quantitative conditions, is the result of calculations involving value judgments, the available evidence is not nearly so convincing. The auditor cannot have anything like a certitude of knowledge.

The entire area of qualitative conditions must be included in those assertions for which certitude is impossible. First, however, it may be well to describe some of the qualitative conditions which are asserted in financial statements.

Included here are both express and implied conditions; that is, some are definitely stated, while others are implied by the classifications and arrangements we find in the statements. The marketability of the securities described as such in the balance sheet is a clearly expressed quality. The availability of cash for the general purposes of the company is a quality which we take for granted if the cash is included among current assets without the disclosure of any restrictions. Thus it is an implied rather than an expressed quality.

The grouping of current liabilities in one section with a total implies that they have one quality or more in common which either permits or perhaps requires their classification together. The listing of current assets in a rough order of liquidity implies characteristics that must be considered qualitative. The omission of contingent liabilities from the money columns of the balance sheet and their relegation to a footnote status imply that they have a different probability from those items which are permitted to remain in the statement itself. The classifications of expenses and revenues in the income statement imply qualities that may or may not be expressed in their titles.

These various express and implied assertions of qualitative characteristics of the things enumerated in the financial statement call for a different kind of evidence than do assertions of physical existence, for example. We cannot see or touch or hear or taste the marketability of securities. Marketability is an abstract quality; as such its assertion requires supporting evidence somewhat different from that required to support the assertion of a characteristic such as physical existence. Clearly the evidence available to support such an assertion cannot be as compelling to the mind of the auditor; for propositions asserting qualitative characteristics, evidence at best can be no more than persuasive.

In addition to propositions that assert existence of quantitative or qualitative conditions, there are a number of assertions in the financial statements that are purely mathematical in nature. The total for a given group of expense accounts asserts that it is the correct sum of the individual items included in the group. The net income figure at the end of the statement of income is an assertion that arithmetically, without regard to the many other factors that may be involved, the net income calculation results in that specific amount. Many of these assertions are the result of a single calculation, the total of a series of amounts or the difference between two amounts; a few, like the net income figure, are the result of a number of subsidiary calculations. In either case, they fall within the class of propositions about which the auditor can attain certitude. By repeating the calculation from which the amount in question was derived, he can determine for himself whether or not that amount is mathematically correct. Having done so, he can know with assurance the truthfulness or falsity of the assertion. Of course, it is always possible that a given calculation would be beyond the abilities of the auditor to test, but the simple nature of the mathematical assertions which now appear in financial statements would make this unlikely. Even if it were a difficult calculation, to maintain professional competence he would have to master the mathematics involved.

Thus mathematical assertions may fairly be classed among those for which the available evidence is compelling.

This brief discussion of the general types of proposition submitted for audit suggests rather forcefully that compelling evidence is available to support only a limited number of financial statement propositions and that a great many other propositions, probably the great majority, are such that the mind of the auditor is not compelled but rather only persuaded of the reliability of the assertion at issue. This idea may be presented in the following outline:

- Assertions for which compelling evidence is available
  - Existence of physical things if present
  - Simple quantitative amounts
  - Mathematical assertions
- Assertions for which compelling evidence is not available
  - Existence of physical things which are not present
  - Existence of nonphysical things
  - Nonexistence of physical and nonphysical things
  - Occurrence of past events
  - Amounts involving value judgments
  - Qualitative conditions whether express or implied

An additional point should be made at this time. The outline above indicates only the general availability or nonavailability of compelling evidence; it does not imply that the auditor is necessarily able to obtain the evidence within the terms of his assignment in every given case. We must remember that time is always an important factor in the collection and evaluation of audit evidence. Thus time may not permit the auditor to take the necessary steps to obtain compelling evidence, even if it is available. Cost is another factor of importance to auditors. Auditing works within a framework of economic usefulness that requires the balancing of cost with benefit derived. If cost and time were not factors, every physical thing asserted in the financial statements could be examined to give certainty of their existence to the auditor. Inventory, no matter how far away or how inconsequential, could be exposed to the physical senses of the auditor so he could assure himself of its existence. But cost and time are important; it would be unreasonable to incur substantial costs to ascertain the existence of assets of inconsequential amounts. It might also be unreasonable to incur substantial costs to prove the existence of assets of even significant amounts if other types of evidence are sufficiently persuasive and more readily available. The difference between compelling evidence and very persuasive evidence may not be sufficiently important to warrant the added cost of obtaining the former. On the other hand, other things being equal, compelling evidence is much the more desirable.

At this point, having faced the fact that an auditor can have certitude on only a limited number of the propositions submitted to his investigation and judgment, and cognizant of the very real influence of time and cost in audit work, we propose a definition of truth in auditing. Earlier in this chapter, truth was defined as "conformity with reality." *Truth in auditing may be defined as conformity with reality as the auditor can determine reality at the time of his examination and with the evidence available.*

Actually this is no real modification of the basic notion of truth at all. No mortal man in any field of professional endeavor attains absolute knowledge. Continuing revisions of man's descriptions of the world as he knows it are accepted in the physical sciences. Courts occasionally reverse the decisions of lower courts and sometimes modify their own positions in given areas of litigation. At best, truth is relative and not always clearly discernible. Auditors have no greater powers of discernment than others. The limitations imposed by their subject matter and the conditions under which they work must be recognized by auditors as by other professional men. A judicious conclusion resulting from a search for evidence which was reasonable in extent and intensity in view of the importance of the question and the limitations of the situation must be considered sufficient to arrive at the truth for auditing purposes. The subsequent discovery of additional evidence or a better understanding of surrounding facts might later challenge or even nullify the original conclusion. Nevertheless, the best conclusion possible at the time approaches truth as closely as can be expected in this field.

This classification of audit evidence has been useful primarily to point out that little audit evidence is such that it can lead to a surety of knowledge and that most of the propositions which the auditor is asked to judge fall in a group for which compelling evidence is not available at any cost. This is true of many other fields of inquiry as well, but we must never forget its importance in auditing. Such a classification as this is not particularly useful for other purposes, such as program planning, actual judgment formation, or introducing novices to the field. For these purposes we need a classification of evidence stated in terms more pertinent to performance of the daily tasks of auditing.

It would be desirable if such a working classification could be prepared to reflect the relative reliability of the different types of evidence included. Unfortunately this is not possible. Only if the classification suggested on page 102 is used can be indicate relative reliability with any substantial degree of accuracy, and we have already decided that we need a more technical classification than this.

A useful classification is one whose terms are familiar to the auditor. If it is also complete and its classes are mutually exclusive it will serve our purposes of examining more closely the nature of the evidence with which auditing is concerned. The simple classification which follows, we believe, has these advantages and two others; it suggests the relative reliability of the evidence included in each class, and it has the important advantage of being directly relatable to the basic audit techniques or ways of obtaining evidence.

Types of Audit Evidence

1. Physical examination by the auditor of the thing represented in the accounts
2. Statements by independent third parties
    - Written
    - Oral
3. Authoritative documents
    - Prepared outside the enterprise under examination
    - Prepared inside the enterprise under examination
4. Statements by officers and employees of the company under examination
    - Formal
    - Informal

5. Calculations performed by the auditor
6. Satisfactory internal control procedures
7. Subsequent actions by the company under examination and others
8. Subsidiary or detail records with no significant indications of irregularity
9. Interrelationships with other data

Auditing in its entirety is made up of two functions, both closely concerned with evidence. The first is the evidence-gathering function; the second is that of evidence evaluation. In many instances in practice, evidence is evaluated as it is gathered so these two functions appear to proceed simultaneously. There is little conscious separation of the two and for the examination as a whole they proceed as one. For judgment on any individual proposition, however, they must be undertaken one at a time and in the order stated. First, the auditor must turn his efforts to obtaining as much evidence as he feels he will need to judge satisfactorily the proposition before him. Having the evidence in hand, he must then examine it critically before he permits it to work on his mind and compel or persuade him to accept the truthfulness or falsity of the proposition.

Here a well-disciplined mind is essential. It is easy to accept evidence on its face, never questioning its reliability. An auditor must refrain from such temptations and school himself in carefully and critically examining the evidence he accumulates before he accepts it. Here his problem is akin to that of any judgment-maker who himself collects or creates the evidence he must then evaluate. Working closely with evidence while collecting or creating it, he may unconsciously be prone to overrate both its significance and its reliability. Only by critically studying evidence in general and the particular evidence before him in each problem can he expect to reach the consistently valid judgments expected of a professional person.

Audit Evidence and the Theory of Knowledge

Auditing, history, and law are among the fields of inquiry which rely upon evidence for settling doubt and obtaining belief.

In studying the nature of historical and legal evidence, authorities have recognized their relationship with the general theory of knowledge.[4] In this section we will study audit evidence from the same standpoint.

The Theory of Knowledge

In their efforts to understand the reality of the universe, philosophers have developed certain basic methods of obtaining knowledge. These have been termed: "sources of belief," "ways of knowing," "organons of knowledge," and "sources of assurance." All these methods have existed together almost throughout the history of philosophical thought, but, usually, one method was dominant at a time or associated with one or another school of philosophy.[5] Today, all these methods are included as a part of regular course work in appropriate fields to train the student in logical thinking.

It is noteworthy that the most influential work in this area was John Locke's *Essay Concerning Human Understanding* in which he set out "to inquire into the origin, certainty, and extent of human knowledge, together with the grounds and degrees of belief, opinion, and assent."[6]

Considerable credit for the analysis and classification of these methods is due American philosophers. Peirce was the pioneer in this area. He urged the study of logic for everyone concerned with reasoning and inferential activities:

---

[4] See for instance, Simon Greenleaf: *A Treatise on the Law of Evidence*, "...it being assumed on the authority of approved writers, that all that men know is referable, in a philosophic view, to perception and reflection. But, in fact, the knowledge acquired by an individual, through his own perception and reflection, is but a small part of what he possesses; much of what we are content to regard and act upon as knowledge, having been acquired through the perception of others." p. 11. See also, George, H. B.: *Historical Evidence*, Oxford University, England, 1909, and Vincent, John Martin: *Historical Research*, New York: Peter Smith, 1929, particularly chapter 21.

[5] For instance, the 17th century, or more accurately, the period starting with Galileo (1564-1642) and ending with Leibnitz (1646-1716), is known as the Age of Reason. The 18th century's philosophy is associated with Locke and Hume's empiricism. Skepticism is particularly attributed to Descartes, and intuition to Bergson.

[6] P. W. Wright, *The Ways of Philosophy* (New York: The Odyssey Press, Inc., 1954), p. 24.

> Few persons care to study logic, because everybody conceives himself to be proficient enough in the art of reasoning already. But I observe that this satisfaction is limited to one's own ratio-cination, and does not extend to that of other men.
>
> We come to full possession of our power of drawing inferences the last of all our faculties, for it is not so much a natural gift as a long and difficult art.

We find Peirce's definition of "inquiry" particularly interesting because it relates directly to the kind of problem faced by auditors. He defined "inquiry" in terms of the basic concepts of "doubt" and "belief ":

> Doubt is an uneasy and dissatisfied state from which we struggle to free ourselves and pass into the state of belief; while the latter is a calm and satisfactory state which we do not wish to avoid, or to change to a belief in anything else. On the contrary, we cling tenaciously, not merely to believing, but to believing just what we do believe.
>
> The irritation of doubt causes a struggle to attain a state of belief. I shall term this struggle, Inquiry.... The sole object of inquiry is the Settlement of Opinion.[7]

Many American philosophers have followed Peirce's work, each advancing his own classification of the sources of knowledge.[8] Contemporary writers, however, are almost unanimous that Montague's treatment of the subject is the most comprehensive. His analysis, evaluation, and objective criticism of the sources of knowledge has made his work outstanding.[9]

---

[7] John Sanders Peirce, "The Fixation of Belief," first published in *Popular Science Monthly*, Vol. XII (1877), pp. 1-15; Edited by Vincent Tomas in *Essays in the Philosophy of Science* (New York: The Liberal Arts Press, 1957), pp. 3-30.

[8] To mention a few:

C. G. Shaw, emphasizes rationalism, empiricism, and pragmatism as the organons of knowledge. *(Logic in Theory and Practice*, New York: Prentice-Hall, Inc., 1935, Chapters 19-21).

P. W. Wright emphasizes authority, observation, reason, empirical method, and intuition as the sources of assurance. *(The Ways of Philosophy*, New York: The Odyssey Press, 1954, Chapter 2).

G. J. Brennan considers authority, intuition, reason, and experience, the typical sources of knowledge. *(The Meaning of Philosophy*, New York: Harper Bros., 1953, Chapter 5).

[9] W. P. Montague, *The Ways of Knowing* (New York: The Macmillan Company, 1953), Fourth Edition, Muirhead Library of Philosophy.

Logic and Audit Evidence

In this section we will proceed on Peirce's theory that logic provides the criteria by which we can settle doubts and evaluate beliefs, whether obtained in the performance of rational thinking or in the regular pursuit of everyday life. We will attempt to apply logic, the most basic of all sciences, to the analysis, classification, and interrelation of audit techniques for obtaining evidence. To point out the essential characteristics of audit evidence we will compare and contrast the factors which govern its collection and use with those recognized in the fields of inquiry which have preceded auditing in the study and use of evidence.

For the purpose of this study we will adopt Montague's definition of logic:

> By logic, then, we shall mean the search for the ultimate criteria by the use of which our beliefs can be validated and true knowledge be attained.[10]

Therefore, we now turn to a brief study of the teachings of logic with respect to evidence and the ways of knowing. Some of these ideas have already been presented in preliminary pages of this monograph. They are included here both for emphasis and to make this presentation reasonably complete.

With respect to evidence, logic teaches:

1. Belief, to be rational, must be supported by evidence.
2. Evidence has varying influences upon the human mind.
3. There are only a few basic ways of obtaining ideas and beliefs.
4. These ways of knowing vary in nature and validity; none of them is sufficient in all cases.

---

[10] *Ibid.*, p. 34.

We should also recognize the attempts of the following writers to apply the principles of logic to accounting:

D. H. MacKenzie, "The Logic of the Cost and Revenue Approach," *The Accounting Review* (January, 1947), pp. 12-18.

L. A. Schmidt, "Practical Uses of Formal Logic in Accountants' Daily Work," *The Journal of Accountancy* (November, 1949), pp. 378-387.

K. B. Berg, *Objectivity and Relevance in Accounting Evidence*, unpublished Ph.D. thesis, University of Illinois, 1952.

W. L. Campfield, *An Inquiry into the Nature of Judgment Formation and Its Implications to the Public Accounting Profession*, unpublished Ph.D. thesis, University of Illinois, 1951.

5. Each method of knowing has special applications in which it is more effective than the others.

The first two statements in this list have been dealt with at some length in this work, but the second merits a little closer scrutiny. Evidence varies in its influence on the human mind in two ways. First, some evidence, as we have seen, is so strong and so vivid that it compels the mind to accept it as truthful, and the mind then reaches a sureness of knowledge; other evidence is not nearly so forceful nor so vivid, and the mind can entertain, along with the evidence itself, the thought that it might not really be so. Such evidence becomes more or less persuasive as it influences the mind to accept or reject the proposition in support of which the evidence has been submitted or obtained. Thus we have differences within evidence itself that help to account for the influence it has on the mind of the judgment-maker.

The second factor which accounts for the varying influence of judgment is the degree of skill and experience possessed by the one using the evidence. A small child will believe almost anything he is told because experience has not taught him to doubt. In the same manner, a novice in any field may easily be misled. A seasoned practitioner with adequate training and a variety of experience is much more difficult to convince. He looks at evidence with a healthy skepticism and a "show me" attitude because he has found from past experience that what appears to be so is not always so. In many ways, the mark of a rational thinker is not only an insistence upon evidence, but the ability to judge the available evidence. Before he concerns himself with what the evidence says about the proposition at issue, he first examines the evidence critically to see whether or not it is acceptable. If it is not, then he cares not what it says about the proposition. The familiar expression "consider the source" is sound advice for anyone who would think logically.

This is a matter of considerable importance in auditing. First, because the auditor gathers his own evidence, there is no one to screen it for him and tell him whether or not it is reliable. His mind is not protected from irrelevant and misleading evidence as is that of the juror in litigation proceedings. Hence he must be alert to variations in the strength and reliability of different types of evidence and skilled in testing evidence before he permits it to influence his judgment. Second, he is a professional judgment-maker; many people rely on his opinion. Any error in his judgment may be compounded many times because others will accept his opinion as that of an expert. Because he claims expertness in the collection and evaluation of evidence pertinent to financial statements and invites others to rely on his judgment, he has a special responsibility to develop and use skill in evaluating the evidence available to him and in forming judgments based on that evidence. He is intimately and professionally involved in acquiring and reviewing knowledge.

Montague points out that there are basically five positive ways of acquiring knowledge.

> As will be seen, the problem of validating beliefs is intimately associated with the problem of ascertaining the source of beliefs. Hence in connection with the logical problem of validity we shall treat to some extent the psychological problems of genesis.
>
> Our ideas and beliefs can be traced to one or more of the following origins:
>
> (1) Testimony of others; (2) Intuition, which is at least partly grounded in instincts, feelings and desires; (3) Abstract reasoning from universal principles; (4) Sensory experience; (5) Practical activity having successful consequences.
>
> Each of these sources may be, and actually has been, accepted as indicating a primary criterion for determining philosophic truth; and thus to the five sources of belief there correspond the following five types of logical theory: (1) Authoritarianism; (2) Mysticism; (3) Rationalism; (4) Empiricism; (5) Pragmatism.[11]

Montague goes on to describe each of these methods, both as a means of determining or obtaining truth and as a basis for a theory of philosophy. He finds no one of them satisfactory in itself as the basis for philosophic theory and recommends the merging of all five types into one all-inclusive philosophy. Our concern here is not so much with the theory of philosophy as it is with the ways of knowing, the ways of collecting and using evidence. It is desirable we give some attention of each of these methods of acquiring ideas and beliefs so that we can relate the types of evidence available in auditing to these basic ways of knowing.

[11] Montague, *op. cit.*, p. 34.

To these five basic ways of knowing Montague adds another which, in contrast to these positive methods, he refers to as a negative method.

> ...there are many propositions which we should all agree can be neither proved nor disproved by any of the above criteria, and which consequently furnish the grounds for a sixth and negative type of logical theory, that of Skepticism.

Let us briefly examine each of these six methods in turn.

Authoritarianism. With respect to authoritarianism, Montague writes:

> We get more of our beliefs from the testimony of our fellows than from any other source. Little of our knowledge of the universe is directly tested by our own intuition, reason, experience, or practice. We accept on trust nine-tenths of what we hold to be true. Man is a suggestible animal and tends to believe what is said to him unless he has some positive reason for doubting the honesty or competence of his informant.[12]

> The weakness of the authoritarian method consists first in the fact that authorities conflict, and that there is consequent an internal discrepancy in the method which makes it difficult of application.... The second and more serious source of weakness is due to the apparent impossibility of treating authority as an ultimate source of truth.[13]

In these few words we get an idea both of the importance of this method of obtaining knowledge and of its shortcomings. If the one from whom we obtain testimony is ill-informed or has any reason to be dishonest, we must accept his testimony with misgiving. And even if he is both honest and well-informed, there is still the possibility that he is in error. Evidence of this kind can never be more than persuasive; it lacks the force of conviction supplied by rational reasoning or sensory perception.

Yet we must make use of authority; we cannot get along without it. At another point, in summing up the various ways of knowing and their usefulness, Montague writes:

> It is necessary for an individual to trust other individuals in matters which he cannot investigate for himself; and unless there is reason to suppose that the witnesses are biased or incompetent, their testimony should be put on a par with his own.[14]

---

[12] *Ibid.*, p. 39.

[13] *Ibid.*, pp. 39-40.

[14] *Ibid.*, p. 225.

This is the attitude taken by auditors in obtaining confirmations from outside parties. A statement from a bank, from a customer, or from a creditor must be accepted because the auditor cannot investigate the fact at issue in any other way. And more than this, he is entitled to rely on this testimony unless there is reason to suppose that the ones returning the confirmation are biased or incompetent. This lends strong support to our confirmation practice. Of course if he does have reason to question the competence or bias of those to whom he sends confirmation requests, he must view their replies with some suspicion.

Mysticism. Knowledge obtained through authoritarianism comes to us from others; knowledge obtained through intuition comes to us from within ourselves. Intuition brings the sudden flash of insight, the quick perception of truth, the unexplained awareness of relationships that we can account for in no other way. The inspiration of the religionist is one with the "genius" of the inventor or the sixth sense that cautions an auditor to beware of irregularities in a given situation. Montague explains intuition as a combination of instinct, imagination, and experience.

The person with a substantial fund of experience, certain inborn instincts which he may have sharpened considerably by skillful exercise, and a lively imagination may combine these abilities to produce innovations that to those who do not possess such talents appear little short of miraculous. All of us have marveled at one time or another at the skill and poise with which someone performs activities which we find difficult, if not impossible. So it may be with the operation of the mind, says Montague; some individuals may have developed their minds to the point where experience and instinct trigger their imaginations to produce ideas which seem most unusual to those with less mental training and skill.

> Our individual experiences are moulded and coloured by this background of inherited tendencies, and many of the intuitions or direct insights that seem inexplicable as products of ordinary perception may well be the spontaneous expression of congenital tendencies. Just as our instincts represent the life habits of our ancestors, so our memories represent the experiences of our own past and constitute an additional background for the intuitive judgments of the moment. It is this joint system of tendencies derived from inherit-

ance and memory which without coming themselves into consciousness largely control our conscious processes and occasionally contribute original ideas and happy inspirations. When the stored-up traces of the past act in this way, we speak, not of memory or instinct, but of *imagination*. We all have a certain amount of imagination; and a characteristic feature of the faculty is the suddenness and spontaneity of its action. Often, after we have been working over some problem and have put it aside as unsolved, the solution will flash suddenly into our consciousness. The movements of all creative art and creative thought, and especially all expressions of humour and wit, have their inception in these flashes of the imagination.[15]

In favour of mysticism as a method of acquiring knowledge, it may truly be said that not only in philosophy, but in art, and even in science, some of the most significant ideas and ideals have originated from the intuitions of the mystic.[16]

The most common application of intuition in auditing is the practice of scanning. An editorial in *The Accounting Review* as long ago as 1934 emphasized the desirability of reducing the effort expended in detailed accounting analyses and increasing the time spent in analytical and comparative review. It reads:

> Field work must be devoted to less routine. Performances should be stressed that utilize to the utmost technical acumen and imaginative resources.
>
> Now scanning does just that. There are accountants who can barely glance at a balance sheet and come away with a good many significant facts in their minds. They are not geniuses. They are exceptionally well-trained scanners. Their peculiar capacity is the fruit of long experience, of many scannings. Not everyone needs to be that expert, but no one should neglect his education in that respect.... A good scanner is a person who sees many things quickly—in their relationship to other things. His judgment has ripened by constant contact with the practical affairs of many business enterprises.[17]

The same idea is expressed in the following:

> To scan means to scruitinize or to examine point by point. In auditing it refers to the critical study of an account, a book of original entry, or any other record or summary of information. If there is any

---

[15] *Ibid.*, pp. 55-56.

[16] *Ibid.*, p. 56.

[17] Editorial, "Scanning," *The Accounting Review*, September, 1934, pp. 257-258.

> technique which approaches the sixth sense sometimes mistakenly attributed to auditors it is that of scanning. An experienced and alert practitioner can frequently look at a given page and almost immediately conclude not only that something is peculiar but also state exactly where the trouble lies. However, there is nothing miraculous about such a diagnosis. The auditor is merely summoning up all his accounting knowledge and experience on that particular type of information to evaluate that which he sees as being either normal and ordinary or as being unusual and therefore subject to suspicion.[18]

Montague accepts both authoritarianism and mysticism as methods of obtaining truth, but he warns against accepting ideas generated by these methods unless there is corroborating evidence.[19] Neither of these methods provides results which can be tested except by recourse to other methods of knowing. Thus authoritarianism and mysticism are useful but not independently reliable methods.

Rationalism. Rationalism consists of reasoning from universals to particulars; it is identified particularly with mathematics and applications of pure logic in which we start with accepted assumptions of universal application and reason from them to conclusions. Thus, in solving an arithmetical problem, we accept the numbering system, the meaning of arithmetical signs and symbols, and proceeding from these we solve the particular problem before us. We use mathematics a good deal in auditing, but recalculation of arithmetical results would not be the only applications of rationalism. When we review a system of internal control and reason from the existence of certain controls that irregularities are or are not likely to occur, we are applying rationalism.

Empiricism. Empiricism consists of basing knowledge on perceptual experience. The empiricist reasons from details to universals. Having observed a large number of cases and found a pattern of some kind in them, he extracts from his experience universal or general ideas. His reliance is on concrete and particular things or occurrences from which he feels safe in drawing

---

[18] R. K. Mautz, *Fundamentals of Auditing* (New York: John Wiley & Sons, Inc., 1954), pp. 55-56.

[19] *Ibid.*, p. 64.

conclusions. The auditor who physically examines inventory or observes a paymaster distributing payroll checks is obtaining empirical evidence.

Empiricism and rationalism are often combined. For example, an auditor reviews internal control and reasons from the description given that it is a good system. Before he can rely on it, however, he wants to examine a number of transactions or events to see if they were actually handled as described. Here the auditor is supplementing his rational conclusion by specific empirical evidence. This may either support or contest his first conclusion. Montague indicates that either of these methods is more likely to be misleading by itself than when combined with the other:

> In short, rationalism and empiricism are complementary criteria for the discovery of truth; neither can be substituted for the other; neither can contradict the other. When there appears, as there often has appeared, to be a conflict between empirical experience and rational reflection, we may be assured that such conflict or antinomy is not due to a defect in either criterion of truth, but only to our misuse of one or the other or of both. It is the function of empiricism to discover through induction the universal propositions that are implied by the analysis of any group of concrete facts. It is the function of rationalism to discover through deduction the particular consequences implied by the synthesis of any group of abstract propositions. Regarding things from the standpoint of "intension" rather than "extension," empiricism is analytic; rationalism is synthetic. Empiricism proceeds from the concrete and particular to the abstract and universal; rationalism proceeds from the abstract and universal to the concrete and particular. The inductions of the empiricist may or may not agree with the theories already established. The deductions of the rationalist may or may not agree with already observed facts.
>
> Pure empiricism gives us unrelated groups of natural laws based upon whatever groups of facts happen to catch the observer's attention, and the gravest danger to which the pure empiricist is subject consists in the possibility of unchecked errors and undiscovered contradictions lurking in his various isolated doctrines. Pure rationalism gives us logical and mathematical systems of consequences which may be wholly irrelevant to the facts of existence; ...When the two methods are joined, the empiricist furnishes propositions implied by facts, and the rationalist, instead of arbitrarily selecting from the whole realm of possibilities whatever suits his fancy, takes the propositions newly discovered by the empiricist, combines them

> with propositions already established, and from this union of old and new, of general and specific, deduces concrete consequences. It is then the turn of the empiricist to verify by observation the hypothetical deductions of his partner. And instead of indulging in haphazard observation, uncontrolled by any systematized interest, he will be influenced by a sense of the relative importance of the facts to be investigated, and will concentrate his observation and experiment upon those portions of the jungle of experienced facts which seem likely to confirm or refute, extend or modify the laws previously established.[20]

Pragmatism. Pragmatism and practice are closely related. The pragmatic believes that what works well must be true; whatever fails to work is not true. Practicability, workability are the tests of truth. The man who believes that accounting principles are developed, not intuitively by flashes of insight, not rationally by reasoning from basic assumptions, but out of the practical experience of a great many accountants and businessmen working in a variety of situations over a considerable period of time is essentially a pragmatist. Montague finds that empiricism and pragmatism have much in common. Both rely on experience, both are means of testing propositions. Empiricism, however, tests belief by present experience. Pragmatism tests beliefs by the consequences that flow from them in the future. Thus pragmatic truth has strong implications of useful, practical consequences; since the usefulness is judged primarily from the standpoint of individuals, it becomes a very subjective type of truth.

In auditing we apply pragmatic methods when we trace the results of transactions or conditions into the future. In considering remittances received after the balance sheet date as evidence of the collectibility of receivables at the balance sheet date, in judging the fairness of inventory amounts by the sales that result from the inventory during the first month or two of the following year, in testing the company's contentions with respect to contingent liabilities by searching for payments made at a later date, we are applying essentially pragmatic methods. It appears apparent from these illustrations that pragmatism has definite limitations as a method of obtaining evidence; it does not have wide applications, especially in auditing where time is of the essence. Rarely is it possible to wait, for example, until the retire-

---

[20] *Ibid.*, pp. 126, 127, 128.

ment of a fixed asset to determine whether the depreciation rate has been established fairly, or until receivables have been collected to ascertain their validity.

Skepticism. To these five positive methods of obtaining evidence in support of ideas and beliefs, Montague adds a sixth and negative method, that of skepticism. The value of this way of knowing is at once apparent to an auditor. Some philosophers have carried skepticism to the point where they are willing to believe nothing, a state of complete doubt. Montague agrees that the human mind is unable to attain absolute certainty in any field of inquiry, yet this does not necessarily lead to a condition of complete doubt.[21] There is still the possibility and even the probability that asserted truths are true; the evidence may be such as will persuade the mind to accept the proposition. If the evidence is thus adequate, the mind is more in error when it continues to doubt than when it accepts. Skepticism is thus an important tool in the thinker's kit only if he uses it wisely. If he tends to question the evidence produced by the other ways of knowing until he has securely established its reliability, skepticism is useful; if he continues to doubt for the sake of doubting long after a reasonable man would be persuaded by the evidence at hand, skepticism has been permitted to get out of bounds.

So it is with an auditor. He should be hard to convince, but not impossible. All evidence should be examined critically and some of it may have to be rejected. None of it should be rejected, however, merely because it is not conclusive. Philosophers disagree whether any evidence provides absolute knowledge, convincing beyond all possible doubt; they agree, however, that if not all, most evidence is no more than persuasive. The auditor must take such evidence as he can obtain and make the best decisions possible. We have propositions to judge; judgments must be made; if compelling evidence is not available, let us judge as soundly as we can with the evidence that is available.

Audit Evidence and the Logical Methods. To gain a better understanding of the nature of the evidence with which an auditor works it may be helpful to classify the types of audit evidence within the general framework of the ways of knowing. This results in a classification as follows:

---

[21] *Ibid.*, p. 209.

- Authoritarianism—evidence based on the testimony of others
  - Testimony of people
    - Statements of independent third parties (confirmations)
    - Statements of officers and employees (representations)
  - Testimony of documents
    - Documents prepared outside the enterprise
    - Documents prepared inside the enterprise
    - Subsidiary or detail records
- Mysticism—intuitively obtained evidence
  - Scanning
    - Books and records
    - Documents
  - Critical review of testimony of others
- Rationalism
  - Recalculation by auditor
  - Existence of internal control
  - Retracing bookkeeping procedures
- Empiricism—perceptual experience
  - Physical examination and count
- Pragmatism
  - Subsequent actions by the company, its officers, employees, customers, etc.

It is interesting to note the considerable amount of audit evidence that falls within the area of authoritarianism. From the standpoint of discovering the truth, this is not a good form of evidence; it can never provide more than persuasion and this may not be strong. Philosophers do not regard authority as one of the stronger ways of attaining valid knowledge. But then, no one of the other methods is completely reliable in itself either; each of them needs support and bolstering from the others.

Combination of the Logical Methods. Once again we can turn to logic, and we find help from Montague on whom we have already relied for a good deal. After giving lengthy consideration to each of the six ways of knowing, he goes on to the federation of these methods, the combinations of methods which might be most effective, the possibilities of strengthening the weaknesses of one with the force of another. This is not a new idea to auditors who have long found it necessary to seek different types of evidence on the same proposition, but it leads us to a most important conclusion. Although evidence is seldom conclusive, the more kinds of evidence we find in support of a given proposition, the more likely that proposition is to be true. Thus if on a given proposition we could muster some of each of the nine kinds of audit evidence and if none of that evidence were in conflict with other, the probability of the proposition's being in error would be so unlikely that we could consider the sum total of the evidence to be little short of compelling. This follows from the fact that these types of evidence are different in nature and cover all the basic ways of knowing. Having exhausted the possibilities with respect to obtaining knowledge about a proposition and having found the available knowledge unanimously to support it, we would be acting irrationally if we refused to accept the proposition as valid.

If some of the types of audit evidence are not pertinent to this particular proposition and therefore cannot be obtained, we lose by just so much the opportunity of becoming convinced. An attack launched from three directions is not as strong as one from nine directions.

Two points require emphasis here. First, it is not just the quantity of evidence; it is the fact that the approaches to the matter of obtaining evidence vary in nature and literally cover all possibilities. Second, there is a great deal of difference between a situation in which one kind of evidence is just not obtainable and a situation in which one type of evidence actually conflicts with or opposes another. In the latter case, the conflict must be resolved; one or the other has not been applied properly or the results have been misinterpreted.

After pointing out that none of the ways of obtaining knowledge is able by itself to provide certainty and that in combination they strengthen one another considerably, Montague carries his analysis a step further. He divides reality, those things which a mind would know, into five domains and points out that one of the ways of knowing is more important than any of the others in each of these domains. This is not to say that the particular domain is the sole prerogative of the related logical method but only that the method is more naturally adapted to that domain than is any other method. Montague's classification is as follows:[22]

---

[22] *Ibid.*, p. 225.

Classes of Knowable Objects	Logical Method
The domain of objects and events that can be experienced only by minds other than our own.	Authoritarianism (testimony)
The dual domain of: (A) Ultimate and noninstrumental values. (B) A supposed ultimate and ineffable truth.	Mysticism (intuition)
The domain of commensurable and abstract relations.	Rationalism (reasoning from accepted and general assumptions)
The domain of particular facts and concrete relations.	Empiricism (perceptual experience)
The domain of individual and social conduct.	Pragmatism (practical results)

Pertinent alike to all these domains is skepticism, the sixth and negative logical method.

> The function of the skeptic is to make us realize that no knowledge attainable by the human mind is absolutely certain. Systems of belief in all of the five domains which we have considered are and must always be open to revision. Even if one and the same judgment could claim the support of the five positive methods, it would acquire thereby, not certainty, but only a high degree of probability.
>
> To retain toward all problems a measure of open-mindedness is as difficult as it is important. We have an almost unconquerable temptation to shun uncertainty, and to commit ourselves definitely either for or against a given proposition, yet it shows at least as much wisdom to suspend judgment when the evidence is insufficient as to hold a definite conclusion when the evidence justifies it. And the former attitude requires the greater courage.[23]

This division of knowable objects and events into domains to each of which one of the logical methods is most applicable helps us to understand more clearly the problem of marshalling evidence to support any proposition, but it also gives us a clue to the relationship between the types of audit evidence and the types of propositions in financial statements.

---

[23] *Ibid.*, pp. 231-232.

Audit Techniques. Audit evidence is obtained through the application of the basic audit techniques in the form of procedures designed to fit the specific situation. These techniques are:

1. Physical examination and count.
2. Confirmation.
3. Examination of authoritative documents and comparison with the record.
4. Recomputation.
5. Retracing bookkeeping procedures.
6. Scanning
7. Inquiry.
8. Examination of subsidiary records.
9. Correlation with related information.
10. Observation of pertinent activities and conditions.

Objections can be directed at this listing of basic audit techniques because there is some overlap among them and because there is not a direct one-to-one relationship with the types of audit evidence. Neither of these seems particularly significant to this study and both grow out of the nature of audit evidence. For our purpose here, which is to develop a concept of audit evidence, this list of techniques will serve satisfactorily.

Using the domains of knowledge presented earlier, we can develop a similar classification of the types of financial statement propositions to which audit evidence and audit techniques are pertinent. The analogy is not a perfect one, but the relationships which this scheme reveals helps us to understand the scope of the basic audit techniques.

In this chart, financial statement assertions are grouped in four classes. The first of these includes assertions of the existence of physical things present for the auditor's examination and simple quantitative enumeration of amounts which likewise can be determined by the auditor through physical examination and counting. For this group, the audit evidence and audit technique are clearly related and they support the assertion directly. The evidence is empirical in nature.

Assertions in Group II are mathematical which places them under the logical method of rationalism. Again the audit technique and the evidence it provides are clearly related.

FIGURE II
CHART SHOWING INTER-RELATIONSHIP OF LOGICAL METHODS, AUDIT EVIDENCE, AND BASIC AUDIT TECHNIQUES

	Logical Method	*Nature of Assertion*	*Audit Evidence*	*Applicable Technique*
		I		
Skepticism	Empiricism	Existence of physical things present Simple quantitative conditions	Examination by auditor Examination by auditor	Physical examination and count
		II		
	Rationalism	Mathematical	Calculation by auditor	Recomputation
		III		
	Authoritarianism	Existence of physical things not present Past events	Statements by independent third parties Authoritative documents Statements by company personnel Subsidiary or detail records	Confirmation Examination of documents Inquiry Examination of records
		IV		
	Authoritarianism Intuition Rationalism Pragmatism	Existence of nonphysical things Nonexistence of physical and nonphysical things Qualitative conditions Value-judgment quantities	Statements by independent third parties Authoritative documents Statements by company personnel Subsidiary of detail records	Confirmation Examination of documents Inquiry Examination of records
			Satisfactory internal control procedures	Inquiry, retracing bookkeeping procedures, examination of documents, scanning, observation
			Subsequent actions by the company and others	Confirmation, inquiry, examination of documents, observation
			Interrelationships with other data	Coordination with related data Scanning

Group III includes but two subgroups of assertions: the existence of physical things not present, such as inventories, or securities, or fixed assets at locations not visited by the auditor, and past events, which include all the transactions entered into by the company under examination prior to the date of the financial statements, and also, to a more limited extent, so-called "subsequent events." A variety of audit techniques are used to obtain a variety of kinds of evidence to support these assertions, and any one of these techniques may apply to assertions in either subgroup. They are all of a kind, however, in that they all rely on the logical method of authoritarianism. Actually the audit techniques are merely variations on the same theme, that of determining from others what apparently exists or took place.

The assertions in Group IV do not have the homogeneity of the preceding three groups, and there is no direct relationship between the assertions themselves and the kinds of audit evidence which may be obtained to support or refute them. Logically and practically, this is the most difficult area of audit evidence, and it requires the greatest skill on the part of the auditor. He must be sufficiently familiar with the available techniques as well as with the potentials of audit evidence to know the technique which in each case will provide the most useful evidence. In many cases he will need to apply more than one technique if he is to obtain all the evidence readily available on the assertion before him.

Because of the variety of techniques applicable here (all except physical examination) four of the positive ways of knowing are involved, frequently in combination with one another.

Skepticism has been indicated at the left of the chart as applicable to all the assertions listed and to be applied in obtaining every kind of evidence the auditor uses. This is the nature of skepticism as a logical method. Its position in the chart suggests that in many ways it is rather an attitude than a method.

One other point mentioned in the chapter can be added. Evidence obtained with respect to assertions in Groups I and II tends to be compelling on the mind of the auditor or, in other words, to give him a certitude of knowledge. The evidence available for assertions in Groups III and IV can at best be persuasive, although, as suggested in this chapter, this persuasiveness can amount to near certainty.

Audit Evidence and Audit Judgment

The Process of Judgment Formation. In the preceding section we have examined the nature of evidence in general and of audit evidence in particular giving recognition to the limitations and applications of the logical methods of obtaining knowledge. Among the conclusions is that audit evidence varies in its influence on the mind of the auditor and that a combination of types of evidence all in support of the same proposition tends to increase the probability that the proposition can be accepted with little danger. It remains now to integrate these ideas with the procedure of judgment formation in auditing. With this completed we will be ready to draw together the essence of this section in a brief summary of a concept of evidence in auditing.

The procedure of judgment formation may be divided into the following steps:

1. Recognition of the proposition to be proved.
2. Evaluation of the proposition as one requiring evidence of a high or moderate degree of probability.
3. Collection of evidence within the given limits of time and cost.
4. Evaluation of the evidence obtained as valid or not valid.
5. Formulation of judgment as to the proposition at issue.

Recognition of Propositions. Most financial statement assertions come in groups rather than individually; this makes their recognition somewhat more difficult. For example, the following statement, included within the current asset section of a balance sheet, incorporates several subsidiary assertions:

Accounts receivable	$125,000.00

Included as subsidiary propositions are at least the following:

The company has amounts receivable from others.

These amounts will yield remittances of $125,000 or very near that sum.

The amounts due are collectible within the operating cycle of the enterprise.

> All items included within this total amount came from ordinary sales to customers unless stated otherwise.

Part of an auditor's task is to recognize the subsidiary assertions contained within any financial statement proposition. Only if these are identified can evidence be obtained to support or contradict each one. Failure to identify all subsidiary propositions is failure to recognize the full scope of the audit problem. This in turn makes the obtaining of adequate evidence and fully rational judgment most unlikely.

Evaluation of Propositions. Financial statement propositions vary in several ways,[24] and certainly they vary a great deal in significance or materiality. The assertion that a company has unexpired insurance of $10,000 has nowhere near the importance of the assertion that it has cash of $100,000. Illustrations could be multiplied many times, of course. Now if we couple this thought with the idea that some evidence is much more compelling or strong than other evidence, we are led to a conclusion that more compelling evidence is required for material assertions than for assertions that are not material. Note that the important point is not the quantity of evidence but rather the quality of evidence. A single piece of evidence may be compelling, whereas a large amount may be only somewhat persuasive; the auditor must be keen enough to judge the evidence before him according to its validity rather than only its quantity.

We have a very useful precedent for this practice in law. In a criminal case a greater preponderance of evidence is required than is expected if the matter at issue is a civil one only.

> The law distinguishes between two degrees of proof: one in which a proposition is established simply with a probability of over one-half, and which is called *preponderance of evidence;* the other requiring a degree of probability differing from certainty by so little, that anyone who acts upon that difference would be regarded as unreasonable—this degree of probability is called *proof beyond reasonable doubt.* The first degree of probability is sufficient in civil cases, while proof in criminal law requires the second.[25]

---

[24] R. K. Mautz, "Evidence, Judgment, and the Auditor's Opinion," *The Journal of Accountancy*, April, 1959, pp. 40-44, at 43.

[25] Morris R. Cohen, and Ernest Nagel, *An Introduction to Logic and Scientific Method* (New York: Harcourt, Brace and Company, 1934), p. 347, Author's Emphasis.

Thus in a civil case a clear preponderance of evidence is required to justify a decision in favor of one or the other of the contending parties. In a criminal case the evidence must provide "proof beyond reasonable doubt" to warrant a conviction. Of course the difference between a "clear preponderance" of evidence and evidence sufficient to prove "beyond doubt" is a matter of judgment and may often be difficult to establish. Yet the justification for requiring more evidence in one case than in the other is clear, and in the great majority of instances the requirement for greater assurance can easily be met. It is recommended here that we adopt a similar type of requirement in auditing.

In auditing, our distinction would not be based on a clear dichotomy between civil and criminal cases but on a much less definite segregation of assertions as more or less material. This makes application of the principle a little more difficult but certainly not impossible.

Materiality has been defined in these terms:

> The materiality of an item may depend on its size, its nature, or a combination of both. An item should be regarded as material if there is reason to believe that knowledge of it would influence the decisions of an informed investor.[26]

In most cases it is relatively easy to determine if a given financial statement assertion is material or not. If it is not, the auditor need obtain only sufficient evidence to persuade (as contrasted with assure) him that the assertion involved is or is not valid. Borrowing the terminology of law, he should require a preponderance of evidence. If the assertion is one that is material, however, he should require considerably stronger evidence. Here he should attempt to eliminate any reasonable doubt. As seen earlier, a combination of all or several of the various types of audit evidence adds to the probability that the auditor's decision on the proposition is valid. This means that for material assertions, the evidence must either be compelling—and this is possible only for existence of present physical things and for mathematical assertions—or a combination of types of evidence must be obtained.

---

[26] Committee on Accounting Concepts and Standards, 1957 Revision, *The Accounting Review*, October, 1957, pp. 538-546, at 543.

Two questions suggest themselves. What if the assertion at issue is more than immaterial but less than definitely material, a borderline assertion? The necessity for judgment and discretion in just such cases as this helps to qualify auditing as a professional activity. The solution seems obvious even if not definite. The auditor should require enough evidence to assure himself that he is not reaching an ill-advised or hasty decision. He should expect more than he would need for an immaterial item, but probably not as much as if the item were unquestionably a material one.

A second and more vital question has to do with the proper course of action for the auditor if he cannot obtain adequate information to remove the possibility of reasonable doubt about a material item. There seems no alternative in such a situation except to refrain from forming a judgment and rendering an opinion. As Montague has pointed out,[27] the human mind prefers a decision, almost any decision, to remaining in a state of doubt with respect to a proposition. But where there is insufficient evidence to remove doubt, the only rational course of action is to abstain from judgment until that doubt can be removed. In science there are a great many hypotheses for which sufficient evidence has not yet been obtained to demonstrate either their truth or falsity. Thus they must remain hypotheses. It seems likely that the same situation might exist in auditing, particularly in view of the fact that time is a matter of such consequence in reaching decisions on auditing matters.

Collection of Evidence. Considerable attention has been given in this chapter to the types of audit evidence, including their applicability to financial statement propositions, and the basic audit techniques have at least been introduced. Since the application of these techniques to specific audit problems as procedures in audit programs has been covered thoroughly in the literature, no further attention will be given to the subject at this time.

Evaluation of Audit Evidence. Because the auditor determines the type of audit evidence pertinent to his needs, then collects that evidence, and finally uses it in arriving at judgments, it behooves him to take special precautions in reviewing it for

---

[27] *Ibid.*, p. 231.

pertinence, credibility, and usefulness. We have already given attention to this subject, but the importance of this step in the process of judgment formation is such that additional attention is warranted. As indicated in the table on pages 92 and 93 there is considerable similarity between the use of evidence in historical studies and in auditing. If we can turn now to the practices of historians in critically reviewing evidence before utilizing it in historical research we will find some parallels that are extremely helpful to us in auditing.

Historical research and auditing have much in common. To a considerable extent, each works with past events although auditing is also concerned with some present conditions as well. Past events cannot be experienced by the judgment-maker, and so he must rely on evidence other than his own perceptual experiences.

Considerable study and analysis have gone into the development of acceptable methods of historical research. Like other serious inquirers, historians strive to determine and reveal the truth. Because of the nature of their field they must rely heavily on testimony and intuition. As we have seen, these methods of obtaining knowledge are in themselves among the least infallible of the ways of knowing. Therefore the historian mixes in a large order of skepticism and reviews critically whatever is made available to him as evidence of the past.

> Since the object of history is to establish as nearly as possible the *true* development of society or of some selected part, it becomes necessary for the historian first to test the data furnished by his predecessor and to determine whether the fragments of information received are themselves true, or what measure of probability should be ascribed to them. These are the duties of historical criticism.
>
> Criticism, however, is not the chief end of historical research. The combination of results, the perception of the relations of events, and the final construction of these into narratives are the great objects of the study, yet these are of no value unless based on scientific criticism. Not until isolated data have been proved and interpreted may the historians draw safe conclusions.[28]

Like the auditor, the historian has no one to screen for him the evidence that is made available to him. Any screening to ex-

[28]John Martin Vincent, *Historical Research* (New York: Peter Smith, 1929), p. 19.

clude unreliable evidence must be performed by the historian himself, just as it must be done by the auditor. This is why rather firm rules of criticism have been developed.

> The processes of criticism fall naturally into two parts. The first important step is to determine whether the given source is at all admissible as evidence, or, in other words, whether the material is genuine or not. Conclusions are worthless and labor is wasted if the document is fraudulent or misjudged. It is necessary to know at the outset whether the chronicle, charter, or relic is in reality what it claims to be, or what it has been esteemed to be. It is important to determine where and when it originated, who was its author, and where he derived his information. The rules of procedure by which these facts are determined in historical research constitute *External Criticism*....
>
> The second part of the critical processes weights the relation of the testimony to the truth. One must decide whether the statements made are trustworthy, and if not absolutely certain, whether they are probable. The degree of probability or possibility must be determined, or, if necessary, the whole cast out as worthless. This is *Internal Criticism*.[29]

Collingwood, an authority on historical research, points out the development of historical criticism and hails it as essential if historical research is to meet the requirements of the scientific method. He emphasizes that acceptance of authority is not justified until the right of the authority to be accepted as a valid source of historical information has been established.

> As soon as it became understood that a given statement, made by a given author, must never be accepted for historical truth until the credibility of the author in general and of his statement in particular had been systematically inquired into, the word "authority" disappeared from the vocabulary of historical method, except as archaistic survival; for the man who makes the statement came henceforth to be regarded not as someone whose word must be taken for the truth of what he says, which is what is meant by calling him an authority, but as someone who has voluntarily placed himself in the witness box for cross examination. The document hitherto called an authority now acquired a new status, properly described by calling it a "source," a word indicating simply that it contains the statement, without any implications to its value. That is *sub judice;* and it is the historian who judges. This is critical history, as it was worked

---

[29] *Ibid.*, pp. 19-20.

> out from the seventeenth century onwards, and officially acclaimed in the nineteenth century as the apotheosis of the historical consciousness.[30]

Two important rules are applied by historians in judging the validity of evidence. The first rule to be observed is that the proof of the genuineness of a document does not prove that it tells the truth.[31] Even though the written record itself may be genuine, it may have been prepared by someone who either did not possess the full facts himself or, because of bias or prejudice, did not record them. This leads to the second rule that, in dealing with written materials of history, the personality of the author is a constant factor to be dealt with.[32] The documents from which the historian derives his beliefs are not themselves witnesses; that are simply the records of others who may have been affected, directly or indirectly, by a number of influences as they recorded their impressions of what happened. Thus the chief factor in historical research is the human being.

> The personality of the reporter is important, for we must know whether he was in position to get reliable information and whether he had any mental or moral bias which would affect his report.... It is necessary to find out how close he stood to the events and how well he was qualified to appreciate and state them correctly; in short, how near he comes to being an eye-witness.[33]

Historians make a strong point that historical research is more than just the collection of facts. The evidence collected must be reviewed and evaluated for its validity before it is used. This, they feel, puts it on a scientific basis although history differs a good deal from some of the other sciences.

> [Assuming that] science means any organized body of knowing...everything that is a science at all must be a science of some special kind.
>
> A body of knowledge is never merely organized, it is always organized in some particular way. Some bodies of knowledge, like

---

[30] R. G. Collingwood, *The Idea of History* (Oxford (England): Oxford University Press, 1949), pp. 258-259.

[31] John Martin Vincent, *Historical Research* (New York: Peter Smith, 1929), p. 120.

[32] *Ibid.*, p. 122.

[33] *Ibid.*, pp. 123-124.

> meteorology, are organized by collecting observations concerned with events of a certain kind which the scientist can watch as they happen, though he cannot produce them at will.
>
> Others, like chemistry, are organized not only by observing events as they happen, but by making them happen under strictly controlled conditions.
>
> Others again are organized not by observing events at all, but by making certain assumptions and proceeding with the utmost exactitude to argue out their consequences.
>
> History is organized in none of these ways. Wars and revolutions, and the other events with which it deals, are not deliberately produced by historians under laboratory conditions in order to be studied with scientific precision. Nor are they even observed by historians, in the sense in which events are observed by natural scientists. Meteorologists and astronomers will make arduous and expensive journeys in order to observe for themselves events of the kinds in which they are interested, because their standard of observation is such that they cannot be satisfied with descriptions by inexpert witnesses; but historians do not fit out expeditions to countries where wars and revolutions are going on....
>
> The business of the historian is not to invent anything, it is to *discover* something...the traditional scheme of arrangement in history is a chronological scheme in which one event is placed before a second if it happened at an earlier time.
>
> History, then, is a science, but a science of a special kind. It is a science whose business is to study events not accessible to our observation, and to study these events inferentially, arguing to them from something else which is accessible to our observation, and which the historian calls "evidence" for the events in which he is interested.[34]

The general problem of the historian is in some respects much like that of the auditor, and we can learn much from the approach and methods of the historical researcher. We must learn to question and evaluate evidence carefully before we are willing to accept it as evidence. We must be careful particularly in our acceptance of authorities and give full consideration to the possibility of bias or self-interest.

Formation of Judgment. Not until the first four steps in the procedure of judgment formation have been completed will the

---

[34] Collingwood, pp. 249-252, emphasis added.

wise auditor undertake the fifth and last. This appears so obvious a requirement that it scarcely bears mention, but the dangers of inadvertenly or carelessly forming an opinion in advance of completing the preliminary steps is a real one. To avoid the easy and tempting practice of making up his mind and then seeking for evidence to support his decision, an auditor, like any other disciplined thinker, must exercise a good deal of mental self-control. He must school himself to see assertions in the financial statements as nothing more than hypotheses until he has determined the kind and extent of evidence he will need to arrive at a judgment, has obtained the evidence, and subjected it to critical review. Only then is he ready to permit that evidence to work upon his mind and lead him either to accept or deny the assertion before him or to decide that with the evidence available he cannot reach a rational judgment.

Summary. From the foregoing discussion of evidence generally and in auditing, it seems reasonable to extract the following conclusions.

Audit evidence includes all influences on the mind of an auditor which affect his judgment about the truthfulness of the financial statement propositions, submitted to him for review.

Audit evidence is obtained through the application of audit techniques and rests upon (1) authority, (2) reasoning from accepted principles, (3) sensory perception, (4) subsequent experience, or (5) intuition. Each of these provides acceptable although not necessarily convincing audit evidence.

In the degree of influence it exerts on the mind of the auditor, audit evidence varies from compelling through persuasive to inconclusive.

No one method of audit evidence is always or completely reliable.

The persuasiveness of audit evidence increases, approaching compulsion, as different types of evidence combine to support any given proposition.

Audit evidence must be reviewed critically with respect to its validity and pertinence as evidence before it is permitted to influence the mind of the auditor with respect to the assertion at issue.

The more material the proposition under consideration, the stronger must be the evidence upon which judgment rests, varying from a merely persuasive preponderance for immaterial propositions to compelling or near compelling evidence for material propositions.

In view of the limitations of audit evidence in the establishment of incontrovertible truth and the influence of time and other conditions under which an auditor works, truth in auditing may be defined as conformity with reality as the auditor can determine reality at the time of his examination and with the evidence available.

Chapter 6

Due Audit Care

It is to be expected that a profession will have difficulty in establishing the limits of its responsibility. The important role which judgment plays in professional practice, and the exercise of judgment is never free from unfortunate consequences, contributes to this. The continuing adaptation of a profession to changes in its social environment and in its own methods and resources require continuing modification of its relationship to clients and others. The difficulty which laymen, and for this purpose all non-practitioners must be considered laymen, have in understanding and appreciating not only the potentialities but the limitations of the profession, also play a part in making the establishment of definite responsibilities a trying and continuing problem.

Another factor frequently contributes to this difficulty and in many ways may be more important than any of the others; this is the reluctance with which practitioners approach this problem. Faced with many opportunities to be of real service to their clients and at the same time with the time-consuming harassment of nuisance suits alleging failure to discharge their professional responsibilities adequately, practitioners tend quite naturally to shy away from a problem, the consideration of which may have adverse effects on litigation in which they or their fellows may even then be engaged. When one is currently engaged in litigation with outsiders on a difficult and abstract subject, it is perhaps expecting too much to require that he sit down quietly with his fellows and solve that problem on an objective and philosophical basis, especially when the solution may work directly to his disadvantage in the current litigation. It may be even more difficult to attack such a problem when fellow practitioners are defending themselves in court.

In this general respect, auditors have much the same problems and tendencies as the members of other professions. As a relatively new professional group they find additional opportunities for service presented to them continually. At the same time, they find themselves engaged in more litigation than they care to think about. It is not surprising, therefore, that, as a group, independent auditors have avoided any positive statements of responsibility. Instead they have relied on protestations which, if accepted at face value, would effectively relieve them of almost any responsibility at all. Although we can understand the pressures and the temptations which have led the profession to adopt this attitude, its efficacy in providing an ultimate solution for the important problem at issue must be questioned, as must the desirability of the effect which it has on the prestige enjoyed by the profession.

To many, these will appear to be rather harsh and unfounded accusations. Let us inquire first whether they are unfounded and second whether they are unnecessarily harsh.

The Profession's Acceptance of Responsibility. Indications of the extent of responsibility which the profession is willing to accept publicly are found in a variety of official and semiofficial publications of the American Institute of Certified Public Accountants. Although there is not complete unanimity on all these points in the literature of the profession, textbooks and other references generally support them strongly. Among the most important sources are the following:

(1) The Rules of Professional Conduct
(2) Generally Accepted Auditing Standards
(3) Codification of Statements on Auditing Procedure.

The Rules of Professional Conduct are explicit with respect to a number of points of good professional conduct which a member of the Institute must not breach. In them we find the most forceful statement of requirements for satisfactory professional practice in the literature of the profession. Certainly they have done much to raise the level of professional practice; the profession is to be congratulated both on their existence and their observance. One can only wish that they were more extensive. In a limited number of restricted areas, they spell out the practitioner's responsibility with a fair degree of specificity. They do not, however, cover a number of other important points such as the auditor's responsibility for the detection of irregularities, for the review of internal control, or for insistence upon full disclosure.

If *Generally Accepted Auditing Standards* had been viewed as a first step in the development of realistic and useful standards for the profession it would have been a milestone indeed. Apparently, however, it is currently accepted as a final and sufficient statement of such standards. In our judgment, a critical reading of these standards finds them unsatisfactory for this purpose. They are not sufficiently specific to provide guidance to any of the several interests in audit work. We are in substantial agreement with the position expressed in the following:

> Standards should provide guides:
>
> (1) For the evaluation of professional performance by practicing public accountants.
>
> (2) To indicate accepted requirements of practice to those outside the profes-sion who have occasion to judge or evaluate the work of practicing accountants.
>
> (3) To suggest the extent and nature of education expected of those preparing for entry into the profession.
>
> Thus generally accepted auditing standards, if they adequately fulfill their function, provide the practicing accountant with a basis for self-review, a means of evaluating his own work so that he may determine whether he is satisfying his professional responsibilities. They should give courts, commissions, and other interested parties a reasonably clear indication of what professional accountants hold as required in the adequate performance of an examination of financial statements. Finally, they should be useful to teachers and students for educational purposes. From the standards it should be possible to determine what a student should know and understand in order to be considered sufficiently well trained to be useful on professional assignments.
>
> A frank evaluation of the ten generally accepted auditing standards finds them generally unsatisfactory for these purposes. Their issuance met the demands of the S.E.C. and satisfactorily fulfilled the immediate need; it is extremely doubtful, however, if they have been effective in raising the level of professional performance in any substantial degree.[1]

It is our considered opinion that the ten generally accepted auditing standards are not sufficient to mark out with any satisfactory degree of accuracy the limits of an auditor's responsibility on any engagement and that only in the most general way do they provide to those outside the profession any indication at all of the quality and extent of performance to be expected from independent auditors. If the ten standards now accepted were satisfactory for their purpose we would not have the pleas for guid-

---

[1]R. K. Mautz, "A Critical Look at Generally Accepted Auditing Standards," *The Illinois Certified Public Accountant*, Vol. 21, No. 1, p. 12.

ance on the extent of responsibility for the detection of irregularities we now find in our professional literature. Surely a satisfactory set of auditing standards would give a more useful guide in this respect as well as in others.

Codification of Statements on Auditing Procedure contains a great deal of useful instruction both to practitioners and to those who rely on their work, and it is unfair to characterize it with a few selected quotations. Thus in fairness both to this useful publication and to ourselves we must emphasize that it is not our intent to suggest that this valuable document be judged by a few selected excerpts. However, there are but a few points on which the Codification takes a firm stand with respect to the auditor's responsibility to others; and since we are now concerned with this particular subject, these points must be given somewhat more attention than they would receive if the Codification were discussed in its entirety.

The first of these points has to do with the acceptance of primary responsibility for the assertions made in a company's financial statements. Both the original Codification and the amendment attribute this responsibility to the company's management. The amended version reads:

> Management has the responsibility for the proper recording of transactions in books of account, for the safeguarding of assets, and for the substantial accuracy and adequacy of financial statements. The transactions which should be reflected in the accounts and in the financial statements are matters within the direct knowledge and control of management; the independent auditor's knowledge is limited to that acquired through his examination. Accordingly, even though the financial statements may show the influence of the independent auditor (for example, as a result of management's acceptance of his advice), the statements are the representations of management. The independent auditor's responsibility is confined to the expression of a professional opinion on the financial statements he has examined.[2]

Except for raising a question about the meaning of "direct knowledge" as used in describing management's awareness of transactions, one can scarcely disagree with this statement of the auditor's position with respect to the financial statements he

---

[2]Statements on Auditing Procedure No. 30, American Institute of Certified Public Accountants, p. 40.

examines and the responsibility he can and does accept. If he is to provide the expert, independent review which our economic society has found so useful, he must first of all remain clear of the preparation of the financial statements so that he can examine them impartially and unemotionally. Second, to the extent that he finds the financial statements unsatisfactory, whether in form or content, he must convey this dissatisfaction to the company and to those who may read his report, unless management accepts his suggestions and improves the statements. He does not deliberately seek to find the management at fault, that is, in the act of issuing unsatisfactory financial statements. In accordance with Postulate Number 2, there is no necessary conflict of interest between the auditor and the management of the company under examination. Both are assumed to be interested in a fair presentation of the company's operations and financial position. Thus the auditor is obliged, first, to report to stockholders and others as accurately and as fully as is usefully possible. If he cannot achieve this responsibility, his second choice must be to point out to those who read his report that in his opinion the statements are deficient in certain specific respects.

His responsibility therefore is to assure that the financial statements are satisfactory if management will cooperate; if it will not, then he must point out in his report the respects in which the statements fall short. We are in complete agreement with the Codification on this point.

We are not in such complete agreement with the position taken on the second point, that of responsibility for the detection of fraud and irregularities.

Through Statements of Auditing Procedure No. 30, the Codification has been amended to eliminate a paragraph which we feel did not appropriately describe the independent auditor's responsibility. The passage to which we refer reads as follows:

> The ordinary examination incident to the issuance of an opinion respecting financial statements is not designed *and cannot be relied upon* to disclose defalcations and other similar irregularities, although their discovery frequently results. In a well-organized concern reliance for the detection of such irregularities is placed principally upon the maintenance of an adequate system of accounting records with appropriate internal control. If an auditor were to attempt to discover defalcations and similar irregularities he would have to extend his

> work to a point where its cost would be prohibitive. It is generally recognized that good internal control and surety bonds provide protection much more cheaply. On the basis of his examination by tests and checks, made in the light of his review and test of the system of internal control, the auditor relies upon the integrity of the client's organization unless circumstances are such as to arouse his suspicion, in which case he must extend his procedures to determine whether or not such suspicions are justified.[3]

This is a frequently quoted passage and one which apparently reflects the attitude and beliefs of a substantial number of independent CPAs. We feel it is a most unfortunate statement of the responsibility independent auditors should accept for the detection of errors and irregularities. To criticize it in any detail is to "whip a dead horse" because, through amendment of the Codification, this paragraph supposedly has been removed from the literature. Nevertheless, it seems desirable to summarize the position apparently supported in the original Codification and to indicate its deficiencies.

The position apparently taken, if we read the paragraph correctly, is:

1. Independent auditors accept no responsibility for the detection of fraud and other irregularities.
2. If the independent auditor were to search for irregularities his examination would necessarily be so extensive that the cost would be prohibitive.
3. Cheaper, although not necessarily better, protection is provided by good internal control and surety bonds.
4. If circumstances in a given examination are such as to arouse the independent auditor's suspicions, he must extend his procedures to some unspecified extent.

If this is a fair summary of the paragraph in question, the original Codification took much too strong a position in relieving the independent auditor of responsibility, and it did so on the strength of assertions and contentions that are difficult to accept as valid. One must question, first, whether independent auditors can absolve themselves of responsibility for the detection of irregularities by a simple declaration to that effect when

---

[3]*Codification of Statements on Auditing Procedure*, The American Institute of Accountants, 1951, pp. 12-13.

there is ample evidence in professional literature that at one time they considered this an important part of their duties; second, whether *some* useful search for irregularities might not be effected without incurring prohibitive cost; third, whether internal control and surety bonds actually do provide a satisfactory degree of protection; fourth, whether the extent of the auditor's responsibility for extension of his work when suspicion is aroused might not be more usefully stated; fifth, whether the over-all attitude toward acceptance of professional responsibility implicit in such a statement is appropriate to the growth and development of a profession.

The position expressed in Statements on Auditing Procedure No. 30 is a substantial improvement in that it apparently accepts some responsibility for the detection of irregularities. However, this responsibility is restricted to those situations in which the auditor's suspicions are aroused, while he is performing his examination in accordance with generally accepted auditing standards, that irregularities sufficiently material to influence his opinion on the financial statements exist. If such suspicion is aroused, he must see that the possible irregularities are subjected to conclusive investigation, either by the client, subject to the auditor's review, or by himself. Suspicion that irregularities of less import exist may be dealt with by referring "the matter to the proper representatives of the client with the recommendation that it be pursued to a conclusion."

The importance of the generally accepted auditing standards in establishing the extent of responsibility here can scarcely be overestimated. Indeed a statement is included specifically limiting responsibility to *clear noncompliance* with auditing standards.

> The responsibility of the independent auditor for failure to detect fraud (which responsibility differs as to clients and others) arises only when such failure clearly results from noncompliance with generally accepted auditing standards.[4]

---

[4]Statements on Auditing Procedure No. 30, American Institute of Certified Public Accountants, p. 41. Apparently for emphasis, the same point is again made in paragraph 8 of this statement:

> The subsequent discovery that fraud existed during the period covered by the independent auditor's examination does not of itself indicate negligence on his part. He is not an insurer or guarantor and, if his examination was made with due professional skill and care, in accordance with generally accepted auditing standards, he has fulfilled all of the obligations implicit in his undertaking.

As stated earlier in this chapter, we do not feel that the generally accepted auditing standards as now constituted are sufficiently specific for this purpose. A clear case of noncompliance would be difficult to establish except in the most flagrant cases. Thus, although the revision of the Codification included in Statements on Auditing Procedure No. 30 appears to be a substantial improvement over the original wording, we feel it does not go far enough. There still appears to be a considerable desire for minimization of responsibility; a defensive attitude prevails throughout. Again without any support, it is contended that internal control and fidelity bonds provide protection against fraud and other irregularities more economically and effectively than do independent audits.

Something more is both desirable and possible. As a profession, independent auditing must accept appropriate responsibility, and it should do so in a positive and courageous fashion. One can have considerable sympathy with the profession's wish to avoid painful and expensive litigation yet believe that a more straightforward acceptance of responsibility is desirable. The remainder of this chapter is devoted to an attempt to develop such a statement.

Approaches to a Statement of Responsibility. In an attempt to develop a statement of the auditor's responsibility for the detection of irregularities, a number of approaches appear to hold promise. Stated differently, there are a number of factors that require consideration before a valid conclusion can be reached. At least the following are included:

1. A careful consideration of the various types of irregularities, searching for characteristics that may provide a clue to those for which the auditor should accept the burden of discovery and those for which he cannot.
2. A consideration of the social responsibility of the profession and the part it can play in reducing the social cost of losses due directly to shortages and resulting indirectly from faulty decisions made on the basis of unreliable data.
3. A consideration of the relationship which irregularities bear to audit evidence, in other words, the possibility and likelihood of detection.
4. The development of a concept of audit care as a possible way of indicating the responsibility the profession should accept not only for the discovery of irregularities but for the performance of its professional duties generally.

Since any serious inquiry should first obtain all available information about the subject, we will do well to thoroughly examine irregularities, their nature and characteristics. A sound understanding of the various kinds of irregularities is of prime importance in arriving at a satisfactory conclusion as to the auditor's appropriate responsibility for their detection.

Characteristics of Irregularities. Perhaps irregularities are so well understood that any attempt to define them is superfluous. Nevertheless, so that we may be in agreement on the subject of discussion in the following paragraphs, it seems desirable to have at least a working definition. An irregularity may be described as any departure from the truth[5] in the financial statements or accounting records or any deviation from established and duly authorized and established company policies. This is probably as broad a definition of irregularities as can be stated, but seems entirely satisfactory for our purposes here.

With this working definition as a base, irregularities have one or more of a variety of characteristics or attributes. These include:

1. Materiality
2. Intent
3. Relationship to internal control
4. Influence on financial statements
5. Extent of concealment
6. Responsibility

Materiality. Materiality is always of interest in auditing. Because cost and time are so important in the performance of an engagement, transactions, events, and even irregularities of little or no materiality cannot be given the attention which must be reserved for material transactions, events, and irregularities. But materiality is always a relative matter and some consideration must be given to the base against which the materiality of the given item is measured.

For example, if fairness of presentation of financial condition and results of operations is the basis for consideration of material-

---

[5]As stated in Chapter 6, "Truth in auditing may be defined as conformity with reality as the auditor can determine reality at the time of his examination and with the evidence available."

ity, a considerable shortage might be viewed as not material. There are a large number of companies in this country which could sustain a defalcation of half a million dollars without any material effect whatever on their financial condition. If we define materiality here as it was defined in the preceding chapter (page 126), we must concede that very few stockholders would be influenced in their investment decisions by knowledge that the company's reported amount for total assets or income was in error by even such a substantial amount. But of course there is another aspect of materiality. There are very few people in this country who would not regard a defalcation of half a million dollars as a serious reflection on the management of the concern in which it had occurred, not to mention the honesty of the perpetrator. We find that we have a somewhat different concept of materiality when we shift our basis from financial condition and results of operations to a notion of acceptable efficiency or honesty.

It should be noted that the difference is both one of kind and one of amount. There are many companies in which a certain amount of petty conversion of company property to personal use is accepted on either an official or semiofficial basis. For example, some companies permit employees to use company automobiles for personal purposes, to make telephone calls at company expense, to draw company postage for private letters, to use company tools for noncompany purposes, and the like. But even under such conditions there are limits. The company car cannot be loaned to relatives or taken off to college by an employee's offspring. The company tools must be returned, or if not, the number taken must be limited; employees are not encouraged to go into a tool rental business with company property. Even the amount of stamps or number of long distance telephone calls must be kept "within reason."

Materiality, as applied to irregularities, is thus an abstract and difficult concept. There are some irregularities which all would agree are material in and of themselves; there are others on which a difference of opinion might arise. A company management which might argue that the capitalization or expensing of a ten-thousand-dollar outlay was not material to its results of operations could well feel that a defalcation in the amount of a few hundred dollars by a petty cash custodian was definitely material. And an independent auditor would be hard pressed to disagree on either point.

From this we may draw three conclusions. First, our idea of materiality with respect to irregularities may be somewhat different from our idea of materiality with respect to financial condition and results of operations. Second, it seems apparent that even within this idea of materiality there may be some irregularities that are sufficiently immaterial to be of little significance to anyone. An error of a few cents in footing a petty cash voucher might be an illustration. Third, there is no sharp line between material and immaterial irregularities.

Intent. Irregularities may be unintentional or intentional, and intentional errors may be subdivided into (a) those intended to conceal only incompetence or inefficiency, (b) those intended either to conceal a shortage or to make one possible, and (c) those intended to influence financial statement readers to actions they might otherwise not take.

The possibility of unintentional irregularities in accounting work is both apparent and serious. An astute management would insist on independent audits even if it had assurance beyond doubt that all its employees were absolutely honest. Inadvertent errors in the mechanics of dealing with large quantities of figures, errors of principle in making accounting judgments, or errors of bias in presenting financial information, are almost certain to occur; and if management is to have confidence in the financial data on which it must rely, review by an independent and impartial expert is important, regardless of the question of employee honesty.

But honesty is always an additional question, both the honesty of employees who must be trusted with the custody of valuable assets and with the integrity of important data, and the honesty of top management which may have reason to misstate financial position or results of operations. A classification of irregularities by intent thus might appear:

I. Unintentional
    - In mechanics
    - In principle
    - Resulting from bias

II. Intentional
    - To conceal incompetence or carelessness
    - To effect or conceal a shortage
    - To mislead readers

This classification can be combined with other classifications, for example with materiality, to obtain a more sophisticated array. Unintentional and immaterial errors in mechanics or even in principle would not seem to be particularly significant. On the other hand, a material and intentional attempt to mislead readers of the financial statements is the very type of irregularity an audit is designed to discover and reveal. In between these extremes, however, lies a variety of combinations on which it is difficult to take a firm position. An accounts receivable bookkeeper, hard pressed with work at the end of the month, might temporarily conceal a difference between her ledger and the control account by forcing an apparent agreement. Later, when time permits, she may seek out the error and correct it so that the difference is eliminated and a valid agreement obtained at the end of the following month. This is the type of irregularity a typical examination of accounts cannot be designed comprehensively enough to uncover, unless we remove both cost and times as important factors: and this we cannot do.

Thus we can only conclude that irregularities vary considerably with respect to the intentions of those responsible and that there is little in such a classification to serve as a clue to the auditor's responsibility for their discovery.

Relationship to Internal Control. A good system of internal control will reduce the possibilities for irregularities and may even reduce the probability to a very small fraction, but it can never guarantee their prevention. For one thing, even the best system may break down, no matter how many precautions and safeguards are worked into it. This is true of a system as a whole and of the several parts of a system and has an important bearing on the responsibility of an auditor for the detection of irregularities. If after a careful and competent review he concludes that the system is an excellent one and curtails his examination accordingly, there is always the possibility that a breakdown in the system, perhaps for only a single important transaction, may result in an irregularity which, if not material with respect to financial condition and results of operations, may still be a material loss.

Within the framework of basic assumptions, the auditor should not be held responsible for the detection of such an irregularity as this. It is conceivable that his examination might find indications of it which would lead to its detection, but that is far different from requiring him to design his examination so that he could appropriately accept responsibility for detection of what must be described as a rare item.

On the other hand, if a system of internal control has a weakness that permits a given type or types of irregularity to occur repeatedly, not because of an improbable and nonrecurring failure but because of an ever present weakness, we have a somewhat different situation. In this case, we tend to expect the auditor's review of internal control to uncover the weakness and his experience and training to make him alert to the potential consequences. Discovery of the irregularity does not necessarily follow, however, because the type of error possible in view of the weakness may not be sufficiently material to warrant spending much time searching for its occurrence. If material irregularities appear likely under the system as it exists, the auditor should at least recognize the possibility.

Thus we find a classification indicating the relationship of irregularities to internal control illuminating but not particularly helpful in reaching a conclusion about the auditor's responsibility for their detection. Irregularities may be:

1. Perpetrated within the scope of the internal control system as determined by the auditor.
2. Effected by circumventing the internal control procedures indicated to be in existence by the auditor's review.
3. Effected at a level beyond the scope of the internal control system.

A word of explanation about the third category may be helpful. In every organization a considerable amount of discretionary authority must be given to those in certain managerial positions. Someone must be able to make decisions, to take action, and to carry on in times of emergency or crisis. We cannot have an effective system if everyone watches everyone else. Ultimate authority for certain transactions and decisions must rest in the hands of someone who for all practical purposes is outside the scope of the internal control system. There are factors of position, prestige, social responsibility, family, income, and character which keep such people honest, but the system of internal control makes very little contribution in this respect. With such a situation there is always the possibility, remote though it may be, that conditions may develop to the point where that person will perpetrate an irregularity. If so, such an unfortunate event would be similar to the rare transaction mentioned previously, although it would result from what must be considered an inevitable weakness in any internal control system. In either event, the independent auditor cannot accept general responsibility for discovering all such irregularities. If a specific irregularity is sufficiently large or perpetrated so clumsily as to be readily detectable, it seems that an independent auditor should discover it in the normal course of his work. If it is not so large or if it is skillfully concealed, the circumstances may be such that he should not be held responsible for its detection.

Influence on Financial Statements. In discussing materiality, one aspect of the relationship of irregularities to financial statement presentation was pointed out, the possible influence on financial position and results of operations. We will now pursue this thought a little farther.

A shortage may result in reducing an asset or increasing a liability, and if the shortage is not recognized by entry in the accounts, the assets will be overstated or the liabilities will be understated in the financial statements. If the shortage is recognized and some attempt is made to conceal it by charging the loss to some expense or income account, the balance sheet may then in effect be considered correct; it does reveal the financial position as it is at the time. The income statement may be considered correct in one respect also; it would indicate the net income for the year with the shortage accepted as a realized loss. But unless the loss has been described for what it is in the income statement, an unlikely eventuality, the income statement is in error in describing the loss improperly. Thus an irregularity may affect either the income statement or the balance sheet or both. There are some who feel that this is a most important distinction.

Because auditing procedures are directed primarily at balance sheet accounts and because balance sheet account balances are things or relationships that exist in the here and now — at least during part of the examination — they can be verified with a higher degree of accuracy than can income statement account balances which are concerned with past events. We can obtain stronger evidence for balance sheet items than we can for income statement items. This has led some to conclude that auditors can and should take a greater degree of responsibility for irregularities concealed in balance sheet accounts than for irregularities concealed elsewhere. The availability of stronger evidence holds true particularly if the error is an overstatement of an asset or an understatement of a liability; it may hold as well for the understatement of an asset or the overstatement of a liability.

To aid in an understanding of these types of irregularities we present the following simple classification:

- Irregularities affecting the balance sheet
  - Overstatement of assets and understatement of liabilities
  - Understatement of assets and overstatement of liabilities
  - Improper description within the balance sheet
- Irregularities affecting the income statement
  - Overstatement of net income
  - Understatement of net income
  - Improper description

It seems clear that a rather clean line separates those irregularities which affect the balance sheet from those which affect the income statement alone. Those involving the misstatement of assets or liabilities, or both, will also have an effect on the income figure. Only those which are concerned solely with improper description or classification within each statement are not in any way concerned with the other statement. It has been proposed that independent auditors base their acceptance of responsibility for the detection of irregularities primarily on this distinction, i.e. that they accept responsibility for irregularities which affect balance sheet accounts and that they deny responsibility for those irregularities which affect the income statement only.[6] Of course the further characteristic of materiality would have to be added, but with a combination of the two, a workable test does appear.

Our objection to this position rests primarily on the ground that it does not sufficiently take into account some of the other

---

[6]Keith W. Dunn, "Clarification of Responsibility for Discovery of Fraud," *The Journal of Accountancy*, August, 1958, p. 53.

important characteristics of irregularities. It is conceivable, for example, that a carefully contrived plan involving the collusion of management and others could escape detection by even a competent and diligent auditor although it affected the balance sheet directly. On the other hand, an ill-conceived scheme buried in the income statement might be easily discovered. A second objection is that, by implication, this test reduces the income statement to second-class status as a financial report. It is difficult to accept the idea that misclassification or improper description in the balance sheet is of some importance whereas the same type of irregularity in the income statement is of no consequence. The notion that an approximately correct figure of net income is the only fact of any real significance in the income statement appears to be gaining support, but it is one which we find as yet unjustified in logic or in practice. In our opinion it would be a serious setback for accounting as well as for auditing if we were to abandon the income statement as an auditable report and concentrate our attention solely on the balance sheet. The interrelationships between the two statements are too important and the income statement has too many uses to justify what amounts to its abandonment.

Extent of Concealment. Shortages and other irregularities may be open or they may be concealed. An open shortage is one in which no effort has been made to conceal the fact that the records do not agree with the realities of the situation. Thus a count of the cash on hand may reveal that there is not as much present as the record indicates. A footing of the subsidiary ledger of customers accounts may result in lack of agreement with the controlling account balance. An inspection of inventories may show that what is claimed does not exist. These are open shortages. A concealed shortage is one for which steps have been taken to reduce the likelihood of its discovery; a considerable variety of methods are available.

To the extent that the system of internal control permits, the perpetrator of an irregularity can either manipulate the records or manipulate documents which provide the basis for the records. He may omit entries from the record, a most difficult kind of coverage to discover, make false entries, effect incorrect results to calculations, or make covering errors in the bookkeeping. He may destroy documents, prepare fraudulent papers, or alter real documents. Of course he can also combine these several opportunities. In outline form a classification of irregularities by method of concealment might appear:

- Open
- Concealed
  - By manipulation of records
    - Omission of entry
    - False entry
    - False footing or other calculation
    - False posting or other bookkeeping procedure
  - By manipulation of documents
    - Destruction of documents
    - Preparation of false documents
    - Alteration of legitimate documents

The skill with which any one of these method is applied, the frequency of occurrence, the amount involved, all have a bearing on the probability and indeed the possibility of detection by the auditor. By itself, this characteristic therefore does not provide any substantial clue to the appropriate extent of audit responsibility.

Responsibility. An irregularity may be caused by an employee or by a member of management; it may be the result of an individual's independent action or it may be a collusive effort. Neither of these separations gives an important clue to the auditor's responsibility. An employee may be resourceful or clumsy in his attempts to convert company resources to his own use; the same is true of an officer. A number of employees or officers working together can devise an elaborate and perhaps an almost foolproof scheme of defalcation, or on the other hand they may overlook the most obvious protective devices. Again there is little in this characteristic taken by itself to provide a useful clue to audit responsibility.

Combined Classification of Irregularities. A moment's consideration will suggest the possibility of combining these several characteristics in a variety of more or less complex classifications. Suffice it to say at this point that we have tried a number of combinations without finding one that provides a rational basis for limiting audit responsibility. As useful as an analytical study of irregularities and their characteristics is, we can discover no apparent pattern in these characteristics that permit establishment of limits to an auditor's responsibility for the detection of irregularities.

One other suggestion should be explored before we pass on to the other approaches to this problem. It may be suggested that in a situation in which an auditor has continuing relations with a client, a single audit is not an appropriate basis for working out a statement of his responsibilities. We know that many audit programs are long-term plans in which different subsidiaries are visited each year, different expense accounts tested, different months used for vouching, and the like. Perhaps we should strive to state the responsibilities of the auditor on some basis which recognizes this rotation of procedures, periods, and emphasis. Perhaps there are irregularities that an auditor might well miss in any single examination but that successive examinations, if carefully planned and performed according to schedule, should disclose. This suggests a classification that might read somewhat as follows:

Detection in single audit expected
Detection in single audit probable
Detection in a series of audits probable
Detection unlikely or impossible

A classification of this kind combined with some of the other classes previously discussed appears to have some usefulness for the purpose at hand. For example, a material, open shortage in a balance sheet account probably should be discovered in a single examination, whereas a less material shortage resulting from collusive action, carefully concealed through the preparation of false documents and charged to an income statement account, might never be discovered.

To give some idea of the nature and usefulness of such a classification, the chart on page 187 has been prepared. It includes a classification of irregularities that takes into account most of the characteristics discussed in this chapter and provides columns at the right of the chart which permit categorizing each type of irregularity according to the likelihood of detection in a single or a continuing series of examinations. We have not attempted to categorize the irregularities ourselves because, for the reasons stated in the following paragraph, we have little faith in this approach as a useful solution to the problem. Nevertheless, it is enlightening to study each irregularity described and consider whether or not a normal audit engagement should detect its perpetration in any given year, in a series of years if the irregularity is repeated, or have little or no change of ever uncovering it.

One difficulty with a classification of irregularities such as this is that it is really no guide at all. How many audits does it take to comprise a "series" in which a given irregularity should be discovered? Must the irregularity occur in every year of the series? With the same or an increasing degree of frequency? There is also still the problem of attempting to characterize the irregularities themselves which would be detected in one or a series of audits. As pointed out in studying these characteristics, the range of possibilities within each class is such that the characteristics discussed offer little real help. Hence, we find this approach useful, not as a solution to the problem of responsibility, but only to indicate the extent and variety of the irregularities with which an auditor may be concerned.

Social Responsibility and Irregularity Detection. Included in the Statements on Auditing Procedure No. 30 is the following:

> If an objective of an independent auditor's examination were the discovery of all fraud, he would have to extend his work to a point where its cost would be prohibitive. Even then he could not give assurance that all types of fraud had been detected or that none had existed because items such as unrecorded transactions, forgeries, and collusive fraud would not necessarily be uncovered. It is generally recognized that good internal control and fidelity bonds provide protection more economically and effectively.

There is a strong implication here of all or nothing. Either an auditor must extend his program to look for all possible irregularities or he can search for none at all. And if he were to look for all, then his examination would become much too costly. But it appears that another course is possible. Perhaps he could extend his examination enough to make a reasonable search for material irregularities, thereby providing his client with a useful service without at the same time extending his audit program to the point where the cost becomes prohibitive. As a matter of fact, this is just about what most practicing auditors are doing today if one can judge from "off the record" discussions.

Once the initial cost of an examination has been incurred, the preliminary negotiations, review of internal control, cost of report preparation, and the like, the additional amount necessary to make some search for irregularities need not be inordinately large. There is a considerable difference between a reasonable search for major irregularities and a complete search for all possible errors. Unfortunately, in discussing this general subject, auditors are inclined to cite only unusual, unlikely, or well concealed irregularities as illustrations. There are indeed a considerable number of irregularities which even an alaborate search might not detect; there are also a considerable number which a reasonable investigation might well disclose.

We should look carefully at the claim that good internal control and surety bonds provide protection much more cheaply. Certainly one cannot quarrel with the desirability of good internal control or with the claim that it provides better protection against irregularities than can an extensive examination by independent auditors. But can the same be said of surety bonds? Knowledge that a company follows a practice of bonding its employees, plus the investigation that a surety company makes of employees proposed for bonding, may have some influence on the honesty of those bonded, but whether it has any significant influence in reducing losses is questionable. Certainly bonding companies pay substantial losses every year.

There are two aspects of the relative cost of bonding versus independent audits as a means of reducing losses by defalcation and similar irregularities. In any given case it may indeed be cheaper to insure against losses, and then recover from the insurer if a loss occurs, than to pay for a more extensive audit. On the other hand, someone must pay for every employee shortage and defalcation. For an individual company, bonding may reduce losses; for business society as a whole it merely spreads them over a larger base. Except for whatever deterrent value bonding may have, and its elimination of some risks by investigation of employees, bonding premiums must equal losses plus the cost of administering the insurance plan. It is as simple as that. Bonding does not prevent losses to any substantial extent; it spreads the burden over a larger base.

> In our world of war, confusion, evil, and suffering, the accounting profession is very much aware of the fact that defalcations and other irregularities have grown considerably in number and amount in recent years. American business losses from these frauds have been estimated to range from one to three billion dollars annually. Contrast this with U.S. police reports to the F.B.I. that the total value of property stolen in 1957 by robbery, burglary, larceny, and auto theft was $272 million. Consider also that the usual embezzlement amounts range from a few to many thousands of dollars and in some instances to millions while the average loss from robbery and burglary in 1957 was only about $200.[7]

One cannot but be impressed with the thought that one to three billion dollars a year would pay for a considerable amount of additional auditing, particularly in view of the fact that the basic costs of the audit have already been incurred in many instances.

Here we have a substantial social cost. Is there anything the profession can do about it? Would a reasonable increase in auditing work have the effect of reducing losses of this kind in an amount equal to the cost of the increased auditing? This is a question and a possibility that warrants serious consideration.

Another consideration of importance is that in many cases bonding falls well short of providing the protection we generally assume it will provide. In many cases the extent of loss is so substantial as to exceed by an important amount the insurance carried. Statistics made available by the Surety Association of America suggest that in many cases reliance on bonding has proved unsatisfactory because losses far exceeded expectations.[8]

We are not prepared to say whether auditing, without an undue increase in audit fees, can have a significant effect in reducing losses due to irregularities, either by discouraging those who otherwise might perpetrate them or by detecting such activities before they become substantial. It does appear, however that here is an important social service that the profession could render the economic community if it would. And of course there is substantial historical precedent for this service. It was not many years ago that leading writers listed the detection of irregularities as one of the

---

[7]Charles A. Stewart, "The Nature and Prevention of Fraud," *The Journal of Accountancy*, February, 1959, p. 41.

[8]*Safeguards Against Employee Dishonesty in Business*, published by The Surety Association of American, New York, 1954, p. 21.

important purposes of auditing.[9] Why should independent auditors as a group abdicate this opportunity and this responsibility? Our claim to professional status carries with it the responsibility of service; independent certified public accountants, if they are truly professional men, are not in business solely for their own profit. Not only do they have responsibilities to their clients and to those who rely on their opinions, it seems reasonable to charge them as a profession with responsibilities to the business community. No other profession, no other type of activity meets this need, the encouragement of employee honesty and the detection of those who fail their trust. There are many who may feel that auditing has failed in its trust if it refuses to be of service here.

Responsibility and Professional Prestige. As important as minimization of responsibility is to professional practitioners at a time when nuisance suits and similar litigation seem to flourish, additional considerations merit attention. Until recently there was substantial acceptance of the idea that an independent audit had as one of its principal purposes the detection and prevention of fraud and other irregularities. Currently we find considerable emphasis on elimination or at least minimization of this responsibility through audit-client agreements, letters, and statements in the professional literature. Whether such agreements and statements offer any real protection we are not qualified to state. Even if auditors can contract away their responsibility for this particular service, serious consideration should be given to the wisdom of so doing. The advantage is an immediate release from what may prove to be an onerous and burdensome responsibility. The disadvantages may far outweigh this. First, the auditor appears to be renouncing his right to an area in which he has competence and in which he can be of service; second, as a professional group auditors are in effect refusing to provide an effective service to the business community; third, auditors are emphasizing to clients and the world at large their unwillingness to accept responsibility, to provide a difficult but useful service, to attempt to cope on even a small scale with an evil force that

[9]See Lewis Lilly, "What Is an Adequate Auditing Procedure?" and J. S. Seidman, "A Case Study of Employee Frauds," both in *Papers on Auditing Procedure and Other Accounting Subjects Presented at the Fifty-second Annual Meeting of the American Institute of Accountants, 1939.*

blights business life in no unsubstantial degree. Such a position cannot but lessen the prestige of the profession, particularly in view of the fact that the service and the responsibility we now deny were, at one time, claimed rather forcefully.

What is needed is a clear and forthright statement of the responsibility which an auditor can and should accept. This responsibility should be defined positively and in such fashion that it will serve as a useful guide to all concerned. No single statement can provide security against litigation; it can do no more than serve as a guide by which litigation can be settled in a reasonable fashion. The man who engages in a profession receives rewards not available to the man who works at a trade. For these rewards he must prepare himself adequately, serve competently, and accept certain risks. Among the risks is that of litigation brought by those who for one reason or another believe he has not fulfilled his professional responsibilities. Part of the price he must pay to hold his position as a professional practitioner is the burden of defending himself against such litigation. By the nature of his work he cannot avoid it and still be a professional man.

Audit Evidence and Irregularities. From the discussion in the preceding paragraphs of this chapter it seems apparent that the extent of responsibility for discovering certain types of irregularities is not at all difficult to determine. At one extreme are those irregularities for which the auditor could not accept responsibility under almost any conditions. These are the immaterial items; the irregularity of which there is no record, such as an unrecorded receipt of cash from some miscellaneous source for which there is no evidence of accountability; the rare transaction which happens once and never again; and extraordinarily well-concealed irregularities perhaps effected through collusion. At the other extreme are certain irregularities that an alert auditor should discover almost as a matter of course. These are open shortages, material in amount; irregularities in balance sheet accounts sufficiently large to influence financial position; and material, recurring irregularities resulting from a known weakness in internal control.

For the first class, those unlikely to be discovered, there is either an absence of evidence or so little chance that the available evidence will come to light that no reasonable person informed of the facts of the situation would hold an auditor accountable. In the second group, those the auditor should discover, there is sufficient available evidence that the irregularity should come to the auditor's attention in the course of a normal examination.

In between these extremes is a considerable gray area which includes a great many types of irregularities with varying characteristics. For all these it is difficult either to charge or relieve the auditor of responsibility. In some cases likelihood of discovery might vary with the circumstances of a particular audit; even the chance selection of a period of testing might have a bearing on the probability of discovery. Other factors pertinent to the probability of discovery include the pressure of time on the auditor to complete his examination, the problem of holding the cost of the examination within the bounds of economic reasonableness, the possibility of discovery by application of the techniques available to the auditor, and the expectations of clients and the public that the auditor will locate any or all irregularities.

A Concept of Due Audit Care. As a solution to this vexing problem, we propose the development of a concept of professional care which indicates in more or less specific terms the considerations which must govern the performance of an examination by an auditor. If his examination is conducted with the care required by this concept he will discover certain types of irregularities, should they be present. Thus he is neither excused from discovering any and all irregularities nor charged with an examination so extensive that it will uncover any and all irregularities. Practitioners are expected, under this concept, to make a reasonable search for irregularities, to provide their clients and business generally with an important service and some effective protection; they are not held for an examination unreasonably extensive or rigorous. At the same time, the concept gives some useful guidance as to the extent of the search they should make.

Of course the statement of such a concept has implications for those outside the profession as well. To the extent that laymen understand the concept they have a satisfactory standard by which to establish their expectations and to measure the results of audit work. The general usefulness of such a concept should be apparent. Even more apparent should be the conclusion that formulation of such a concept is an appropriate, even an essential undertaking for a profession, to state fairly and clearly the responsibility which its members accept without equivocation or understatement.

Development of a concept of due audit care can be divided into two parts; the first calls for establishment of the idea of a prudent practitioner, the second for an indication of the care with which he will perform under varying conditions.

The Prudent Man. In every profession, indeed in almost every area of activity in which one comes in contact with others, there is at least an implicit image of a prudent, reasonably competent practitioner whose degree of skill is taken as the standard measurement whenever the quality of performance of a fellow practitioner is questioned. This prudent practitioner is related to the "reasonable man" whose supposed activities and caution help to establish the bounds of negligence in any type of activity in which the unintentional failings of one are asserted to be the cause of harm or injury to another.

> We come next to inquire into the nature of the standard below which conduct must not fall if it is to avoid being negligent. This is ordinarily measured by what the reasonably prudent person would do under the circumstances. As everyone knows, this reasonable man is a creature of the law's imagination. He is an abstraction....
>
> Now this reasonably prudent man is not infallible or perfect. In foresight, caution, courage, judgment, self-control, altruism and the like he represents, and does not excel, the general average of the community. He is capable of making mistakes and errors of judgment, of being selfish, of being afraid — but only to the extent that any such shortcoming embodies the normal standard of community behavior. On the other hand, the general practice of the community, in any particular, does not necessarily reflect what is careful. The practice itself may be negligent. "Neglect of duty does not cease by repetition to be neglect of duty." Thus the standard represents the general level of moral judgment of the community, what it feels ought ordinarily to be done, and not necessarily what is ordinarily done, although in practice the two would very often come to the same thing.[10]

---

[10]Fowler V. Harper and Fleming James Jr., *The Law of Torts*, Boston: Little, Brown and Company, 1956, pp. 902-903.

The prudent man has certain attributes; and although they cannot be spelled out with any substantial degree of precision, some brief attention to them will aid us in gaining an understanding of the nature of due care.

The prudent man is:

(1) Required to exercise judgment equal to that of the level of his community whether that judgment is concerned with the perception and appreciation of risk or the choice between selfish and altruistic interests. He is not expected to be omniscient, nor is his judgment to be criticized on the basis of advantageous hindsight. He must exercise as sound judgment as would another possessed of the same extent of information available to him at the time.[11]

(2) Required to use with reasonable intelligence the knowledge which he has. He is considered to have as much knowledge of the basic facts and laws of nature, of his own abilities and limitations, of life in this country, of normal hazards and the dangerous properties of objects, animals, and so on as would be acquired by any reasonable man. If he acts within a given sphere or comes into relationships with people or things which would give a reasonably intelligent person specialized knowledge or experience, he is presumed to have such knowledge. Further, as science advances, more knowledge becomes available to all, and the prudent man is expected to keep up with his community both in general and in specialized knowledge.[12] In using the knowledge and experience he has acquired, the prudent man is considered to have average ability to perceive risks and their consequences. He is expected to be aware of his own ignorance and to perceive the risk of proceeding or acting in a state of ignorance of potential hazards.[13]

(3) Assumed to possess and exercise reasonable skill in his ordinary and occupational activities. In this respect he is

---

[11] *Ibid.*, p. 906.

[12] *Ibid.*, p. 916.

[13] *Ibid.*, p. 916.

required to exercise the degree of skill possessed by the general class of people engaged in that activity or line of work. This holds whether he is a beginner or not; as long as he acts in a given capacity he is held to the standards of those who are reasonably skilled and experienced in that capacity.[14] To the extent that the prudent man has physical defects or infirmities, he cannot be required to act as if he did not have such limitations, but he can be required to conduct himself as would a reasonable man who has the same infirmities. That is, he must employ the safeguards which a reasonable person would employ under the same conditions.[15]

(4) Required to recognize and give due consideration to his experience. If, for example, a reasonable man has found himself or others to be "accident-prone," he would take extra precautions to avoid accidents and injury. The prudent man is expected to show the same caution.[16]

In appraising the reasonableness of the judgments and actions of a prudent man, the general test is whether a reasonable person possessed of the same amount of knowledge would have foreseen the risk and taken steps to avoid it. Three factors are of importance. In Justice Learned Hand's words: "The degree of care demanded of a person by an occasion is the resultant of three factors: the likelihood that his conduct will injure others, taken with the seriousness of the injury if it happens, and balanced against the interest which he must sacrifice to avoid the risk."[17]

Probability of injury, amount of potential injury, and cost of avoidance, these three must be weighed and a reasonable balance reached. As the probability and extent of injury increase, the cost of avoidance becomes less significant. A reasonable man would not be expected to pay a great price to avoid an injury which at worst was quite improbable and of small consequence if it did occur. On the other hand, if his actions or inactions seriously threatened others with substantial damage, he would be

---

[14]*Ibid.*, p. 918.

[15]*Ibid.*, p. 920.

[16]*Ibid.*, p. 924.

[17]Conway v. O'Brien, 611 F. 2d at 612 (Federal Reporter-Second Series, Vol. III, p. 611, at 612).

expected to provide suitable safeguards even if this required a considerable sacrifice on his part.

Based on this brief summary of the legal concept of a prudent man, two conclusions seem warranted. First, it is an eminently reasonable and fair doctrine, holding each of us to a standard that provides necessary protection to others without burdening anyone with unjust responsibilities. Secondly, it provides a substantial measure of protection as well as responsibility to the prudent man, because it indicates the level of performance beyond which he is not required to go. If one discharges the responsibility of a prudent man he has done enough; he cannot be held for more.

There is nothing in this concept which gives specific rules of conduct or action. If specific rules were possible, no doctrine of a prudent man would be needed. When relationships, actions, and judgments vary so much from situation to situation that specific rules fail, then a concept such as that of the prudent man provides the only workable solution.

The Prudent Auditor. The independent auditor's responsibility for the detection of irregularities falls in just such an area as this, an area which as we have seen, does not lend itself to precise rules based either on classification of irregularities or on outright denial of any responsibility whatever. The solution here is development of the idea of a prudent practitioner, an auditor who represents the average of his profession. The action of any actual practitioner in any given case can then be compared with the anticipated actions of our assumed prudent practitioner in the same circumstances to determine whether the standards of the profession have been met. This prudent practitioner, because he is a member of a learned profession, can be held to standards of performance and judgment somewhat higher than those of an ordinary person. On the other hand, such standards must not be unduly rigorous or the profession will find them intolerable and society will suffer through loss of its services.

Development of a complete concept of a prudent practitioner must wait upon the expressions of leaders in the profession and the results of litigation over a period of years. Indeed, such development must be a continuing matter as conditions and our notions of social responsibility change; thus we may never have a "completed" concept. At this point, however, the following thoughts might be incorporated into a tentative concept of a prudent practitioner.

(1) The prudent practitioner will take steps to obtain any knowledge readily available which will enable him to foresee unreasonable risk or harm to others. This requires a thorough review of internal control, not one unduly circumscribed by doubtful technical distinctions. It further suggests a review of such matters as the company's program of insurance protection, of employee selection and supervision, and of the procedures for internal audit and reporting. To the objection that these are outside the scope of many standard audits as now performed we must reply that these are services the independent auditor can perform without adding substantially to the audit cost, that no other profession has the opportunity or the requisite training for the performance of these socially desirable activities, and that the concept of an audit should be expanded to include them as standard practice. We feel strongly disposed to a concept of due audit care which calls for serious effort by the auditor to acquire all readily available knowledge that might lead to perception of any substantial financial risks accepted deliberately or unknowingly by the company under examination.

(2) To the extent that audit experience, the auditor's own or that of others, or the history of the company under examination suggests the existence of extra risk in connection with the work of any employee, department, type of transaction, or asset, the auditor should give that risk special attention. A reasonable man is expected to provide special safeguards for particularly dangerous activities or for accident-prone persons. An analogy in financial and accounting activities is provided by situations in which the risk of an irregularity is great or an employee has a bad or doubtful record, in other words, an irregularity-prone situation or employee. That this idea already has some acceptance appears from the considerable emphasis on cash, marketable securities, receivables, and inventories in audit program planning. On the other hand, if experience indicates that the company's internal control procedures are particularly effective, a reasonable man, i.e. our prudent practitioner, would give less attention to the account, department, or employee concerned.

(3) Any unusual circumstances or relationships should be taken into consideration by the auditor in planning and performing his examination. Not infrequently, the circumstances surrounding an engagement are such that, in effect, they put the auditor "on notice" that extra care is required. A bond indenture provision calling for a minimum ratio of current assets to current liabilities, an audit specifically for credit purposes, strained relations between management and shareholders, a "one-man operation" in a given department or activity, and in some cases even the existence of a profit-sharing arrangement would suggest to a prudent practitioner that a little extra care and caution are advisable. These conditions suggest an additional incentive for the perpetration of irregularities or perhaps only less than usual restraint on bias and judgment. Unconscious bias resulting from unrecognized pressures may influence the judgment of the most honest business manager or accountant. A prudent practitioner must be aware of this, note the potentialities in the examination before him, balance risk with the cost of extending his procedures, and act accordingly.

(4) The prudent practitioner must recognize unfamiliar situations and take such precautionary measures as are warranted by the circumstances. It is not unusual for an auditor to find situations where terminology, practices, or relationships are somewhat out of the ordinary and quite unfamiliar to him. Sometimes insufficient information is made available. Any time the prudent practitioner finds himself concerned with strange or unusual conditions, it seems reasonable to assume that he should adopt extra precautions. That this is considered a normal requirement is suggested by the following:

> On the other hand, he did not attempt to translate the pound and bale figures in these confirmations into dollars for comparison with the inventory recapitulation, which was among the working papers. Indeed, he was not familiar with the market price of silk and never inquired concerning it, accepting Marien's pricing without question, and relying entirely upon Marien's representation that the total inventory figure agreed with the corporation's own records.[18]

---

[18]In the Matter of Interstate Hosiery Mills Inc., 4 S.E.C. 706, at 713.

(5) The prudent practitioner will take all appropriate steps to remove from his own mind any doubtful impressions or unanswered questions concerning matters material to his opinion. Harper and James point out that a man may be held for his impressions and beliefs if they are not unreasonable in the circumstances.

> One further matter may be brought up appropriately here. Not all of a man's conscious sensations and beliefs accurately reflect objective reality. But even his mistaken impressions and beliefs are to be taken into account in judging a man's conduct, and allowance will be made for them provided they are not unreasonable in the light of his background and experience.[19]

In the preceding chapter on evidence, the acceptance of intuition as a method of obtaining knowledge was noted. Montague, it will be recalled, attributed much of intuition to a combination of instinct, experience, and imagination. A professional man should have all the components mentioned, and it is not unreasonable to assume that he will develop knowledge intuitively. To permit him then to ignore the promptings of his intuition would be unfortunate indeed. A careful investigation of his intuitive feelings about the situation at hand would seem to be essential to a professional examination. That the courts may agree is indicated in a Canadian case as follows:

> In holding the defendants liable for their negligence in not discovering the defalcations, the court placed emphasis upon the fact that the defendant auditors had at one point suggested to another manager the position of power held by the latter, and the opportunity afforded him for any possible fraud, but had failed to communicate to their employers, the shareholders, the danger which existed, and had not taken any steps to discover whether or not he was in fact taking advantage of his position.[20]

In an American case the court found fault with the contention of an auditor that he was not certain of the managerial position of an employee bookkeeper who had also become a stockholder. Had the auditor taken the necessary precautions to learn the standing and responsibilities of the employee-stockholder in question, he might have avoided the censure that followed:

---

[19]Harper and James, *op. cit.*, p. 917.

[20]International Laboratories, Ltd. v. Dewar (Manitoba), 54ALR2d, p. 342, at 342 (American Law Reports, Annotated, Second Series).

> Defendants seek to justify their acceptance of Zastrow's [the bookkeeper's] list of accounts on two grounds; That Zastrow was present during the audit for 1944 and 1945 when Becker [the president] gave his list of accounts not to be confirmed, and, That Zastrow had become a stockholder of the plaintiff.
>
> Neither ground is tenable....Acceptance of a list of accounts not to be confirmed prepared by him [Zastrow] without the knowledge of Becker or other officer was inexcusable negligence for which defendants are liable.... The trial court did not err in rejecting the defense of contributory negligence.[21]

Anyone who reviews the audit work of others is almost certain to be distressed by notes and questions in the work papers which suggest that the auditor who wrote them into the papers had questions which, so far as can be told from the papers, were never answered. A prudent practitioner will insist that such matters be dealt with in the only appropriate manner, by requiring that the auditor who wrote them obtain sufficient information to satisfy himself on each one which has any material consequence. This holds for the prudent practitioner who first encounters the difficulty as well as the auditor who performs the review.

(6) The prudent practitioner will keep abreast of developments in his area of competence; he will seek knowledge of methods of perpetrating, concealing, and detecting irregularities. As a professional man, the auditor must give acceptable evidence of attainment of satisfactory skill before he is permitted to practice, or at least practice on his own account. To keep that skill at a satisfactory level, he must take such steps as are necessary to familiarize himself with developments in auditing. No reasonable man would expect to maintain his competence in a dynamic and growing profession without continuing study and effort.

(7) The prudent practitioner will recognize the necessity for review of the work of his assistants and will perform such review with full understanding of its importance.

> The importance of audit review grows out of the related facts, first, that the audit work papers are both the basis for the audit report and the proof that an adequate examination has been made by each person assigned to the engagement; second, that accounting and auditing are of such a nature that errors in the handling of

---

[21]Cereal Byproducts Co. v. Hall, 8 Ill., app. 2d, 331 at 336.

> figures or in judgment as to the best treatment of a given item are not only possible but may also be significant in their effect. Audit review is directed at both of these points. First, there is the need for insuring that the work papers are as complete and as useful as possible. Second, there is the requirement that errors be eliminated or at least reduced in so far as possible.[22]

The legal concept of a prudent man holds that beginners must meet the standards of the average practitioner in the field. The auditor in charge of an engagement must hold his assistants to the same standards he would expect of the average independent auditor. He must exercise considerable care and effort, first in instructing his assistants as to the nature and purpose of each assignment he makes, second in reviewing their work and their conclusions to satisfy himself that they performed satisfactorily and comprehended his instructions. Audit review includes steps to insure not only that all portions of the audit program have been completed but that they were performed intelligently and alertly. Of course the auditor in charge cannot stand over his assistants like an overseer throughout the audit, but he should find time to discuss with them the work they are doing, to point out its importance, and to determine whether they understand both how to perform the required procedure and what its purpose is. Not all of this need be done on the job. A prudent man would see to it that his assistants are urged to keep up to date with new developments and that opportunities are provided for self-improvement through training programs, availability of professional literature, and discussions with experienced practitioners.

As noted earlier, these suggestions for some of the characteristics of a prudent practitioner can be no more than tentative at this time. We feel strongly, however, that such a concept is not only important to the improvement of the profession's general level of performance, it is at the present time the most likely solution to the problem of responsibility for the detection of irregularities as well as for establishing responsibility for performance generally. Due audit care is the care which a prudent practitioner would exercise in planning and performing an audit. If an auditor has failed to perform with due audit care, he has fallen short of professional

---

[22]R. K. Mautz, *Fundamentals of Auditing*, New York: John Wiley & Sons, Inc., 1954, p. 326.

standards because the concept calls for at least average performance. If he has performed with due audit care and has acted as would a prudent practitioner having the same amount of information available to him, he has met the standards of the profession and has no further obligation in this respect.

Summary. In this chapter we have tried to establish a concept of due audit care as the basis for judging the responsibility of independent auditors in the performance of their professional duties. This concept is based on an assumed prudent practitioner and the knowledge, skill, caution, and responsiveness that could be expected from him under the circumstances at issue. The usefulness of such a concept seems clear. If it can be developed, it will give to all concerned with the subject a more explicit statement than is now available in the literature.

The difficulty of formulating such a concept is closely related to the problem of irregularity detection. There are some irregularities which should be discovered in any standard examination; the obligation of discovering certain other irregularities would be so onerous a burden as to be unbearable. Between these extremes are perhaps innumerable cases varying from one extreme to the other. We are unable to find in the characteristics of irregularities themselves any significant clues which permit a precise statement of audit responsibility for detection. This leads us naturally and inevitably to consideration of the legal doctrine of a prudent man and its application to auditing.

It must be recognized that a concept of due audit care, founded on the legal concept of a prudent man acting reasonably with average knowledge and average judgment in the specific circumstances, cannot give us objective advance answers to the question of responsibility in any given case. We feel it does give a useful criterion to the auditor himself and to those who must judge the quality of his work, a criterion which will increase in usefulness as experience sharpens and strengthens the concept itself.

We also believe that a statement indicating the extent of responsibility accepted can be formulated in a manner that will make its usefulness apparent, both to practitioners in their daily affairs and to the profession as an indication of acceptance of its just and fair responsibilities. Like development of the concept of due audit care, this may take some time, but it is a worthy endeavor and will repay the effort. As a beginning, we suggest the following summary. It will be apparent to the careful reader that its component ideas have been borrowed from a variety of sources.

Independent auditors should accept responsibility for the discovery and disclosure of those irregularities which the exercise of due audit care by a prudent practitioner would normally uncover. A prudent practitioner is assumed to have a knowledge of the philosophy and practice of auditing, to have the degree of training, experience, and skill common to the average independent auditor, to have the ability to recognize indications of irregularities, and to keep abreast of developments in the perpetration and detection of irregularities. Due audit care requires the auditor to acquaint himself with the company under examination, its method of operation and any significant practices peculiar to it or the industry of which it is a part, to review the method of internal control operating in the company under examination by inquiry and such other methods as are desirable, to obtain any knowledge readily available which is pertinent to the accounting and financial problems of the company under examination, to be responsive to unusual events and unfamiliar circumstances, to persist until he has eliminated from his own mind any reasonable doubts he may have about the existence of material irregularities, and to exercise caution in instructing his assistants and review their work.*

Due Audit Care and the Review of Internal Control

The relationship of internal control to auditing has long been recognized and it has become axiomatic that the effectiveness of the system of internal control must be taken into account in determining the extent and nature of the audit procedures appro-

*Some readers may find in this summary little that differs from their interpretation of Statements on Auditing Procedure No. 30. Others may find significant differences. This is not surprising. Much of our concern with that statement results from its reliance on generally accepted auditing standards as an adequate base for indication of responsibility. In interpreting the present standards in terms of specifics, some will reach conclusions quite different from others. Until auditing standards themselves are such that substantial variations in interpretation are much less likely than at present, a statement such as the one suggested here is needed.

priate in a given examination. The second standard of field work included in the ten generally accepted auditing standards requires consideration of the existing internal control in these words:

> There is to be a proper study and evaluation of the existing internal control as a basis for reliance thereon and for the determination of the resultant extent of the tests to which auditing procedures are to be restricted.[23]

Modification of the audit program because the system of internal control in effect is either more or less effective might seem to imply the existence of both a "standard" audit program and a "standard" system of internal control. If the internal control meets the standard, then the standard audit would appear to be satisfactory. Actually this is not the case at all; there is neither a standard system of internal control nor a standard audit program. True, there are standards which an effective system of internal control should meet, but the infinite variety of ways in which the requirements of these standards can be satisfied nullifies the false assumption of any standard system. The same is true of an audit program. There are standards accepted by the profession which establish more or less specific requirements for any audit. But again there is a considerable variety of auditing procedures, plus many alternative possibilities for emphasis and timing of application of the procedures, which effectively eliminate the applicability or usefulness of a standard audit program.

The relationship is well expressed in our Postulate Number 4:

> The existence of a satisfactory system of internal control eliminates the *probability* of irregularities.

Note the use of the term "probability" rather than "possibility" in this statement. Irregularities are always possible, no matter how good the system of internal control may be, because any man-made and man-operated system may break down when subjected to sufficient pressures or interference. Internal control, therefore, can eliminate only the probability of irregularities and it does this in proportion to its effectiveness. Thus in the complete absence of internal control, a situation difficult to imagine, irregularities, unintentional and intentional, would be very prob-

---

[23]American Institute of Accountants, *Generally Accepted Auditing Standards*, 1954, p. 13.

able indeed. As various useful procedures are installed and the system becomes better and better, the probability of errors decreases until finally the system becomes so effective that probability disappears. The possibility of irregularities, remote although it may be, always remains.

Thus each audit poses an individual situation. From the infinite variety of possible internal control procedures, which ones are employed here and how well are they functioning? To what extent have they added to the reliability of the financial data to be examined? To what extent have they made irregularities less likely? Having answered these questions, the auditor can then select from the large number of available audit procedures those which are peculiarly suited to the purposes of his examination under the conditions of internal control discovered to exist.

Purpose of the Review of Internal Control. Just as there is general agreement on the importance of internal control in auditing, so there is agreement on the purpose or purposes of the auditor's review. His review is undertaken to provide a basis for determining the extent of his examination and for making constructive suggestions about improvement of the system.

Each of these purposes may be viewed as an application of the concept of due audit care. A prudent practitioner will not plan his audit program until he has a reasonably satisfactory conception of the dangers and difficulties present in the situation he faces. He cannot determine how much work to do or what kind of work to do until he has become familiar with the strong and weak points of the internal control system which protects the enterprise resources and provides the data on which he is asked to present an opinion. Until he has studied and evaluated the system of internal control he cannot determine the extent of potential damage to his client inherent in the situation and thus cannot act intelligently to reduce that potential. As a prudent practitioner, therefore, he must first review the internal control and then plan accordingly.

Once having reviewed the internal control, the auditor will have acquired certain information, the possession of which he cannot ignore. If he learns of deficiencies in the system of internal control which constitute sources of potential injury to his client, he has an obligation to make these known to the client.

Surely no professional man would neglect to inform his client of dangers discovered in the course of serving the client. To the person who would point out that notification of the client with respect to weaknesses in internal control is an excellent way of obtaining additional accounting assignments, we must reply that, although this is true and the desire for additional business may be influential in the auditor's thinking, it cannot be permitted to become his primary motive in keeping the client informed. As a responsible professional practitioner, the auditor has a duty to report sources of potential injury to his client regardless of whether or not he himself stands to profit thereby.

The Nature of Internal Control. Although there is considerable agreement on the auditor's interest in internal control and its importance to auditing, there is still some controversy over the nature of internal control itself, particularly as that term is used by auditors in such statements as the second standard of field work. The essence of the controversy is found in the breadth of the definition of internal control published in 1949 by the American Institute of Certified Public Accountants:

> Internal control comprises the plan of organization and all of the coordinate methods and measures adopted within a business to safeguard its assets, check the accuracy and reliability of its accounting data, promote operational efficiency, and encourage adherence to prescribed managerial policies.[24]

As pointed out in the publication containing this definition, the definition goes well beyond the accounting and financial activities to which many accountants think internal control is limited.

> It recognizes that a "system" of internal control extends beyond those matters which relate directly to the function of the accounting and financial departments. Such a system might include budgetary control, standard costs, periodic operating reports, statictical analyses and the dissemination thereof, a training program designed to aid personnel in meeting their responsibilities, and an internal audit staff to provide additional assurance to management as to the adequacy of its outlined procedures and the extent to which they are being effectively carried out. It properly comprehends activities in other fields as, for example, time and motion studies which are of

---

[24]"Internal Control," A Special Report by the Committee on Auditing Procedure of the American Institute of Accountants, New York: 1949, p. 6.

an engineering nature, and use of quality controls through a system of inspection which fundamentally is a production function.[25]

The breadth of this definition seems apparent; it is difficult to conceive of a more inclusive statement. At the same time, the definition helps us to understand the purposes of internal control and the types of practices and procedures which can be included within a complete system.

Another attempt at explaining the nature of internal control sets forth the basic techniques available to an accountant in the construction of an accounting system as follows:[26]

1. Organization
2. Review
3. Reporting
4. Records
5. Training
6. Protective devices
7. Clerical proof devices

A description of the way in which each of these techniques of system construction can be employed provides a general operational definition of internal control; a description of the way they are employed in any given situation would be an operational definition of the internal control in that situation.

What amounts to a general operational definition of internal control is found in the following statements which purport to summarize the standards by which any system might be judged:

1. Authority for the performance of all activities essential to enterprise objectives and responsibility for performance of such activities should be clearly established and specifically prescribed.

   1A. Duties requiring performance of acts or operations should be assigned to employees other than those who authorize, record, or review those actions or operations; duties requiring custodianship of or access to property should be assigned to employees other than

---

[25] *Ibid.*

[26] R. K. Mautz and R. E. Schlosser, "Techniques of Internal Control," *The Journal of Accountancy*, October, 1957, pp. 43-48, at 44.

those who keep records of that property or review or approve discharge of the custodial responsibility.

2. Sufficient reliable and pertinent operating and financial data to permit informed decisions by responsible officers and employees should be supplied on a timely basis.
   2A. Proof devices, electronic, mechanical, and other, should be employed in the accumulation and processing of data to reduce to a reasonable minimum the possibility of inadvertent errors and intentional irregularities.
3. Actions, events, and transactions, both projected (potential) and completed, should be reviewed sufficiently to give reasonable assurance that transactions essential to enterprise objectives are effected and that unauthorized and otherwise irregular transactions are prevented or discovered.
   3A. Provision should be made for a system of reports indicating acceptance of responsibility for all important transactions, custodial activities, reviews, and approvals.
4. Provision should be made for the performance of all necessary activities by employees who are qualified as to training, experience, ability, and integrity for the discharge of their responsibilities, and whose replacement, temporary or permanent, is provided for in case of inability or unwillingness to perform.
5. The risk of loss of valuable assets and records should be reduced by precautionary measures insofar as reasonably possible.[27]

This operational definition, like the Institute definition quoted previously, is extremely broad because internal control itself is an extremely broad subject. When we combine these definitions with the requirement for review of internal control in the second standard of field work, it becomes apparent that the duty thereby assigned to the independent auditor extends well beyond his area of capacity. Few, if any, independent auditors would claim the

---

[27]R. K. Mautz and R. E. Schlosser, "Necessary Standards of Internal Control," *The Controller*, September, 1960, p. 148.

competence to review the effectiveness of training programs, time and motion studies, and quality controls.

Responsibility for Review of Internal Control. Acceptance of such a broad definition of internal control for auditing purposes has been pointed out to be undesirable because it implies onerous and unfortunate legal consequences.[28] Although professional practitioners must not shirk their reasonable responsibility, there are limits to the responsibilities which society can place on any profession if it is to continue to receive the services of that profession. Auditors cannot be expected to exceed their professional competence by invading fields foreign to their training, such as engineering and production; neither should they exceed their professional competence by accepting responsibility for accounting actions which are beyond their abilities. It must be recognized that the evaluation of internal control is at best a difficult and subjective weighing of imponderables. Although we talk of a "system" of internal control, we must remember that objective measurement of its effectiveness is an impossibility.

To borrow a phrase, "internal control is people." A system of internal control is made up of people and procedures, procedures in which people are expected to perform and report in a normal fashion. But unknown to the reviewer, the pressures which motivate the people in the "system" may change sufficiently that they cease to act in an expected fashion, where-upon the internal control procedure loses its effectiveness. An appeal for sympathy may cause a superior to overlook an assistant's failings; pressure by an older or higher-ranked employee, even if from another department, may be sufficient to keep an employee from reporting a suspicious occurrence; an offer to help with a heavy load of work may effectively circumvent a review procedure; collusive action by apparently unrelated individuals in different departments may offset an essential and apparently effective checking procedure; temporary substitution during vacation periods or during an emergency because of the illness of one or more employees may make division of duties a mockery; changes in an internal control system during a year may make answers given during the review at the end of the

[28]Saul Levy, "Internal Control and Legal Responsibility," *The Journal of Accountancy*, February, 1957, pp. 29-33, at 33.

year inappropriate for much of the year's activities; even a temporary relapse by a reviewing employee because of illness on the job may permit an irregularity to slip by unnoticed. There are so many events and relationships which can work to offset the most effective internal control measures and which at the same time would be neither apparent to nor necessarily discoverable by the independent auditor that acceptance of responsibility for the review and evaluation of internal control is hazardous at best. Nevertheless, it remains an essential preliminary to the development of an intelligent audit program and an area in which the auditor can be of great service to his client.

To some extent the problem here is similar to the problem of acceptance of responsibility for the detection of irregularities, in that the auditor's appropriate duty does not lend itself to statement by rule or to uniform measurement. And here again the solution is to be found in the concept of a prudent practitioner. What considerations would govern the actions of a prudent practitioner confronted with the necessity of reviewing the internal control of a company in connection with an audit? What would he review? How would he review? To what extent would he review?

First, it must be emphasized that a prudent practitioner strives continually to keep caution and cost in reasonable balance. He is neither so cautious that he forgets all notions of time and effort nor so complacent that he refuses to undertake necessary investigative steps. Neither undue extension nor undue limitation of the review is desirable, but rather a reasonable response to the situation he discovers.

In identifying those matters which would normally be reviewed by a prudent practitioner, we find the following statement helpful:

> In summary, if the purpose of the audit review of internal control is to provide a basis for development of an audit program, it must as a minimum be extensive enough to permit the auditor to come to conclusions with respect to the organization, policies, activities, and personnel of the financial and accounting departments, and it must go beyond these departments to determine the extent of physical safeguards and alternative control measures in use as well as to investigate the reliability of data supplied to the accounting department by other divisions of the enterprise.[29]

---

[29] R. K. Mautz and R. E. Schlosser, "Standards for the Review of Internal Control," *The Journal of Accountancy*, July, 1958, p. 30.

Internal control, like irregularities, does not lend itself to any simple classification or characterization on the basis of which review can be limited. The auditor, if he is to perform responsibly, must give consideration to any procedure which tends to increase the reliability of the reported data or tends to decrease the probable incidence of irregularities. This principle is suggested in the following proposed standards for the review of internal control by independent auditors:

1. The formal and informal organization of the company under examination is to be studied sufficiently to enable the auditor to conclude:
   a. Whether authority for the performance of essential financial and accounting activities is clearly established and specifically prescribed.
   b. Whether responsibility for the performance of financial and accounting activities is fixed.
   c. Whether the authorization, recording, review, or approval of financial and custodial activities are accomplished by persons other than those who perform such activities.
2. The financial and accounting procedures in use by the company under examination are to be studied sufficiently to enable the auditor to conclude:
   a. Whether completed transactions have been reviewed sufficiently to give reasonable assurance that financial transactions have been effected as authorized and that unauthorized and otherwise irregular transactions have been discovered.
   b. Whether mechanical and other proof devices are utilized sufficiently to reduce errors and irregularities in operating and financial data to a reasonable minimum.
   c. Whether reports are required and prepared to indicate responsibility for the authorization, performance, review, and approval of financial and accounting duties and transactions.
3. The work of the employees in the financial and accounting departments of the company under examination

should be reviewed sufficiently to enable the auditor to conclude whether they discharge their assigned duties in a satisfactory manner.

4. The protection given valuable assets and records by the company under examination should be studied sufficiently to permit the auditor to conclude whether the risks of destruction, theft, violation, or other loss have been reduced to a reasonable minimum.
5. If financial or accounting department procedures are considered unsatisfactory for internal control purposes, sufficient investigation should be made of related or supporting procedures outside those departments to enable the auditor to conclude whether the apparent weakness is offset by other procedures.[30]

These standards, of course, must be applied with reason and with full awareness of the probabilities as discussed in this chapter. The auditor cannot make a systems survey within the scope of an audit and even if he could, there would still be possibilities for breakdown in a system that appeared sound and effective. The auditor should do what a prudent practitioner would do, that is, make a reasonable investigation and, if weaknesses are found, search for balancing features. If the system appears sound and his tests, discussed in the following section, find no apparent violations of the control as provided, he may consider the system to be adequate.

A recent release by the Committee on Auditing Procedure of the American Institute of Certified Public Accountants describes the extent of the auditor's review of internal control in somewhat different terms but arrives at substantially the same conclusions as found in these standards.[31]

Method of Review. Our concern here is primarily with theory rather than procedure and because the methods of reviewing internal control have been discussed at some length in the literature

---

[30] R. K. Mautz and R. E. Schlosser, "Standards for the Review of Internal Control," *loc. cit.*, pp. 27-31.

[31] See: "Statement on Auditing Procedure No., 29, October, 1958," The Committee on Auditing Procedure of the American Institute of Certified Public Accountants.

of the profession, we will not dwell long on the procedures for review at this point. It should be noted, however, that a prudent practitioner will draw upon his knowledge of evidence and how it can be obtained in reviewing internal control just as he would for any other phase of his examination. All the basic audit techniques are available to him and should be used as applicable. He cannot rely completely on any one of them. Thus he will not only ask questions of informed employees and read whatever manuals and charts are available; he will also examine documents, review subsidiary records, and trace bookkeeping procedures as necessary. It may be desirable to devise specific tests and procedures to facilitate the review. In addition, his review of internal control is completed only with completion of his examination. He will make a preliminary review, of course, in advance of preparing his audit program, but throughout the examination he must keep alert to signs that the internal control is either more or less effective than his preliminary review indicated. To the extent that he finds such indications, as a prudent practitioner he will extend his investigation and tests to determine whether his initial review and evaluation were in error and, if so, the extent to which his planned program should be modified.

Extent of Review. Because the extent and effectiveness of internal control is so important in audit programming and performance, a prudent practitioner will tend to give this phase of the examination a full measure of emphasis. At best, internal control is a rather amorphous subject and difficult to comprehend and reduce to satisfactory work paper notes. Yet no part of the examination is more important than his review and evaluation of internal control. Also, there is no area in which he can be of more real assistance to his client than by scrupulously examining and reporting on the client's control procedures. His professional training should qualify him to perform this service in a way that practitioners of no other profession can equal. He owes it to his clients not to miss the opportunity.

Because of the difficulty of a satisfactory and reasonably thorough review and evaluation of internal control there may be a tendency to give this important part of audit work somewhat less attention than it deserves. Any such tendency should be resisted vigorously. A prudent practitioner will know why he performs every step in his audit program, why procedures are applied at the times they are performed, and why certain procedures have been selected over alternative possibilities. The answers to such questions are likely to be found in the extent and effectiveness of the internal control, and only a thorough and intelligent review will provide them.

Thus a prudent practitioner will review the internal control of a company under examination sufficiently to familiarize himself with the procedures and practices in effect. He will meet the standards suggested in the preceding section. To the extent that he has questions or doubts in his mind about the effectiveness of the control in any material respect, he must continue to investigate and test until he has removed any reasonable doubt from his mind. Two points might be mentioned here.

Although we speak of internal control as a "system," our valuation must be more concerned with the parts or divisions of that system than with the system as a whole. It is not enough that we judge a given system as satisfactory or unsatisfactory; we must know the specific respects in which it is satisfactory or less than satisfactory. For example, good control over cash receipts cannot balance weak control over cash disbursements. The strong features of control over receipts may protect the receipts from misappropriation and the data respecting receipts from material error, but they provide no protection whatever to disbursements and the related data. Evaluation of internal control cannot be effective if it is stated in terms of averages. "In general the internal control is satisfactory" is not an appropriate conclusion unless it is followed immediately by a specification of the individual points at which it is less than satisfactory.

In developing an audit program for a given examination, the auditor must have intimate knowledge of the strong and weak points of internal control. How else can he determine what steps to apply, when to apply them, or how extensive to make his tests? His claim to expertness in his field, to professional competence, is a claim that he will neither waste his time and efforts unduly nor omit reasonable consideration of conditions which the average practitioner would consider potentially dangerous to the client. Here, as elsewhere, he must exercise due audit care and he can do so only if his review has pin-pointed the specific weakness in the system of internal control under examination.

The second point is that we should not confuse the review of internal control with the application of auditing procedures where the control has been found to be something less than satisfactory. In an ideal situation, one in which the internal control appears to be excellent and in which testing of the system finds it to be excellent in fact, the audit program itself might be little more than a test of the internal control system as described. In a less ideal situation, one in which the internal control neither appears to be nor is in fact excellent, the audit program will be expected to go beyond a testing of the system as described and on into some investigation of the actual incidence of the potential irregularities. In the first case, the ideal situation, it may be impossible to separate the review of internal control and the audit program; in the second case, the distinction should be clear. Once the auditor has satisfied himself as to the fairness of his understanding of the internal control system, any steps taken to discover the extent of potential irregularities is part of the audit program separate from the review and tests of internal control.

Responsiveness of Auditor to Internal Control Situation. Once the auditor has completed his review and evaluation of internal control, he has obtained information which his client should have made available to him. A strong point is made by independent auditors of the responsibility of the management of a company for development and maintenance of adequate internal control.[32] Whatever the auditor's legal responsibilities in this connection, surely he has an important professional duty to acquaint his client with significant potential dangers and to do this as forcefully and emphatically as the particular dangers warrant. In this connection, the suggestion has been made that the auditor should comment on the effectiveness of internal control in his audit report.[33] This, we feel, is a proposal that should be viewed at the present time with considerable caution.

---

[32]See, for instance: "Internal Control, A Special Report by the Committee on Auditing Procedure," The American Institute of Accountants, 1949 and Philip L. Defliese, "Auditing when Internal Control is Inadequate," *The Journal of Accountancy*, September, 1959, pp. 37-43.

[33]See: Norman H. S. Vincent, "Reliance Upon Internal Control," Chapter 16 in *CPA Handbook*, American Institute of Accountants, 1953.

The argument against expressing an opinion on the effectiveness of internal control does not raise the question of the propriety of such an opinion. There is little question in our minds that the auditor has a responsibility to keep his client informed on the actual state of internal control practices and procedures discovered by the auditor throughout the course of his examination. Nor is it a question of knowledge, because if the auditor makes the type of review and evaluation suggested in this chapter, he should certainly be qualified to express an informed opinion. The real difficulty is whether such an opinion can be expressed in terms which will not be misunderstood. As suggested earlier in this chapter, it is extremely difficult to evaluate a system of internal control as a system. At one extreme is an excellent system of internal control; to merit this description, all phases of the system must be effective and operating. Anything less than this automatically includes certain existing or potential dangers. If all phases of internal control except that dealing with cash receipts are excellent, how does one describe the system? On the average, a saucepan with but one tiny hole in it is good, but as a matter of fact it leaks and is worth nothing at all until the leak is repaired. Of course this is not a direct analogy with a system of internal control, but there are important resemblances. It is extremely dangerous to attempt to describe an entire system of internal control in such terms as "good," "fair," or "satisfactory." Can there be a satisfactory system of internal control which is short of the excellence found when all parts are functioning effectively? As yet, the individual components or parts of a system of internal control have not been stated in such a way that a "piecemeal opinion" of their effectiveness can be given. As noted earlier in this chapter, standards for evaluation of a system have been proposed, but these have not been authoritatively accepted, nor were they designed for the purpose at issue. Until an authoritative basis is developed for offering an opinion on divisions, parts, or components of the system of internal control, auditors will do well to refrain from offering opinions on the effectiveness of systems of internal control taken as a whole.

It might be pointed out that the expressions of opinion on a system of internal control taken as a whole and on a set of financial statements taken as a whole are not at all similar. Returning again to the analogy of the leaky saucepan, we find that a weakness in internal control has implications substantially different from those which any deviation from fact in a balance sheet or income statement item would have. Furthermore, the concept of qualified and piecemeal opinions is well developed with respect to financial statements. It is not developed at all for internal control. This is not to say that expression of such opinions as to effectiveness of internal control would not be useful and cannot be worked out. On the contrary, such opinions would be extremely useful, and with sufficient background work in the analysis and description of internal control, its techniques, procedures, and standards, we think that methods of reporting not only can but should be developed. At the present time, however, that essential background work is only just beginning and we feel it unwise to express opinions about the effectiveness of internal control systems until it is much more advanced.

How then does the auditor discharge his responsibility to his client and to those third parties who rely upon his report and opinion? At the present stage of development, his responsibility to his client can best be accomplished by reporting directly to the client any weaknesses in internal control worthy of the client's attention. This should be done in writing, of course, and to reach a level sufficiently high to assure a suitable response preferably should be directed to those to whom the regular opinion itself is sent. If the responsibility for maintenance of good internal control is placed on management, then failure to assure that such control is maintained is a management failing and should be reported to those who in turn are responsible for keeping management in its present position. To report to any lower level is to permit management to cover its deficiencies. If the auditor permits this, he fails those who look to him for professional guidance. If the auditor is ever to move into a position in which he reviews management skill, competence, and judgment, it would seem that acceptance of responsibility for reporting on the effectiveness with which management discharges its internal control responsibilities might well be a first step.

The responsibility of the independent auditor to other interests in the enterprise with respect to the efficacy of the internal control system is a closely related although separate matter. Some of the differences between the two are noted in the following:

> From the foregoing, it seems apparent that many accounting officers of business organizations believe public accountants can and should expand their reports to express an opinion on the effectiveness of internal control. We are inclined to agree with them as to the value of an accountant's opinion in that respect to those concerned with the management of the company. However, we doubt that it is a matter which should ordinarily be brought to the attention of those outside management. It is seldom a matter which can be dealt with adequately without considerable explanation, and is a matter which relates primarily to the management function. It seems to us, therefore, that it is an appropriate subject for inclusion in a detailed, long-form report, or for a special memorandum for the use of management or board of directors, but it is not generally an appropriate subject for comment in the short-form report or certificate.[34]

Although we are in general agreement with the position expressed in this quotation, the question must be raised: Under what conditions would the auditor's opinion on the internal control situation become an appropriate subject for comment in the short-form report or certificate? A statement that "generally" it is not appropriate leads to the conclusion that in some cases it is appropriate. Just what circumstances would provide sufficient justification for an exception to the general rule?

The answer to this question, as to any question dealing with wording of an auditor's opinion, is governed primarily by the materiality of the point in question. If the weakness in internal control were such that knowledge of it might deter a reader of the financial statements from taking action which he otherwise would take or would cause him to take an action that he otherwise would not take, it appears that this should be disclosed. If, for example, a company under examination had no internal control whatever, would an auditor be wise to issue any opinion at all? In this extreme case, it appears that even if he had performed a detailed audit the auditor would have no sound basis for offering an opinion on the fairness of presentation because unrecorded transactions are more than merely possible. Furthermore, it is

---

[34]Carman G. Blough, "Auditing Practice Forum," *The Journal of Accountancy*, May, 1950, p. 430.

doubtful that he should give an opinion even on the balance sheet, although he may have satisfied himself that as of the date of examination it was substantially accurate. The complete absence of internal control suggests that after that date anything might happen to the company's assets. The situation is such that post balance sheet events cannot be adequately reviewed; those who read the statements tend naturally to project them forward to the date of reading, a dangerous projection if internal control is missing and one the auditor should not encourage. The only satisfactory solution to such a situation would seem to lie in appropriate disclosure of the situation in the financial statements and, if necessary, in the auditor's report.

If we assume a less extreme situation, one in which, for example, the company has a completely inadequate insurance program and refuses to do anything about it, must the independent auditor disclose such a situation in his report? It seems reasonable to conclude that there are situations in which he would. If we assume that investment transactions which involve a substantial portion of the company's assets and activities are under the exclusive control of one individual who also keeps the records of investments, perhaps a less clear-cut situation appears. No easy rule can be propounded for such assumed cases, but it appears entirely within reason to recommend that an independent auditor disclose to all concerned any weaknesses in internal control which in his opinion are sufficiently important to influence the judgment of one reading and acting on the financial statements.

Program Modification. In another expression of our views,[35] we have offered what we consider a reasonable summary of the possibilities for the modification of audit programs in view of conclusions reached in the review and evaluation of internal control. We believe these statements, with some minor revisions, are pertinent here.

1. The system of internal control provides the basis for planning and modifying the audit program, and the existence of specific strong points and weaknesses in the system of internal control should be reflected in the audit program.

---

[35]Hussein A. Sharaf and R. K. Mautz, "The Internal Control Standard and Program Planning," *The Illinois Certified Public Accountant*, Vol. 20, No. 2, Winter, 1957-58, pp. 30-33.

2. However effective the system of internal control may be, there exists a "minimum" audit program which must be applied.
3. Program planning is essentially a problem of allocating scarce resources as effectively and economically as possible among the competing demands of not only a specific audit engagement but all examinations making up the auditor's practice.
4. In the allocation of audit resources, the significance of the irregularities possible under the given internal control situation is of primary importance.
5. Modification of the minimum audit program to meet the needs of a specific internal control situation can be obtained by:
   a. Appropriate timing in application of procedures.
   b. Appropriate assignment of personnel.
   c. Appropriate selection of techniques and procedures.
6. Even in the absence of specific weaknesses in internal control, the application of audit procedures and the search for complementary evidence through supplemental procedures will be extended in certain instances such as the following:
   a. In areas where the transactions or financial data are particularly subject to irregularity. (Examples are receipts of currency by mail, unclaimed wages, petty cash disbursements, financial statement classifications, disclosure of contingent liabilities.)
   b. To functions which hold a standing temptation and therefore tend to invite dishonesty and possibly collusion. (Examples are custody of valuable assets, commission calculations, approval of expense accounts.)
   c. For transactions sufficiently unusual in nature not to be provided for in the ordinary routine of internal control. (Examples are sales of scrap, sales of retired assets, income from securities, employees' loans.)
   d. To accounting processes controlled by employees about whom the auditor gets an impression of moral weakness, excess spending habits, etc., through his observations during the course of the examination.

7. A major factor to be considered in determining the desirability of extending audit procedures in the length of time during which the auditor has examined the company and the degree of intimacy attained.
8. Although many deficiencies in an internal control system can be met by a reasonable adjustment of audit time, careful use of personnel, or selection of appropriate procedures, other deficiencies may require program changes that are not economical or may be of such a nature that they cannot be remedied under conditions as they exist. In these cases a disclaimer of opinion may be required.
9. Audit review procedures should give special attention to weaknesses in internal control and to the program modifications required thereby.

Conclusion. As a professional man, the independent auditor must have a concern for any internal control measures which increase the reliability of the data in the financial statements or reduce the probability of irregularities, and his review must be broad enough to discover these. Having reviewed and evaluated the internal control sufficiently to form an opinion as to its effectiveness with respect to specific areas of transactions and resources, he will have obtained information which he must then use as any prudent man would. This means that any weaknesses which represent a potential for significant injury to the client should be reported to the client at a level sufficiently high to assure a constructive response. Any weaknesses sufficiently material to influence the judgment of those who read and rely on the financial statements and the auditor's opinion should be revealed in the auditor's opinion. In addition, as a prudent practitioner, the auditor should modify his audit program by altering the timing, emphasis, and choice of procedures, and by using the available time and personnel as effectively as possible.

APPENDIX TO CHAPTER 6
Illustrative Classification of Irregularities Providing for Indication of Probability of Detection

Type of Irregularity	Probability of Detection in a "Standard" Audit				
			Probable in		
	Expected in a single examination	Expected in a continuous series of examinations	Single examination	Series of examinations	Impossible or unlikely of detection
Unintentional irregularities					
Material in amount					
Affecting balance sheet accounts					
Erroneous record					
Omission of entry					
Erroneous entry					
Erroneous calculation					
Erroneous posting or other bookkeeping procedure					
Loss or omission of document					
Affecting income statement accounts					
Erroneous record					
Omission of entry					
Erroneous entry					
Erroneous calculation					
Erroneous posting or other bookkeeping procedure					
Loss or omission of documents					
Immaterial in amount					
(The same sub-classes apply here as under material irregularities.)					
Intentional irregularities					
Perpetrated within scope of internal control system					
Material in amount					
Not involving collusion					
Affecting balance sheet accounts					
Open shortages, differences, etc.					
Concealed shortages, differences, etc.					
Manipulation of records					
Omission of entry					
False entry					
False calculation					
False posting, etc.					

APPENDIX TO CHAPTER 6 – *(Continued)*
Illustrative Classification of Irregularities Providing for Indication of Probability of Detection

Type of Irregularity	Probability of Detection in a "Standard" Audit				
			Probable in		
	Expected in a single examination	Expected in a continuous series of examinations	Single examination	Series of examinations	Impossible or unlikely of detection
Manipulation of documents					
Destruction of documents					
Introduction of false documents					
Alteration of legitimate documents					
Affecting income statement accounts					
Manipulation of records					
Omission of entry					
False entry					
False calculation					
False posting, etc.					
Manipulation of documents					
Destruction of documents					
Introduction of false documents					
Alteration of legitimate documents					
Affecting income statement accounts					
Manipulation of records					
Omission of entry					
False entry					
False calculation					
False posting, etc.					
Manipulation of documents					
Destruction of documents					
Introduction of false documents					
Alteration of legitimate documents					
Involving collusion					
Affecting balance sheet accounts					
Open shortages, differences, etc.					
Concealed shortages, differences, etc.					
Manipulation of records					
Omission of entry					
False entry					
False calculation					
False posting, etc.					

APPENDIX TO CHAPTER 6 – *(Continued)*

Illustrative Classification of Irregularities Providing for Indication of Probability of Detection

Type of Irregularity	Probability of Detection in a "Standard" Audit				
	Expected in a single examination	Expected in a continuous series of examinations	Probable in		Impossible or unlikely of detection
			Single examination	Series of examinations	
Manipulation of documents					
Destruction of documents					
Introduction of false documents					
Alteration of legitimate documents					
Affecting income statement accounts					
Manipulation of records					
Omission of entry					
False entry					
False calculation					
False posting, etc.					
Manipulation of documents					
Destruction of documents					
Introduction of false documents					
Alteration of legitimate documents					
Immaterial in amount					
(The same sub-classes apply here as under material irregularities.)					
Manipulation of documents					
Destruction of documents					
Introduction of false documents					
Alteration of legitimate documents					
Involving collusion					
Affecting balance sheet accounts					
Open shortages, differences, etc.					
Concealed shortages, differences, etc.					
Manipulation of records					
Omission of entry					
False entry					
False calculation					
False posting, etc.					

APPENDIX TO CHAPTER 6 – *(Continued)*
Illustrative Classification of Irregularities Providing for Indication of Probability of Detection

Type of Irregularity	Probability of Detection in a "Standard" Audit: Expected in a single examination	Expected in a continuous series of examinations	Probable in: Single examination	Probable in: Series of examinations	Impossible or unlikely of detection
Manipulation of documents					
Destruction of documents					
Introduction of false documents					
Alteration of legitimate documents					
Affecting income statement accounts					
Manipulation of records					
Omission of entry					
False entry					
False calculation					
False posting, etc.					
Manipulation of documents					
Destruction of documents					
Introduction of false documents					
Alteration of legitimate documents					
Immaterial in amount					
(The same sub-classes apply here as under material irregularities.)					
Perpetrated by violating provisions of system of internal control					
Material in amount					
Not involving collusion					
Affecting balance sheet accounts					
Open shortages, differences, etc.					
Concealed shortages, differences, etc.					
Manipulation of records					
Omission of entry					
False entry					
False calculation					
False posting, etc.					

Chapter 7

Fair Presentation

Auditing is concerned with the faithfulness with which reported financial data portray the realities of an enterprise's operations and financial condition. In the language of the profession, this relationship of reported data to reality is expressed as "presents fairly," and the expression occurs in every standard short-form auditor's report. It is interesting to note that through statements on Auditing Procedure No. 27 and No. 28, this idea of fair presentation is extended to information beyond that included in the customary financial statements and by implication to any data which the independent auditor is asked to examine for propriety.

The essence of auditing is found in the service the auditor performs in expressing his expert judgment with respect to the fairness of presentation of financial statements, and certainly the vindication of his professional status is found in the responsibilities he assumes in expressing that judgment. Thus the concept of fair presentation is a crucial one in auditing and merits intensive analysis along with the other basic concepts.

In our view, the concept of fair presentation is composed of three sub-concepts, which, although they are closely related, require independent consideration. These are:

1. The concept of accounting propriety.
2. The concept of adequate disclosure.
3. The concept of audit obligation.

Although these subsidiary concepts are often confused in discussions of this subject, we believe much will be gained by an effort to identify and separate them so that each may receive the attention it merits.

Accounting Propriety

In Chapter 1, the close relationship of accounting and auditing was noted, although the point was made that auditing is not properly considered a subdivision of accounting but rather is to be viewed as a separate and closely associated field of knowledge and effort. Auditing has its primary roots in logic, not in accounting. It draws ideas and concepts from accounting as it does from a number of other fields, but it has its own identity and existence distinct from each of these.

From accounting, auditing has borrowed generally accepted accounting principles and all that this expression implies.[1] This includes the ideas (1) that there are accounting principles, (2) that there is general agreement and some authoritative support for these principles, and (3) that their application in any given case not only improves the financial presentation but raises it to a satisfactory standard of quality. However, an auditor does not borrow accounting principles blindly, he accepts them with reservations. He must be aware of the fact that being what they are, generally accepted accounting principles may not always realize in application a satisfactory standard of quality. When he finds this to be the case, he may find it necessary to develop principles to meet the given situation. To understand this point we need both a better understanding of the relationship of auditing and accounting and an understanding of the nature of generally accepted accounting principles.

The Relationship of Accounting and Auditing. Much of the confusion in our thinking about these two fields stems from the fact that so often the same individual serves both as an accountant and as an auditor. The independent certified public accountant holds himself out as an expert accountant who is available for employment either as an auditor, an accountant, or both. Because little attention has ever been given to developing auditing as a distinct discipline, most practitioners probably give little conscious thought to whether a given engagement is an accounting or an auditing assignment. As suggested in the following chapter, this distinction is extremely important to maintenance of the auditor's independence, and definite steps may be necessary to establish the difference clearly and effectively.

All auditors are first accountants, or at least trained as accountants, because one cannot effectively verify accounting data unless he has some understanding of how they were gathered,

[1] Throughout this chapter the term "principles" is used in the same sense that it is currently used in the standard short-form auditor's opinion, that is as an equivalent to "practices."

summarized, classified, and presented. He must know the procedures and practices of accounting and be familiar with its devices and techniques. Thus accounting provides a necessary background for the study of auditing. Only if one has competence as an accountant can he have competence as an auditor. Yet when a practitioner, no matter how much accounting training or experience he has had, acts in the capacity of an auditor he is doing something above and beyond the activities of an accountant. Although he may use his accounting training and experience, he is auditing, not keeping accounts.

An analogy may be helpful here. A judge must have a sound knowledge of the law if he is to be a successful jurist. Certainly the overwhelming majority of judges will have had a thorough legal education and probably substantial legal experience as practicing attorneys. But when a man sits as a judge, he no longer is a lawyer; he has an entirely different task to perform and a substantially different calling. He must bring to his new calling a different point of view, a sense of detachment, an impartiality that would have been out of place when he acted as an attorney.

So it is with the auditor. Although he must make use of his accounting background, as an auditor his attitude and point of view must be quite different; he must develop a sense of detachment; he must strive for impartiality in his search for and weighing of evidence. The auditor reviews the work of accountants. Where they have been free to innovate and experiment, to attempt new presentations, perhaps of necessity to develop new practices, the auditor merely reviews and evaluates. He measures the innovations and experiments, the new presentations of the accountant, against generally accepted accounting principles. If they do not meet the requirements of generally accepted accounting principles, he finds them deficient.

But his evaluation is more than just a comparison of the accountant's work with accepted principles. The auditor must also evaluate the principles and their applicability in the specific instance. As a matter of fact, if he approaches his assignment responsibly, he will first establish the propriety of generally accepted accounting principles in the case at hand and then measure the specific accounting methods and results against the principles. Either or both the principles and the accounting may be deficient, and he must not hesitate to criticize and call for the improvement of either or both. Thus the auditor borrows generally accepted accounting principles from accounting but he accepts them with reservations. If they do not meet the needs of the case at hand, he must reject them and develop what in his judgment is a proper solution.

It should be emphasized here that rejection is not based on a disinclination to accept practices which others find satisfactory. Rejection is based, rather, on the sober belief that important aspects of the situation at hand remove it from the category to which generally accepted principles do apply. There is something sufficiently unusual about the situation to make generally accepted principles inapplicable. Principles by nature apply to a variety of situations. Not all of them, however, can apply to all situations. It is in the unusual situation that the auditor may find generally accepted accounting principles unsatisfactory.

The Nature of Generally Accepted Principles of Accounting. The assertion that an auditor can reject generally accepted accounting principles if he feels they are not appropriate to the problem at issue may seem to give the auditor undue power for determining accounting propriety. Actually, the auditor has no alternative to this position. The fault is in what we now refer to as generally accepted accounting principles.

At the time of this writing there does not exist any authoritative, comprehensive system of accounting principles.[2] Committees of the American Accounting Association have made repeated attempts to develop comprehensive statements of principles or standards; but whatever success attended these efforts, they have not received any important degree of authoritative support. On the other hand, individual or groups of principles less than comprehensive in scope have received authoritative support from such influential bodies as the Securities and Exchange Commission through its Accounting Series Releases and the American Insti-

[2] The American Institute of Certified Public Accountants has recently embarked upon a program of research which is intended to produce both a comprehensive and an authoritatively established system of accounting principles. If such a system existed, auditing could perhaps adopt it with less reservation than it must now maintain with respect to the principles that are available to it.

tute of Certified Public Accountants through its Accounting Research Bulletins. The incomplete system which results from recognizing the rather odd assortment of authoritatively established principles is presumably what auditors now refer to as generally accepted accounting principles. A brief examination of their significant characteristics may be helpful. In our judgment, the following are the more important characteristics:

1. Incompleteness of the "system."
2. Relative rather than absolute authority.
3. Nonrequirement of unanimous or even majority support for establishment as generally accepted.
4. Development in response to business events commonly on an "after the event" basis.
5. Presumptive rather than established ability to display financial events and conditions.

Incompleteness of the System of Generally Accepted Accounting Principles. The lack of substantial authority for any of the published attempts at statement of a complete system of accounting principles leaves us with what at best can be described as a fragmentary system. The authoritative statements of the American Institute of Certified Public Accountants together with pertinent S.E.C. Accounting Series Releases provide us with a substantial number of specific principles but they do not in any sense make up an integrated and comprehensive system. This could be remedied to some extent if either one included some basic statements of purpose or fundamental principle to serve as a guide for evaluation of problems for which no specific formal statement has been made. But this has not been done. Whether it is felt that such a statement is unnecessary because most accountants already understand the purposes of accounting and financial statement presentation or that such a statement is too fraught with hazards is not clear. At any rate, we now have neither complete coverage with specific rulings nor broad principles which provide guidance in the absence of specific rulings.

This presents a considerable problem to both accountants and auditors. In dealing with situations in which no specific ruling applies, recourse must be had either to custom and convention or to innovation and experiment. To a considerable extent, custom has provided the solution, and a great part of what we now consider to be generally accepted accounting practice has its support solely in custom with no formal statement by any authoritative body. Yet new accounting problems continually appear in business, and frequently neither custom nor stated rulings provide a ready answer. In such cases it must be the judgment of the individual auditor which guides.

> It is not to be expected that there will ever be compiled one body of authoritative, exhaustive, and permanent accounting principles against which the auditor may weigh all of the practices he encounters. The reason is inherent in the nature of accounting, which must be readily adaptable to changes in business practices as well as to conditions under which business operates. The application of accounting principles to the infinite variety of business situations is a matter for judgment of the experienced accountant rather than for mechanical application of a set of fixed rules.[3]

Relative Rather than Absolute Authority. None of the authoritative statements currently accepted as principles are binding upon all accountants under all conditions. A strong feeling exists that the circumstances of individual cases may made deviations from stated principles both necessary and desirable. Hence there has been almost no tendency on the part of professional bodies to impose their ideas on others.

> Except in cases in which formal adoption by the Institute membership has been asked and secured, the authority of opinions reached by the committee rests upon their general acceptability. The committee recognizes that in extraordinary cases fair presentation and justice to all parties at interest may require exceptional treatment. But the burden of justifying departure from accepted procedures, to the extent that they are evidenced in committee opinions, must be assumed by those who adopt another treatment.[4]

Any position short of absolute authority for accounting principles opens the door to a range of opinions among individual accountants. That individuals accept the authority of these principles with varying reservations is indicated in the following quo-

---

[3] Norman J. Lenhart and Philip L. Defliese, *Montgomery's Auditing* (Eighth Edition, New York: The Ronald Press Co., 1957), p. 77.

[4] Accounting Research Bulletin No. 43, The American Institute of Accountants, 1953, p. 9.

tations which probably are typical of the feelings of a good many. In the first selection, concern is expressed that they may have a stifling effect on the individual judgment of the practitioner; in the second a strong argument is made for their acceptance whether the individual agrees with them or not.

> It is hardly conceivable that the accounting profession will ever reach a position where certain groups of individuals will be empowered with authority which will permit them to decide definitely and exclusively all matters of principle and procedure. While rejecting (professional) authoritarianism as a goal to be sought, one must acknowledge that there are groups and individuals whose opinion on accounting matters are to be highly regarded. When the collective judgment of the members of the profession expressing the substantial agreement of its members with respect to principle comes into conflict with the opinion of the individual, there is a strong but not an absolute presumption supporting the position of the group. However, the members of a profession should avoid letting others do all their thinking for them. As long as accountancy remains an art, there will always be place for a certain amount of individualism—individualism should be encouraged rather than stifled.[5]

> In conclusion it should be stated forcefully that the profession should recognize that the pronouncements of the committee on accounting procedure point the way to better accounting; that they have been drafted, after mature and objective consideration, by men who, while not infallible, are able men of wide experience; and that the pronouncements have not been issued idly, but that each has a purpose. Where an accountant has an opinion contrary to a pronouncement of the committee, he should realize that he has not had the experience of the committee as a whole, nor has he had the opportunity for such extensive consideration as was given the problem by the committee before issuance of its opinion. It should be obvious to him that the opinion of the committee is the more reliable, and that it justifies his acceptance.[6]

Nonrequirement of Unanimous or Even Majority Support. It is unfortunate that the word "general" was selected for use in describing the extent of acceptance of accounting principles, because it carries a connotation of consensus or majority rule that is not intended in the customary use of the expression "generally

---

[5] Brother LaSalle, "Basic Research in Accounting," *The Accounting Review*, October, 1959, pp. 603-608, at 604.

[6] Anson Herrick, "A Review of the Work of the Accounting Procedure Committee," *The Journal of Accountancy*, November, 1954, pp. 627-638, at 638.

accepted accounting principles." As currently used, the term merely means that there is some substantial support for the given practice; it does not in any way claim that a majority or more of those concerned with the problem follow that practice. This use is unfortunate because the dictionary meaning of the term "general" suggests just such a majority view. One of its synonyms is "universal," which certainly is not the meaning independent auditors intend to give the term when they use it in their opinions.

Even a casual review of published annual reports of business corporations would reveal a number of relatively uncommon practices which still are described as "in accordance with generally accepted principles of accounting." The simultaneous existence of a variety of alternative practices, all equally in accord with *generally* accepted principles, presents a problem to anyone reading financial statements. In discussing the necessity for research in the area of accounting principles, Mr. Louis H. Penney, then President of the American Institute of Certified Public Accountants, stated:

> If divergencies are so wide that they merit mention in radio advertising and yet still comply with accepted principles, it is entirely understandable that the layman on the street or even a pretty sophisticated businessman might wonder, when we use the term "generally accepted accounting principles," whether we really know what we are talking about.[7]

As a specific illustration of the range of practice permitted by present principles, Mr. Penney described the following situation:

> All of you probably know that the tax laws permit intangible drilling costs to be charged to expense for income tax purposes when incurred. Virtually all companies claim the tax deduction. Some of the companies prepare their financial statements on the same basis. The majority of the major oil companies whose stocks are listed on the New York Stock Exchange, however, deduct the intangible drilling costs for federal income tax purposes, yet capitalize them in their financial statements to be allocated against income by some appropriate method over the expected life of the wells.
>
> One, at least, of these major companies reflects in its financial statements the deferred income tax liability it must pay when the capi-

[7] Louis H. Penney, "Why Research?", *The Accounting Review*, January, 1960, pp. 1-7, at 7.

talized expenses, which have already been deducted for income tax purposes, are eventually charged against income on the books. The other companies do not make such tax provision in their statements and perhaps properly so, under the bulletins of the Committee on Accounting Procedure, if there is a presumption that the differences between the tax returns and the income statements will recur regularly over a comparatively long period of time.

The financial statements of all these companies are examined by practicing certified public accountants and presumably all the opinions are to the effect that they are presented in conformity with generally accepted accounting principles. The question is, are there, or should there be, different accounting principles that can be applied with equal propriety to the same set of facts with the results reflecting substantial differences of ten, or even a hundred, million dollars.[8]

Development in Response to Business Events. The establishment of accounting principles through the issuance of pronouncements either by the Securities and Exchange Commission or the Committee on Accounting Procedure of the American Institute of Certified Public Accountants has always lagged behind the problems which they purport to solve. This almost inevitably follows from a procedure of developing individual rulings rather than a comprehensive system. As problems appear in practice, immediate attention will be given to them. Because of limited research and committee facilities, the immediate problems consume all or almost all the effort available, and there is little time or energy remaining to foresee and consider the problems which although not yet present already loom on the horizon.

In some cases, of course, specific problems can be solved quickly and easily and so the lag between appearance of the problem and official pronouncement of its solution is brief indeed. In other cases, such as the perennial one of the influence of inflation on reported data, the problem has been with us for many years with no real solution yet in sight.

Presumptive Rather than Established Ability to Display Financial Events and Conditions. The nature of business transactions and enterprise financial condition is such that it cannot be clearly and completely reported by quantitative data alone.

[8] *Ibid.*, p. 3.

Yet accounting reports rely heavily on quantitative data in their attempts to present financial position and the results of operations.

> Accounting procedures and reports are based on the premise that quantitative data provide an effective means of description and are basic to the communication of qualitative information about the enterprise. Although many of the significant facts of business can be dealt with in accounting, others cannot be expressed in financial terms within the scope of accounting reports. Therefore accounting data ordinarily are most useful if supplemented by other types of statistical data and by relevant non-quantitative information.[9]

Because there is much that is subjective in one's interpretation of any enterprise transaction, it would be unreasonable to contend that any given financial statement was "correct." At best, financial reports can give but an approximation of what took place in the enterprise. The necessity for summarizing diverse transactions, of classifying items together which are significantly different, of ignoring minor differences to emphasize major points of similarity, of dealing with an immense quantity of information, all make accurate and detailed reflection of actual events and conditions impossible. Thus it is that the expression "present fairly" seems to be a thoroughly realistic way to express the attainment of accounting propriety.

Effect of the Characteristics of Accounting Principles. Perhaps other significant characteristics of accounting principles could be noted and discussed, but these seem adequate for the purpose here. What is their effect? It seems to us that any careful analysis of the nature of generally accepted accounting principles, as the term is used at the present time, unavoidably stresses the auditor's duty to accept them with care and caution. Because they are not complete, have no absolute authority, do not require even majority support, tend to lag behind the appearance of the problems they are intended to solve, and can no more than presume to reflect actual events and conditions, he must never accept and apply them blindly. To do so would be a violation of his professional responsibility to bring to his work the benefits of his judgment and experience.

---

[9] "Accounting and Reporting Standards for Corporate Financial Statements—1957 Revision," *The Accounting Review*, October, 1957, pp. 536-546.

Surely an auditor will welcome the existence of established principles because the collection and evaluation of evidence in itself is a sufficiently difficult assignment to tax his abilities. But until accounting principles are established on a more secure basis than now exists, an important part of his assignment must be to evaluate the principles applied in the accounts and statements he reviews. Whether they produce data that measure up to his concept of truth must be the question he undertakes to solve, not merely whether the reported data are in accord with what someone contends are accepted accounting principles.

Admittedly this leaves the auditor with a difficult burden. If he cannot rely on generally accepted accounting principles as a standard against which to measure the data submitted to him for examination, what can he rely on? But of course the problem is not at all that difficult. First, a great many accounting practices and procedures exist for which majority if not near-unanimous support can be found, and these are well known to the experienced auditor. Second, although not often stated in the literature, there is an accounting philosophy or point of view supporting generally accepted accounting principles which provides an additional guide when an auditor finds it necessary to evaluate innovations or unusual situations. That is, from the pronouncements of authoritative bodies and from the customarily accepted practices, one can, if he will, extract a theme or pattern which gives a clue to the aims and purposes of accounting. An awareness of this theme or pattern permits an auditor to deal competently and confidently with unusual situations.

To make this point clear, we may again draw an analogy from the position of a judge in legal cases. The first duty of a judge is to decide controversies between individuals or between the state and individuals as they come before him in the regular course of his official duties. Although the auditor does not decide similar controversies, he does sit in judgment on accounting presentations and must decide whether they are fair in the circumstances. Cases brought before a judge may be classed as usual and unusual. The former present disputes simply as to facts and in which there is no difficulty of law; the latter involve novel situations of fact or changed conditions which raise a question of law. Auditing decision likewise may be routine, or they may be unusual in that they proceed from novel business transactions or relationships and raise new questions of accounting principle.

When unusual cases arise in court they call for a process of reasoning by analogy from similar cases and from broad principles extracted from previous litigation. When they arise in audits, again they call for reasoning by analogy from similar audit situations and from broad principles based on previous applications of generally accepted accounting principles.

> In the unusual case, involving some novel situation of fact, judges will generally reason by analogy from cases resembling the controversy before them. Even though their reasoning be by analogy and hence inductive in nature, they have a way of stating their decision in terms of deductive logic as if their conclusions were drawn from universal principles. By this process of analyzing the facts, reasoning by analogy and then stating their conclusions as deductions from broad pre-existing principles, judges are enabled not only to decide the controversy pending before them but to aid in the growth of the law to meet new situations of fact in a changing world. Thus the decision in any given controversy not only disposes of the case, but states the rule that will govern in future cases of the same sort. Accordingly, it will be seen that judicial reasoning is by no means the judges' own personal thinking alone. They are concerned with the problem before them in the light of the law that has been developed in earlier cases and with due regard to related cases that may arise in the future.[10]

Many contributions to generally accepted accounting principles have been produced in the same way, by auditors faced with a new set of facts who, reasoning by analogy and in accord with the general tenor of accounting principles, have devised what they consider to be a satisfactory solution. It is likely that, as long as business continues to develop new types of transactions and relationships, auditing will continue to face this type of problem and to solve it in this way.

The Essence of Generally Accepted Accounting Principles. In an effort to summarize the concept of accounting propriety, that is conformance with generally accepted accounting principles, it is helpful to attempt to abstract from accepted accounting practices what appears to be the essence of the principles now before

[10] Arthur T. Vanderbilt, "*Judges and Jurors: Their Functions, Qualifications and Selection* (Boston: Boston University Press, 1956), p. 4.

us. Such principles as we now have seem to be concerned with two broad areas of accounting work; the first may be called accounting methods, the second financial statement presentation. Accounting methods include such practices as account classification, transaction analysis, the practice of capitalizing the cost of long-lived assets and subsequently amortizing these costs through depreciation charges, the use of accruals and deferrals, the consideration of inventory in income determination, methods of pricing inventories, and the like. Unless acceptable accounting methods are followed, reliable data will not result. Financial statement presentation is concerned with balance sheet classifications, the treatment of unusual gains and losses for income statement purposes, the disclosure of contingent liabilities, indication of valuation bases in the balance sheet, and similar matters. Even with reliable data, unsatisfactory financial statement presentation may conceal useful information or even be misleading and deceitful.

In each area, the goal of generally accepted accounting principles is to provide financial statement data which faithfully portray the realities of enterprise operations and financial condition. We feel the essence of these principles can therefore be presented in the following statements:

1. Acceptable accounting methods are those which realistically recognize enterprise transactions and their effects as they occur, and which, through the use of the accrual system, relate efforts (costs) and accomplishments (revenues) on the basis of their pertinence to one another within time periods.
2. Acceptable financial statement presentations are those which, without favoritism or bias, report as fairly as possible data obtained through acceptable accounting methods to those having a legitimate interest in the results of enterprise operations and enterprise financial position.

In these statements we find the basic ideas of the concept of accounting propriety. To the extent that the presentations submitted to an auditor meet these requirements, they can be said to "present fairly," to meet the requirements of accounting propriety. But if he finds that they fail to meet these requirements he must reject them and call for their improvement. The auditor's concern must be with the goals of generally accepted principles, not with their letter. An approach sometimes followed is one that finds acceptable any method or presentation that is "not misleading." Such a negative attitude should not be condoned and certainly does not satisfy the concept of accounting propriety. Surely the auditor should insist upon something more constructive than the mere absence of injury; unless a practice actually aids and furthers understanding, it should be held deficient.[11]

As a conclusion to this section, it should be noted that the determination of accounting propriety is ultimately a matter of audit judgment. Although the auditor borrows generally accepted accounting principles from the field of accounting, he does so with full recognition that he may have to reject their application in some cases. To the extent that they are satisfactory in bringing about a realistic portrayal of the facts of business activity and conditions he is grateful for them; to the extent that they fail, he must draw upon his knowledge of their goals and develop solutions which his experience and judgment tell him are constructively useful.

The concept of accounting propriety will be greatly aided by the development of more specific and more authoritative accounting principles, but it is unlikely that in the foreseeable future the auditor will ever be able to rely on them completely and without reservation. His position is such that he must judge their applicability and effectiveness in specific cases before accepting them.

Adequate Disclosure

The concept of accounting propriety discussed in the preceding section was concerned with the manner in which financial statement data portray the realities of financial condition and transactions. It was concluded that the standards for judging reported data are provided by accounting and borrowed by auditing, although auditing necessarily has certain responsibilities in connection with the use of such standards. First, auditing must determine whether the given presentation does meet the requirements of generally accepted principles of accounting; second auditing must determine whether the application of generally ac-

[11] Harper and James, *op. cit.*, See Chapter 7 on Due Audit Care.

cepted principles of accounting in the particular case does result in a satisfactory reflection of the truth as truth was defined in Chapter 5. The concept of adequate disclosure, as that term is used here, is not directed at the reflection of truth in reported data bur rather at the extent of the financial data to be reported. The kinds and amounts of information to be disclosed provide the substance of this concept.

As pointed out by Griffin and Williams, the expression "full disclosure," which is commonly used in discussions of the amount of information to be revealed, has some unfortunate implications.[12] Disclosure does not necessarily improve with the provision of more information. A plethora of detail, like too much of almost anything, can be more harmful than helpful. Use of the term "full disclosure" also neglects the idea that not only the quantity of disclosure is important but also the kinds of information to be revealed. Actually, the subject of adequate disclosure involves the following:

1. The extent of detail to be disclosed.

   One of the tasks of accounting is to reduce the tremendous mass of detailed information contained in a company's business papers to manageable and understandable proportions. To present the reader with so much detail that he is unable to extract from it the essential information about enterprise activities and conditions is to do him a real disservice. On the other hand, the summarization and condensation may be carried to such an extreme that useful comparisons and distinctions are lost or concealed. Obviously, either too much or too little detail may be harmful.

2. Scope of information to be disclosed.

   a. With respect to possible harmful results.

      It seems reasonable that disclosure of certain information about a company which may be useful to financial statement readers conceivably could do serious injury to the company and thus the various in-

[12] Charles H. Griffin and Thomas H. Williams, "Measuring Adequate Disclosure," *The Journal of Accountancy*, April, 1960, pp. 43-48.

terests in it. Secret processes, research in progress, formulas, perhaps even planned advertising programs may be such that their disclosure would be more detrimental to the company than beneficial to legitimate readers of the statements. Thus excessive disclosure as well as inadequate disclosure seems to be a real possibility.

b. With respect to the limitations and bounds of accounting and auditing.

   Accounting typically restricts itself to information reportable in a normal set of financial statements, that is, a balance sheet, statement of income, and statement of retained earnings, together with various footnotes and supporting schedules. Although a published annual report may include information about plans, new products, projected capital expenditures, and the like, this is generally presented in such a way that it is definitely separated from the ordinary financial statements. Auditing likewise restricts itself to an examination of and an opinion on the information in the ordinary financial statements, often expressing this by specific reference to statement titles or page numbers. We think subsequent paragraphs of this chapter will raise interesting questions as to whether such statements can constitute adequate disclosure and whether auditing should be so restricted.

Present Solution to the Disclosure Problem. Current standards of reporting tend to deal with the disclosure problem, first, by assuming a "reasonably informed investor" as the person for whom financial reports are prepared, and second, by restricting the responsibility for disclosure of accounting data to information in the typical financial statements.

In discussing the meaning and importance of disclosure, the 1957 Revision of Accounting Concepts and Standards Underlying Corporate Financial Statements states:

> The use by investors of published financial statements in making investment decisions and in exercising control over management should be considered of primary importance. It seems reasonable to assume

> that those using financial statements for these purposes will be willing and competent to read them carefully and with discrimination.[13]

Support for this point of view is found in the fact that almost all published annual reports are described as "Report to Stockholders." Along with this attitude is an implied understanding that the informed investor will read the financial statements himself and make his investment judgments accordingly. Thus the data included should be intelligible to him and sufficient to permit him to arrive at an informed judgment on the relative desirability of a "buy, hold, sell" decision. A rather extreme position expressing this general view may be found in the remarks of Mr. Edward T. McCormick, permit him to arrive at an informed judgment on the relative desirability of the American Accounting Association.[14] In rather forceful terms, Mr. McCormick pointed out what he considered to be deficiencies in present reporting practices which he felt were not at all satisfactory for use by the great army of American shareholders.

The second part of the solution to the disclosure problem, restriction of the accountant's disclosure responsibility to the material in the typical financial statements, is so well established as to appear almost beyond question. Even a hurried survey of published reports would indicate that auditors feel the three standard statements with their footnotes and occasional supporting schedules, although these are by no means required, provide all the information for which the accountant and auditor can be held. If for no other reason than that this solution to the disclosure problem is so well established and has been held for so long, we feel that it should be given careful reconsideration.

There are other reasons as well. In the last thirty years, substantial changes have occurred in the financial market, changes so significant that in our view they require important changes in our ideas of adequate disclosure. The remainder of this section will be devoted to an examination of these changes and their implications for auditing and for the auditing concept of fair presentation.

---

[13] Committee on Accounting Concepts and Standards of the American Accounting Association, *The Accounting Review*, October, 1957, pp. 536-546, at 542.

[14] Edward T. McCormick, "Reporting to Stockholders," *The Accounting Review*, April, 1960, pp. 223-227.

Evolution in the Securities Market. Anyone familiar with the financial scene in America is conscious of the fact that great changes occurred between the decade of the 1920s and that of the 1940s. Perhaps less spectacular yet still important changes are still occurring, and there is some question whether the combined significance of all these changes for the concept of adequate disclosure has been sufficiently emphasized.

In the 1920s the securities market was free almost to the point of being completely without control. The Federal Reserve Board did not then have the power to fix margin requirements for trading in securities, a deficiency which some economists allege was partly responsible for the excessive speculations which led to the 1929 crash.[15] Certainly some control was provided by the New York Stock Exchange, but this was far from adequate as evidenced by two different investigations prior to World War I and considerable criticism of the Exchange and its workings.[16] Little provision was made for the required release of reliable information. The formation of pools was common, and false information about the prospective operation and profitability of corporations circulated freely. Gullible investors relied on rumors and newspaper stories, some of which had absolutely no foundation whatever in fact.[17] Out of this, and of course other factors, came the financial catastrophe of 1929 and the consequent regulations of the 1930s.

The decade of the 1930s brought the first serious efforts to control the investment market. No single act could possibly have remedied all the evils of the market; but as the weaknesses of successive acts became apparent, new legislation was forthcoming to stop the loopholes. Gradually the effect of legislation accumulated to the point at which the free and open market of a few years before became a regulated one. Along with this, and almost as important, occurred a substantial reorganization of the

---

[15] See for instance, John Kenneth Galbraith, *The Great Crash of 1929* (Boston, Massachusetts: Houghton Mifflin Co., 1955), p. 37.

[16] These were the Hughes Committee investigation of 1909 and the Pujo investigation of 1912, see George L. Leffler, *The Stock Market* (New York: The Ronald Press Company, Second Edition, 1957), p. 104.

[17] See Arthur M. Wickwire, *The Weeds of Wall Street* (New York: NewCastle Press, Inc., 1953), Chapter 2.

New York Stock Exchange itself. The movement toward reorganization was initiated by the S.E.C. in 1935; need for the revision of exchange operations is expressed in the following:

> Operating as private membership associations, exchanges have always administered their affairs in much the same manner as private clubs. For a business so vested with public interest, this traditional method has become archaic. The task of conducting the large exchanges (especially the New York Stock Exchange) has become too engrossing for those who must also run their own business.... Their management should not be in the hands of professional traders but in fact, as well as nominally, in charge of those who have a clearer public responsibility.[18]

Finally, and certainly not without opposition, the reorganization was accomplished:

> On March 17, 1938, the Exchange Governing Committee expelled Richard Whitney, former President of the Exchange; on the same day, by an overwhelming vote, it adopted the new plan of reorganization. The Whitney scandal was a bitter dose for the Exchange. Out of the reorganization fight, however, the Exchange emerged an organization with greater public responsibility than ever before and with rules which should make another Whitney scandal impossible....[19]

Included in the new form of exchange organization were provisions for:[20]

1. A full-time, paid president.
2. An entirely new board of governors with representation for non-member brokers and out-of-town members.
3. Public representation on the board.
4. A drastic revision of the committee system.
5. Definite rules governing the activities and responsibilities of members.

The president of the New York Stock Exchange describes the differences between the uncontrolled market of the 1920s and the present situation in these words:

> In addition to the difficulty encountered in attempting to compare 1929 and 1954 stock prices I personally find it very difficult, if not

---

[18] William O. Douglas, quoted from the *New York Times*, November 24, 1937, by Leffler, *op. cit.*, p. 108.

[19] *Ibid.*, p. 109.

[20] *Ibid.*

> impossible, to make valid comparisons between market conditions then and now; the social and economic contexts in which the two markets are imbedded are so completely different.
>
> The present market is a well-regulated market. The rules of the exchange have been revised and elaborated for the protection of the public. The self-policing of the exchange itself goes far beyond the regulation of the Securities and Exchange Commission. The Securities Act of 1933 provides for full disclosure concerning new issues of securities publicly offered in interstate and foreign commerce, and through the mails. The Securities Exchange Act of 1934 makes mandatory adequate disclosure of information, and registration with the SEC of all securities listed on national exchanges; it bans all manipulative operations.
>
> The Federal Reserve Board is now charged with the responsibility of preventing the excessive use of credit in the securities market.
>
> In addition a new profession—devoted to exploring and assessing every obtainable fact bearing on the value of a security—has arisen in the last two decades. The security analyst, whose services are essential now in the offices of our member firms, provides the public with a tremendous flow of accurate information.
>
> In short, endeavors have been made to protect the investor against virtually everything but himself.[21]

But regulation alone does not explain all the changes in the investment market which have a bearing on our ideas of disclosure. Concurrently with the imposition of regulation, both internal and external, and certainly to some extent dependent on such regulation, has come a professionalization of investment activities. Not only are the exchanges managed and governed by responsible professionals, but a number of affiliated specialists have developed whose influence on investment practices is beneficial and highly significant to accounting and auditing. Financial analysts, investment counselors, and public relations experts in the field of finance contribute a great deal to the functioning of the investment market.

This change in the financial environment in which auditing exists, from a free and uncontrolled market thirty years ago to a

[21] Statement of G. Keith Funston, President of the New York Stock Exchange, Submitted to the Committee on Banking and Currency, 84th Congress, First Session, Published in *Stock Market Study* (Washington: U.S. Government Printing Office, 1955), p. 102.

regulated and professionalized market today, has some important implications for auditing. These can be understood best by considering the development of the following significant market factors:

1. The rise of institutional investors.
2. The appearance of professional financial analysts.
3. The appearance of professional investment counselors.
4. The appearance of public relations experts in the field of finance.

The Rise of Institutional Investors. There is almost unanimous agreement among the observers of the investment market, both in the United States and abroad, that the growth of institutional investors is one of the important features of the financial market in the 1950s. Foundations, insurance companies, pension funds, investment companies, and the like have come to be huge enterprises with vast sums to invest, and these institutions are turning more and more to common stocks and away from the traditionally "safe" bonds in which such institutions once tended to specialize. Some indication of their importance in the market may be obtained from this statement by the President of the New York Stock Exchange before the Senate Committee on Banking and Currency:

> At the end of 1954, it is estimated that insurance companies, pension funds, investment companies, foundations and endowment funds, and mutual savings banks owned stock valued at $28 billion, and personal trust funds administered by banks own stock worth another $38 billion—for a total market value of $66 billion held by institutions compared with $32 billion in 1949. About eighty per cent of this increase is accounted for by a rise in market value, with the balance representing net additional purchases. Of this $66 billion in stock owned by institutions, approximately $48 billion are common and preferred stocks listed on the New York Stock Exchange. These institutional holdings constituted 28 percent of the total market value of all shares now listed on the exchange. Net stock purchases by institutional investors in 1954 totaled approximately $3 billion, of which about $2 billion were stocks listed on the New York Stock Exchange.[22]

[22] Statement by G. Keith Funston, President of the New York Stock Exchange, "Hearings before the Committee on Banking and Currency," United States Senate, 84th Congress, First Session, March, 1955, p. 97.

An English writer, concerned with the same development in his country, writes:

> One of the most significant features in the investment world, both at home and abroad, has been the rise over the past quarter of a century of the importance of the institutional investor. In this country the phenomenal growth of pension and life insurance schemes has channelled, and will continue to channel, vast sums of money into relatively few vessels. The proprietary and mutual companies, and the self-administered pension funds in the United Kingdom alone, are now investing at the rate of over a million pounds per day. In North America not only have pension funds grown, but there also has been the vast expansion in the mutual or unit trust funds. Although it may take a long time before the North America levels are reached, the unit trust movement in this country appears to be set fair for a considerable expansion.[23]

A final quotation from an American analyst helps us to comprehend the place which the institutional investor has claimed:

> In a very real sense, then, the institutional investor has filled the shoes of the wealthy individual as an important supplier of new equity money. When pension funds currently invest $800 million a year in equities instead of $100 million a year, as they did a decade ago, the increase is equivalent to almost a third of the average new money raised through common stock flotations during recent years. The contribution of mutual funds to the process of replacing the historical source of new equity capital is equally impressive. A large part of the new money assembled from middle-income groups by these organizations would not otherwise have been made available to the stock market. There can be no question of the influence in a quantitative sense of these new suppliers of equity money. Without them it is difficult to see how the stock market could have functioned effectively during the years of postwar prosperity. A market starved for funds received timely and substantial nourishment. The individual investor was not crowded out, but he found a new and active partner. This is a fact of the 1950s.[24]

Just what is the importance of this development in the financial market? Why is a rise in the amount of institutional investment significant to auditors and to a concept of adequate disclosure? The answer to these questions is found by contrasting the

---

[23] A. R. English, "What the Investment Analyst Would Like to See in Company Reports and Accounts," *Accountancy*, Vol. 71, No. 798, February, 1960, p. 66.

[24] Roger F. Murray, "Institutional Influences on the Stock Market," *The Analysts Journal*, May, 1958, p. 15.

nature of the institutional investor with the traditional view of the reasonably well informed individual investor. An institutional investor of the kind included in the statistics given will be a substantial enterprise with competent management, large sums to invest, and a recognition by its management of the institution's fiduciary nature. This will enable and encourage such managements to obtain the advice of investment specialists. Their resources are such that they can afford the best, and their responsibilities such that they can settle for little less. Obviously, skilled financial analysts and investment counselors will require more in the way of information than might an individual investor, unable to comprehend and utilize any great quantity of information. To the extent that such information is not made available to them, they may seek it for themselves; and, because of the funds which they control, such information will likely be forthcoming.

It seems a reasonable conclusion, therefore, that the rise of institutional investors will be of influence in expanding our ideas of adequate disclosure. Their appearance gives us reason to question the validity of our approach to disclosure based on the idea of a reasonably informed investor who will use the data himself. Instead of investment decisions by individuals who read published data and make their own investment decisions, we have important investment decisions made on the advice of professionally trained and responsible specialists. The nature and extent of the disclosure which these specialists feel is desirable will appear in the following section.

The Appearance of Professional Financial Analysts. It seems apparent that large institutions would be able to afford and would require investment advice on a scale unlike that desired by individual investors. It is probable that the rise of institutional investors, therefore, has had a great deal to do with the development of financial analysis as a profession. But whatever the contributing factors, we can hardly escape the conclusion that this new profession does exist and is an influential factor in the investment market.

> Twenty-five years ago, management could afford to ignore security analysts as a tribe. The securities market was quite different from that of today. Contrary to the popular belief, small investors were

relatively few in number. The little fellow was usually looking for a speculative killing, and he neither sought nor conceived much real investment information. Institutions such as pension trusts, endowment funds, insurance companies, and bank trustees invested chiefly in "safe" bonds and mortgages. Big speculators in common stocks often depended on feedbox tips from within companies. The market, lightly regulated, could be manipulated by large operators, and the public considered it no place for the average man.

Now, stock ownership has broadened into many American homes.... Meanwhile, the hold-down on yields of bonds and other fixed-interest securities has sent institutional investors into stocks....

Both the individual and institutional investor rely on security analysts. And management, both by legal requirements and by choice, sees that the analysts know about the companies that are traded in the market.[25]

It is not our intention here to enter into debate about the requirements for professional status of financial analysts or any other group. It is sufficient to point out that there are local organizations of financial analysts in several of the large cities in this country and that a national federation has been formed with professional standards for its members.[26] Since 1945 *The Analysts Journal* has been published as a monthly and has obtained general recognition for contributing substantially to professional development in its area of influence.[27]

As a group, financial analysts have a keen interest in corporate information. Their literature indicates that they are not satisfied with the information found in the traditional accounting statements, but that they desire additional data as a basis for advancing others on investment opportunities. In this connection, a report by a subcommittee on the Adequacy of the Annual Reports of the Chemical Industry is enlightening.[28] The subcommittee divides information it would like to find in annual reports into three categories: (1) essential, (2) desirable, and (3) useful, as follows:

---

[25] "Nowadays Their Opinions Count," *Business Week*, June 30, 1956, p. 43.

[26] A. Moyer Kulp, "National Federation to Set Professional Standards," *The Analysts Journal*, July, 1959, p. 65.

[27] Editorial, *The Analysts Journal*, November, 1958, p. 3.

[28] Report of the Subcommittee on the Adequacy of the Annual Reports of the Chemical Industry, *The Analysts Journal*, Second Quarter, 1950, pp. 67-68.

(1) Essential features

Summary of year's operations

Full income account (current year and previous year recommended)

Balance sheet (current year and previous year recommended)

Operating review

(2) Desirable features

Breakdown of sales by divisions

Breakdown of sales by industries served

Capital expenditures

Research expenditures

Total wages (including benefits)

Ten-year record (on comparable basis)

Foreign investment

(3) Useful information

Index of selling price

Index of wages

Future plans for capital expenditures

Total number of employees

Description of operating divisions

Summary of products made

Description of management

Charts

The usefulness of all this information to a competent and trained financial analyst is apparent, and one wonders how soon items in the second two categories will be added to the "essential" group. As financial analysts become more important they will be in position to exert more influence and to get more and more information. In this they will certainly have the support of institutional investors, a fact that will increase their influence considerably.

> These institutional accounts are tough to get, and unless the registered representatives are backed by research departments of the first water they don't stand much chance of landing them.[29]

---

[29] Russel R. Clevenger, "Are Institutions to Become the Important Stockholders?" *The Commercial and Financial Chronicle*, Vol. 174, Dec. 20, 1951.

That financial analysts are discriminating in the kind of information they desire is indicated in an article by Mr. William G. Maas, the president of the Investment Analysts Society of Chicago. Entitled "What to Tell Security Analysts," the article was published in *The Public Relations Journal* and deals frankly with the subject of what a business executive should and should not tell a financial analyst in search of information about the executive's company.[30] Mr. Maas states that the financial analyst is not interested in a long corporate history, a re-hash of the annual report, an enumeration of plants and properties, industry statistics and figures (unless otherwise unavailable), flag waving, sales talk, and visual presentations. In brief, factual material available from other—and perhaps more reliable—sources, information not pertinent to the analyst's needs, and unfounded opinions are of little benefit. On the other hand, a considerable amount of information not found in published reports and statements is desired. Enumerated by Mr. Maas are the following:

> 1. Financial information: Sales ... In all cases profit margins are one of our most important facts used in financial analysis of a company's operations. As a result of some completely legitimate accounting treatments, earning figures alone can actually be misleading to stockholders.
>
> 2. Interim statements: Much can happen within a year's time; the interim statements give a worthwhile clue as to the trend of a company's operations between annual reports.
>
> 3. Sales breakdowns: (a) by major divisions; (b) by types of operations, and (c) by customer classification.
>
> 4. New products: ...Discussion of new products means much in appraising the progress made by a company, particularly under competitive conditions. The analyst is always conscious of the "growth possibilities" of an organization. What is its competitive position? Is an expansion program justified? New products mean "life" to the organization. Next to a description of new products themselves, it is important to know when they will become commercially available.
>
> 5. Research: A favorite question among financial analysts is "How much is spent on research?" or "What proportion of sales is expended on research?" It is even more important to learn how the

---

[30] William G. Maas, "What to Tell Security Analysts," *Public Relations Journal*, March, 1955, pp. 5-6, and 26.

research organization is set up. What type of research is done? Is it aimed at development of new products? Improvement of existing products? Is there a centralized research organization? How broad is its scope? What has the research department developed commercially?

6. Plant expansion and modernization: Is a company keeping up with its competitors in both expansion and modernization?... How far ahead is the planning schedule? And what are the proposed capital expenditures?... Of equal importance is the method of financing.

7. Management: ...It would be more interesting to hear how the so-called "management team" is set up—with an aim toward proving its "depth" and continuity—if that exists. A description of responsibilities—with particular reference to younger "second line" men could be given. Something might well be said on the subject of management incentives—bonuses, special compensation, retirement provisions, and the like.

8. Existing problems: If problems exist, executives should admit them and not gloss over them. Every corporation has them. And the good financial analyst will learn about them eventually. Executives should be frank—and explain what is being done to solve the problems.

9. Forecasts: A corporation management need not fear to make some types of forecasts within reason—both of sales and earnings. Such forecasts need not be too specific and mention can be made of such uncertainties that do exist. The good analyst is not going to take an executive to task if there turns out to be some variations when the final figures are available, if the forecast was made honestly.[31]

Just as the rise of institutional investors casts doubt on our image of a reasonably informed investor as the one for whom audited financial statements are prepared, so the recognition of the advent of financial analysts as an important factor in the investment market casts doubt on the adequacy of traditional financial statements to supply the information needed for investment decisions. Here we have a responsible professional group, a group at least as competent as auditors to establish the bounds of necessary disclosure for investment decisions, and this group has indicated a desire and a need for information not now covered by auditor's reports. This poses a sharp and certainly a vital

[31] *Ibid.*

question. Have auditors reached the limit of their service with the examination of the information in the traditional forms of financial statements and the expression of an opinion thereon? If the answer is affirmative, financial analysts must either rely on unverified data in arriving at investment judgments or find someone else to give them the same kind of assurance of reliability for such data that auditing presently gives to traditional financial statement information. In either case, the implications for auditing are unpleasant. If financial analysts can rely on unaudited data in large part, why not then for all the information they use? Even more likely, if they find they want an independent expert to verify all the information supplied to them, and auditors refuse to step beyond the bounds of their traditional role, is it not possible that the new verifiers will extend their work to the financial statements as well?

Professional Investment Counselors. Relatively few people have either the ability or the interest to make the type of analysis and investigation that should precede the investment of any substantial amount of money in the securities of business corporations. On the other hand, those who invest on the basis of mere tips or hunches are likely to find themselves involved in companies which fail to return even the original investment, much less give any prospect of gain. The combination of these two factors has led to the appearance of professional investment counselors, experts who either employ financial analysts or themselves are competent to perform the necessary analytical work and who serve their clients in a variety of ways. That this service has become significant in our economy is evidenced by the fact that as early as 1940 investment advisers were recognized by law. The Investment Advisers Act of 1940 was passed to regulate the offering of such services and to place them under the control of the Securities and Exchange Commission:

> ...it is hereby found that investment advisers are of national concern, in that, among other things—
>
> (1) their advice, counsel, publications, writings, analyses, and reports are furnished and distributed, and their contracts, subscription agreements, and other arrangements with clients are negotiated and performed, by the use of the mails and means of instrumentalities of interstate commerce;

(2) their advice, counsel, publications, writings, analyses, and reports customarily relate to the purchase and sale of securities traded on national securities exchanges and in interstate over-the-counter markets, securities issued by companies engaged in business in interstate commerce, and securities issued by national banks and member banks of the Federal Reserve System; and

(3) the foregoing transactions occur in such volume as substantially to affect interstate commerce, national securities exchanges, and other securities markets, the national banking system, and the national economy.[32]

Section 202, paragraph 11, of that act sets forth the definition of an "investment adviser" and distinguishes his activities from those of other individuals who may be engaged in similar work:

"Investment adviser" means any person, who, for compensation, engages in the business of advising others, either directly or through publications or writings, as to the value of securities or as to the advisability of investing in, purchasing, or selling securities, or who, for compensation and as part of a regular business, issues or promulgates analyses and reports concerning securities; but does not include: (a) a bank ... which is not an investment company; (b) any lawyer, accountant, engineer, or teacher whose performance of such services is solely incidental to the practice of his profession: (c) any broker or dealer whose performance of such services is solely incidental to the conduct of his business as a broker or dealer and who receives no special compensation therefor; (d) the publisher of any bona fide newspaper, news magazine or business and financial publication of general and regular circulation;...[33]

It is interesting to note that an attempt has been made to distinguish between "investment advisers" and "investment counselors," the latter organizing themselves into a professional body known as the Investment Counsel Association of America.

...*An Investment Counselor* is an individual or firm engaged in no other business but that of rendering investment advice. This advice can, and does, go beyond merely advising on securities. An investment counselor generally does not take custody of securities; does not trade in securities; does not participate in new offerings; and does not provide brokerage facilitics.

---

[32] *United States Statutes at Large*, Vol. 54, Part I, Washington: United States Government Printing Office, 1941, pp. 847-857, at 847.

[33] *Ibid.*

An Investment Adviser, on the other hand, may be engaged in a business other than the rendering of investment advice, such as a lawyer, or a bank, or such as in the case of my firm, which by reason of being a member of the New York Stock Exchange and other Exchanges, can provide facilities for custody of securities and consummation of brokerage transactions.[34]

Investment counselors make available to the individual investor the benefits of careful financial analysis which large labor unions, trust companies, insurance companies, and other institutional investors are able to provide for themselves. Because many banks provide investment counsel for their customers, relatively few investors find themselves without expert guidance readily available. Investment counselors themselves are agreed that careful and exhaustive research is the key to success; they make use of every reliable tool available to render an objective informed service.[35]

In this connection it may be interesting to note some recent developments in communications theory, a field which is not as foreign to auditing as some might expect. The dissemination of financial information to the thousands of present and prospective investors in American business corporations is an exercise in mass communications, and we will do well to consider carefully the applicability of some of the ideas of mass communications to the field of financial reporting and to auditing. It seems to us that the thoughts expressed in the following rather lengthy quotations have direct applicability to an auditing concept of adequate disclosure as we will try to make clear in subsequent paragraphs.

Mass communication, by our definition, is directed toward audiences that are relatively large and heterogeneous and whose members are anonymous so far as the communicator is concerned. These three audience characteristics help, in part, to distinguish mass communication from other more limited, directed, and personal forms.

The term "mass audience" connotes just such qualities of size, heterogeneity, and anonymity. But in its earlier technical and current common usage, "mass audience" also implies something more. It suggests that audiences share many or all of the sociological characteristics of a special type of human activity, a *mass*.

---

[34] T. E. Lennon, "Factors in Investment Management," *The Commercial and Financial Chronicle*, Vol. 172, September 21, 1950, p. 1086.

[35] *Ibid.*, p. 1107, see also: J. P. Sullivan, "Value of Professional Investment Management," *The Commercial and Financial Chronicle*, Vol. 184, November 15, 1956, p. 2076.

What is a mass? One sociologist, Herbert Blumer, isolates four sociological components which, taken, together, identify a mass:

> First, its membership may come *from all walks of life*, and from all distinguishable social strata; it may include people of different class position, of different vocation, of different cultural attainment, and of different wealth.... Second, the mass is an anonymous group, or more exactly, is composed of *anonymous individuals*. Third, there exists *little interaction* or exchange of experience between members of the mass. They are usually physically separated from one another, and being anonymous, do not have the opportunity to mill as do the members of the crowd. Fourth, the mass is *very loosely organized* and is not able to act with the concreteness or unity that marks the crowd.

The reader will note that this concept of the mass, if applied to audience members, would regard them as not only heterogeneous but also anonymous and isolated from one another. In short, they are like separate atoms which together comprise the mass audience.

Usually accompanying this concept of a mass audience is an image of the communications media as acting directly upon the individual audience members—reaching each member or not, influencing him directly or not. This view of mass communication has been called "hypodermic needle model,"—each audience member being personally and directly "stuck" by the medium's message, along with the rest of the people in the mass audience. Once it has stuck him, the communication may or may not influence him, according to whether or not it is potent enough to "take."

Recently both concepts of a mass audience and the "hypodermic needle model" of the communication process have been subjected to theoretical and empirical challenge. As sociological research developed during the past two decades both concepts were modified along several lines.

For one thing, a conception of the audience has emerged in which greater notice is taken of the social context within which each audience member operates. The individual (although he is anonymous to the communicator) is rarely genuinely anonymous in his social environment. Ordinarily, he is a member of a network of primary and secondary groupings—his family, friendship groups, occupational circles, and so on—which influence his opinions and attitude. Inevitably, they affect the way in which he is exposed to mass communication, how he interprets or reacts to any specific communication, and the extent to which he will or can modify his behavior is compliance with the message.

> ...There is growing evidence, in fact, to support the hypothesis that mass communication messages do not always reach all members of their ultimate audience directly (hypodermic needle model). Sometimes, through a two-step process, they first reach one layer of society (called opinion leaders or influentials) who, in turn, either pass the message on by word of mouth to persons who consult them or utilize the message in the advice or information which they pass on to their circle of influences.[36]

The concepts of "opinion leader" and "two-step flow" of communication may be seen more clearly from the following:

> 1. Some individuals seem to serve as personal transmitters for others. Without these relay individuals, messages originating from the mass media might not reach otherwise unexposed people. This, of course, is the major part of the opinion leader idea; we call it the *relay function* of interpersonal relations.
>
> 2. Furthermore, personal influence seems to be singularly effective. When a mass media influence-attempt coincides with an interpersonal communication, it appears to have much greater chance of success. We call this the *reinforcement function*.[37]

This explanation of the role of opinion leaders is especially descriptive of the role which investment counselors and investment advisers play in the securities market. It seems unlikely that very many serious investors commit their funds solely on the strength of the information they find in published annual reports. It seems much more likely that they rely on others who have access to more information and have greater competence to deal with it effectively.

> While the Stock Exchange and Curb facilities for disseminating the SEC data are indeed used, the inquirers comprise but a tiny fraction of the 5 or 10 million stockholders in the listed companies, with much of the daily clientele even including repeaters. Investigation reveals that the users consist mostly of professionals, as security analysts, statistical service researchers, and credit departments of banks. An estimated 80 per cent peak load comes in the spring months of annual report issuance, substantiating the conclusion that the investing public does not deem it worthwhile to use the

---

[36] Charles R. Wright, *Mass Communication, A Sociological Perspective* (New York: Random House, 1959), pp. 49-52.

[37] E. Katz and P. F. Lazarsfeld, *Personal Influence* (Glencoe, Illinois: The Free Press, A Report of the Bureau of Applied Social Research, Columbia University, 1955), pp. 82-83.

detailed information in connection with making its new market commitments throughout the year.[38]

The purchase of securities is a different type of transaction from the purchase of retail goods. Prospective buyers, particularly nowadays when they are besieged with advice to be wary in such dealings, may still operate as "impulse buyers," but it seems more reasonable to believe that most of them will turn to someone for advice, their broker, banker, or a local investment counselor. Of course there will always be a number of investors interested in the "hot tip" and the chance for quick and easy profits, but these people cannot be helped by annual reports or any other type of disclosure. Serious investors, those who want sound information as a basis for making investment decisions, will more and more turn to those who can give them help, to the influentials and opinion leaders.

Recognition of these facts of mass communication seems to make the concept of a reasonably informed reader even less pertinent to the audit concept of adequate disclosure. We find it very difficult indeed to agree with the position taken by Mr. McCormick of the American Stock Exchange that efforts should be made to simplify financial reports so that they can be understood by the average investor.[39] We agree, of course, that the average investor has a legitimate interest in financial information, but simplification, in our opinion, is not the way to help him. We believe he takes his advice from investment advisers who themselves are quite competent to deal not only with financial statements as now prepared, but also with substantial amounts of other financial information. The greatest service auditors can render to these investors is to urge the disclosure of more rather than less information and to develop ways to verify that additional information so that it may be considered reliable by the opinion leaders who advise and influence the small investors. Thus it seems to us that the small investor, under this concept of opinion leaders, needs and will benefit by information similar to that indicated as desirable by the financial analysts discussed in the preceding section.

---

[38] A. Wilfred May, "Must the Stockholder be Spoon-fed His Company Information?", *The Commercial and Financial Chronicle*, Vol. 170, December 22, 1949, p. 5.

[39] Edward T. McCormick, "Reporting to Stockholders," *The Accounting Review*, April, 1960, pp. 223-227.

Financial Public Relations Men. As any organization grows in size and complexity, the difficulty of expressing its purpose, motives, and general image in terms the public can understand becomes more difficult. Thus it is not surprising that we live in an era of the public relations man, when corporations, government agencies, baseball teams, universities, and even individuals employ specialists to make communication between themselves and the rest of the world not only easier but more productive of the impression they wish to create. And neither is it surprising to find this development reaching even into the financial affairs of business corporations.

One of the real problems of a major business is the development and maintenance of satisfactory relations with the various influentials in the investment market. This is borne out in the following:

> How to cultivate, and keep informed the investing public and the professional investment advisers who influence their opinions, has become a primary concern of management in the increasingly competitive financial markets.
>
> ...Today, there are several tested methods available to reach and influence the financial community and the investing public. Many case stories could be cited to provide the evidence of progress. However, I am convinced that the combination of a well-planned financial public relations program and a continuing financial advertising campaign will produce the most lasting results in broadening stock ownership.[40]

Apparently, financial analysts find it necessary to rely on the financial public relations man for a considerable amount of information. In fact, any information used by financial analysts that is not verified by independent auditors must be taken on faith by the financial analyst. This suggests that a relationship of mutual confidence must be established between the two parties. As a matter of fact, it appears that such a relationship is already well established in many cases as indicated by the following program recently offered by a recognized public relations consultant.

> We can begin with the public relations practitioner whose job it is to communicate information to the financial community for its use in evaluating a company's performance and its plans for the future. It would seem that the public relations practitioner, in exchange for

---

[40] Weston Smith, "Building a Profitable and Effective Corporate Image," *The Commercial and Financial Chronicle*, Vol. 188, July 24, 1958, p. 313.

the information that he has made available, has every right to expect the following from a security analyst:

1. That the financial analyst will welcome efforts to keep him informed of the affairs of companies in which he has a present or potential interest.

2. That the financial analyst will utilize the information he has been given in a manner that reflects the best interests of the company concerned as well as his employer.

3. That the financial analyst will check questionable information with the public relations representative or other reliable authority before using it.

4. That the financial analyst will consider the public relations representative as a source of information but not as a substitute for the analyst's own judgment.

The legitimate role of the public relations specialist is in the field of supplying accurate and useful information—not the areas of giving counsel, forecasting earnings, offering conclusions, or advising analysts when to but or sell securities, for these are strictly the province of the broker who is compensated for doing these things and carries full responsibility for the outcome.

In accepting the role of being a source of information to the financial community, the public relations practitioner automatically assumes certain responsibilities. Financial analysts would seem to be fully within their rights in expecting public relations practitioners to observe these responsibilities:

1. That the public relations representative will present an accurate picture of the company's affairs, including unfavorable as well as favorable news.

2. That the public relations representative's understanding of his company's affairs will be thorough.

3. That the public relations representative's objective is to help assure an appraisal that is based on a sound understanding of the facts, and to that degree will present information but will leave forecasts and evaluation up to the analyst.

4. That the public relations representative will not release more data to one party than to another if both parties have an equal right to information.

5. That the public relations representative will withhold only that information which would jeopardize the best interests of the company or would violate accepted standards of good taste and decency.

> It is in the best interest of both security analysis and public relations that the quantity and quality of corporate information be constantly upgraded. A major step in this direction can be accomplished if both security analysts and public relations practitioners take a new look at the relationship they have established and search for ways in which they can be strengthened and made more useful.[41]

That the material supplied by the financial public relations representative includes information beyond the audited statements is clear from this statement:

> Assuming a basic communication format is conceived, what should it include?
>
> Certainly not only facts and routine balance sheet figures. Substituted are certain intangible corporate assets, which are presented in a tangible way. Included in this category are forecasts and plans, personnel achievement records, corporate dividend philosophy, interpretive factors behind sales news, management attitudes toward executive succession, corporate research programs, the company's labor policy, its community relations program, and record compared to its competitors. The secret, of course, is how these items are correlated and presented in proper perspective.
>
> The success of presenting this data to the investing public lies in knowing what interests the professional investor and what is likely to be misinterpreted by him.[42]

Two important conclusions may be drawn from this apparently happy relationship between public relations experts and financial analysts. The first is one that has already been mentioned; there is a considerable amount of information required and obtained by financial analysts beyond that included in the standard audited financial statements. The second is rather surprising; we find financial analysts apparently relying on unaudited financial information. Much of the information they require and use is not of the type which auditors are accustomed to verifying and therefore is not covered by the examinations and opinions of independent auditors. Yet financial analysts find it useful in their work. Just what is the significance of this? Two possibilities present themselves.

---

[41] T. C. Thomasen, "Improving the Flow of Corporate Information," *The Analysts Journal*, May, 1958, pp. 73-74.

[42] Sidney A. Hunt, "Successful Corporate Relations with the Investment Community," *The Commercial and Financial Chronicle*, Vol. 188, July 31, 1958, p. 414.

The first thought is that if unaudited information of this type is satisfactory for the purposes of financial analysis, then perhaps unaudited information of the financial statement type is also satisfactory for the purposes of financial analysis. The second is that analysts accept unaudited financial information only because they have no way now of getting such information verified. Of course the second possibility has an obvious appeal to the mind of an auditor, but there is every reason to think that even unbiased minds would reach the same conclusion. Surely financial analysts, well-trained and competent as they are, recognize the dangers of unintentional bias, not to mention the hazards of deliberately misleading information and over-enthusiasm on the part of those issuing such data. As responsible professionals, does it not stand to reason that they would appreciate the review of independent experts to assure them that the financial data made available to them present fairly what they purport to represent? Here the danger to the auditor is not so much that analysts will find unaudited financial statement information is satisfactory for their purposes as it is that the development of other ways of verification may effectively bar to him this new and growing opportunity for the exercise of his talents and the performance of his traditional service as the verifier of financial data.

Public relations men have an additional part to play in the disclosure picture. They also serve as a vehicle to convey to the business enterprise the requests of financial analysts and investment counselors for investment information. Thus they provide not only a means of getting information to the market but a means of getting requests for information from the market back to business corporations. This "feedback" function has undoubtedly had considerable effect in increasing the amount of available information and will continue to do so.

The S.E.C. and the Stock Exchanges. There is no intention here to underemphasize the importance of the Securities and Exchange Commission and the listing requirements of the stock exchanges in establishing standards of disclosure and in influencing the development of accounting and reporting practices. These are so well known as to be taken almost for granted. Certainly there would be general agreement that they are an important factor in the determination of adequate disclosure. Too often, indeed, independent auditors find it necessary to rely on the prestige and influence of the S.E.C. to obtain concessions with respect to reporting which could perhaps be obtained in no other way. In this chapter, however, we have deliberately stressed those influences and factors which we think have been overlooked by most accountants. As the S.E.C. and the stock exchanges are not among these, we have perhaps given them less attention than they otherwise deserve.

Interrelationship of the Financial Market Professionals. At this point, the comparison of two charts will aid in pointing up the change in the securities market. The first illustrates the relationship on which our present ideas of disclosure are apparently based. Here information is made available to the investor by the enterprise through the medium of audited financial statements. The information goes directly from the enterprise to the investor with but one intermediary, the auditor who reviews the information and offers his opinion. But this interpretation is hardly adequate to describe the functioning of the securities market of today.

The second illustration, somewhat more complicated, is a more realistic picture of the current situation. The corporate management and its staff prepare and present the data, but two different classes of data must be recognized: those included in the typical financial statements and other information such as capital expenditure budgets, descriptions of research facilities and accomplishments, and explanations of management organization. In deciding what data to present, management is influenced by such agencies as the Securities and Exchange Commission and the stock exchanges with their listing requirements which tend to establish a minimum disclosure standard for their specific purposes. It is also influenced by the advice of its public relations experts who are in touch with financial analysts, investment counselors, and other influentials in the investment market.

Of the information released by the corporation, only a part goes to the independent auditor for his review. In reviewing statement data, independent auditors give attention to whether the disclosure requirements of the S.E.C., stock exchanges, and their own profession have been met, and whether the reported information meets the requirements of generally accepted principles of accounting. But, to repeat, this review is of financial statement data only. Nonfinancial statement data are not submitted to the review of independent auditors and flow on in their "raw" form.

All the data, audited and unaudited, made available by management is used by financial analysts in arriving at their evaluations of the company's investment potential. As remarked previously, these are well-trained specialists, entirely competent to utilize technical and detailed information.

The conclusions of the investment analysts are then passed on to investment counselors and financial advisers of different types who advise their clients, or other interests dependent on them for information, on investment and other financial matters. The ultimate beneficiaries of the information released by corporate management may never see that information in the form in which it is released. Their only contact may be the advice they receive, directly or indirectly, from financial advisers.

This description presents quite a different view of the investment market and the flow of information within it. To some extent the diagram is an idealized representation, but it is far more realistic in terms of today's operations than the simpler presentation in Figure III. We feel it is a much more accurate portrayal of the present market and, even more, a better indication of the trend that investment practices will follow in the future.

FIGURE III
ASSUMED FLOW OF DATA IN INVESTMENT MARKET

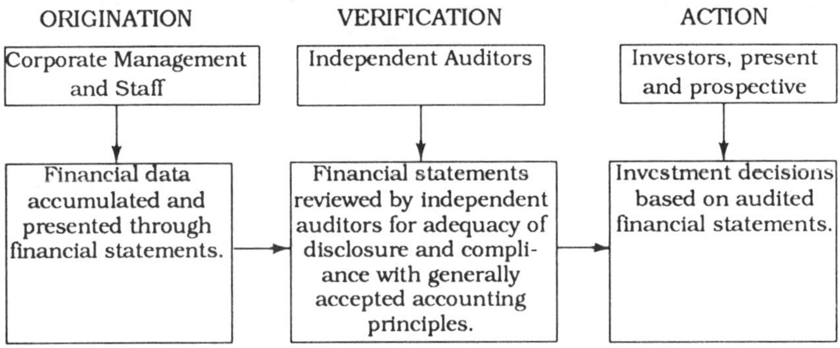

FIGURE IV
DIAGRAM SHOWING FLOW OF FINANCIAL INFORMATION IN PRESENT INVESTMENT MARKET

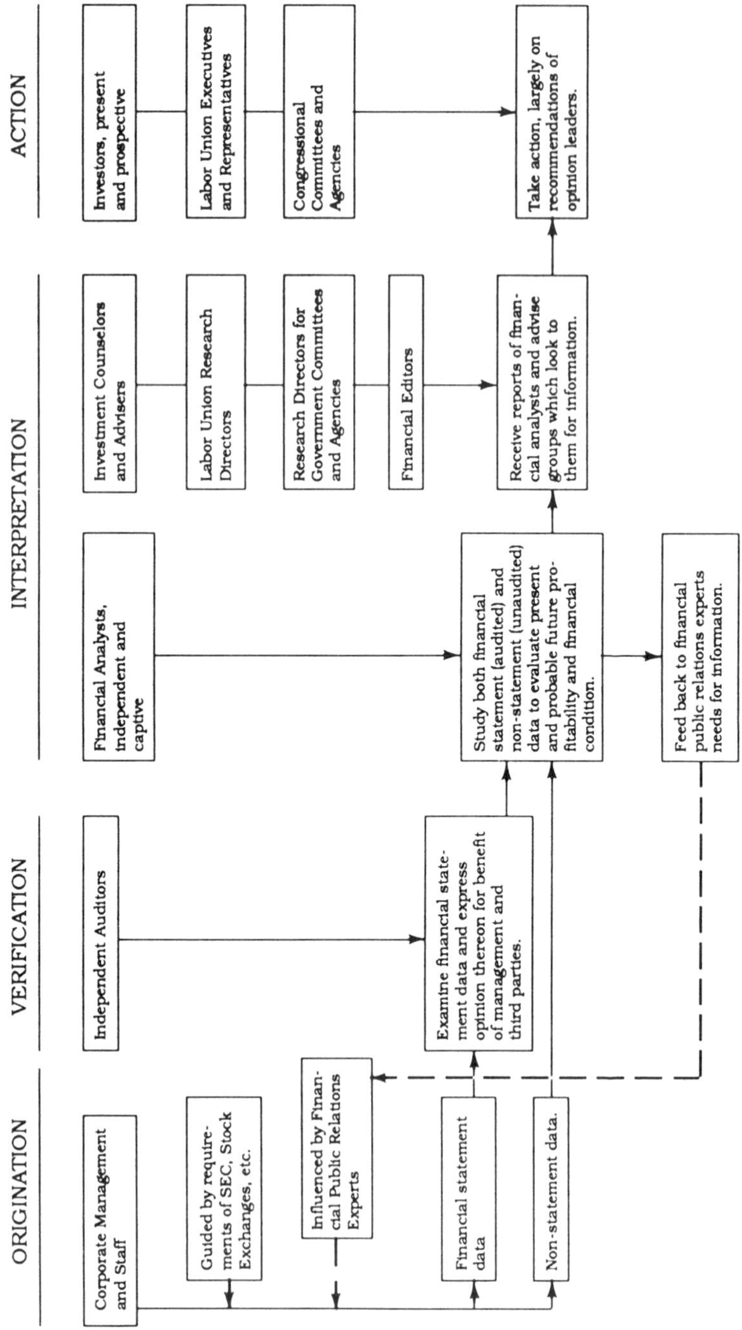

In this picture, the auditor does not have either as important a position as he had in the past or as he should in the future. Here we see a new concept of disclosure developing: not the presentation of the data a reasonably informed reader can use to make up his mind about an investment opportunity, but disclosure of the information which a thoroughly competent and skilled analyst can use and must have to discharge his professional responsibility to those who rely on his judgment. It seems obvious that the auditor should not be the sole judge of what should be disclosed. He does have standards for financial statement disclosure which he insists must be met if he is to attach his "fair presentation" stamp of approval to the statements, but his disclosure standards fall short of the disclosure on which investment decisions are being made. Other professionals have moved in and now have a voice in deciding just how much information is to be disclosed. This in itself is not an unfortunate development; indeed, the independent auditor might find it advantageous to have someone share with him the burden of establishing standards for adequate disclosure. A much more serious matter is that a substantial portion of the information now required by those making investment decisions is not at present submitted to the independent auditor for verification. Where previously, all, or almost all, information passed through his hands for his review, now only a portion of it benefits by his services; and it seems a fair prophecy that unless the trend is halted, more and more unaudited information will find its way to the opinion leaders in the investment market.

Auditable and Unauditable Financial Data. The obvious question at this point is whether the various kinds of nonstatement information can be audited. Auditors have a natural and understandable reluctance to extend the area of their responsibility by increasing the scope of their examinations to include verification of such data as budgets, financing plans, and capital expenditure programs. Yet the basic question must be one not of limiting responsibility but of extending service. Such information is needed by the opinion leaders on whose judgments investments are made. Review by an expert would add reliability to such information. Can auditors develop methods and standards of verification that will permit them to express an opinion as to whether such data have any basis in fact, any standing at all beyond the claims of those who issue them?

We contend that any assertion having a basis of corporate action and planning can be subjected to useful verification and confirmed or negated by more or less convincing evidence. As the chapter on evidence concluded, the auditor deals in probabilities. To invade this new area of service, he need but extend his probabilities a little further. The same techniques will apply, the same kinds of evidence will be found, the same problems of judgment will be met. Certainly auditing should move slowly and with caution in accepting such assignments because there are substantial difficulties to overcome. Yet it is a service which auditing must perform soon or find its opportunities usurped by others. As analysts and investment counselors strengthen their positions, their demands for necessary information will increase until they have all they feel is necessary. Then, inevitably, their call will be for better information. And what feature of the information supplied by the public relations expert could be more important to them than to have it subjected to an independent review?

Management's Attitude Toward Disclosure. In many ways, auditors are the laggards in this matter of extent of disclosure. Management itself has indicated a new and growing interest in making information available to shareholders and others. Indeed, there appears to be an entirely new attitude developing on the part of corporate management in this respect.

> The president of a big company stood up at a luncheon meeting in Wall Street last week and made a speech he wouldn't have dreamed of making ten years ago. He was Philip M. Zenner, president of the Royal McBee Corp., and he was speaking to 150 members of the New York Society of Security Analysts.
>
> The group listened intently as Zenner revealed facts about his company that management would have kept closely secret a decade ago.[43]

A study published in 1955 pointed out that a majority (as indicated by a selected random sample of companies) of top man-

[43]"Nowadays Their Opinions Count," *Business Week*, June 20, 1956, pp. 43-44.

agements believe that reporting to stockholders alone no longer meets the needs of business. Enterprise activities are now reported to a much wider circle of interests than they used to be; this is suggested by the following question and the answers from the published survey results:[44]

Question: To whom do you send your annual reports?
Answer:

	Number of companies replying	Per cent of total replying
Stockholders	203	99.0%
General public	194	94.6
Government	147	71.7
Creditors	144	70.2
Employees	117	57.0

Not only are annual reports distributed more widely than they once were, but there apparently is a feeling that they should contain information going well beyond that included in the typical financial statements. The same study reports the following question and answer:[45]

Question: Which of the following do you believe should be the objective of your annual report?

	Number of companies replying	Per cent of total replying
(a) To furnish a report of business activities to stockholders, creditors, employees, government, and general public.	154	75.1%
(b) To furnish a report of the business activities to stockholders only.	55	26.8
(c) To enhance public understanding of the economic facts of life.	41	20.0

It is interesting, and perhaps surprising too, that as many as twenty per cent of those queried indicated an interest in using annual reports to enhance public understanding of the economic

[44]Robert D. Hay, "Management Thinking Concerning Corporate Annual Reports," *The Accounting Review*, July, 1955, p. 444.

[45] *Ibid.*

facts of life. If over three-fourths of business managements feel they have a responsibility to keep stockholders, employees, creditors, government, and the general public informed with respect to the activities of the enterprise they manage, there certainly is an emphasis on disclosure and information not previously effective in this country.

To what factors may we charge this increased emphasis on disclosure of facts about corporate activities? It would seem that perhaps three are of primary importance. First, the pressure from financial analysts and other investor representatives for information essential to intelligent investment decisions has awakened management to the needs of investors and accustomed it to making information generally available. Second, a growing tendency appears on the part of corporate management, to accept a great deal more in the way of social responsibility than was the case even a few decades ago. Third, management realizes more and more that there are relatively few business secrets and to keep information from the legitimate interests in the enterprise is to do them a real disservice when, at the same time, those who want that same information for improper purposes have ways of obtaining it. The first of these factors has already been dealt with at length in this chapter; the second must be taken on faith and, for the purposes of this discussion, may be so taken because it is not an important consideration in our conclusions; the third may require some support.

One would be naive indeed to believe that such a thing as industrial espionage is nonexistent. The attempts of corporations to keep operating information secret from competitors or from labor unions, a fairly traditional attitude of the past, are almost certain to fail. In 1959, nine students at the Graduate School of Business Administration at Harvard University investigated the problem of business espionage in the United States. The investigators stated the motive and justification for their research as follows:

> Very little had been written about corporate spying; but the few articles published on this activity indicated that it represented a significant portion of the total amount of intelligence collected about competitors....

> In the fall of 1958, we became interested, not only in what some people call business espionage, but in the entire area of how companies collect information about their competitors. We wanted to know how much importance businessmen attach to the knowledge of competitors' operations as a guide in the decision-making process of their own organizations.[46]

Information in this report was obtained from about 200 business executives, on a vice-presidential level or higher, and 187 corporations ranging in size from some of the largest American corporations to those with less than 100 employees. We need not describe the findings of this research in detail; but it is sufficient to quote two of its basic conclusions:

> 1. Most businessmen interviewed indicated the need for developing competitive information. They considered business spying unethical and immoral, yet, very few made any attempt to define what they meant by *unethical* or *immoral*.
>
> 2. Investigators believe that corporate spying is increasing. The executive frequently underestimates the importance of this activity in his own industry. Since undercover operators are seldom discovered, the executive is often unaware that spying may actually have been directed against his company.[47]

In discussing the sources from which labor unions obtain corporate information, another report quotes research directors of labor unions as follows with respect to their sources of information:

> One Union research director said, "I make it a practice to have two luncheon engagements a week with people in the industry who are 'in the know.' You would be surprised how much of the financial affairs of the industry or of a particular company I can learn over a cup of coffee."
>
> Still another means of gaining necessary knowledge was disclosed to the interviewer by a research director. "If I want certain figures bad enough...we steal them....I have friends on the other side of the fence, too....I do not care to reveal the methods I use, for the information is too valuable to me."[48]

---

[46] *Competitive Intelligence: Information, Espionage, and Decision-Making*, Watertown, Massachusetts: C. I. Associates, 1959, p. 3.

[47] *Ibid.*, p. 63.

[48] Wilbur F. Pillsbury, *The Use of Corporate Financial Statements and Related Data by Organized Labor*, University of Indiana, Bureau of Business Research, School of Business, 1954, p. 18.

It is no wonder that a business executive warns his fellow managers against the consequences of permitting labor unions to gather information where and how they can. He takes the more enlightened view that management should supply such information as is needed for bargaining purposes:

> Management has to recognize that unions now have research departments and in many cases they have more information than we have. Many times they come to the conference table better prepared than we are, and we must remember that. Information which unions have forms a basis, at least a part of a basis, for the demands that they make on management. We must recognize the danger of misinformation. Management's position will be strengthened by accurate information covering the points that are going to be talked at the conference table.[49]

An Audit Attitude Toward Adequacy of Disclosure. In introducing this section on adequacy of disclosure, we pointed out that a change had occurred in the investment market, a change that makes our present attitude toward disclosure at least obsolescent. Auditing can no longer base its ideas of fair presentation on the concept of a reasonably informed investor who reads the published financial statements and makes his investment decisions accordingly. Today the investment market is a controlled market; further, it is one in which a number of skilled professionals all play highly integrated and highly important roles. The financial public relations man, the financial analyst, and the investment adviser or counselor all act to serve the interests of both the corporation needing funds and the investors with funds to commit. The auditor has a place to play in this professionalized market organization too, but if it is to be one that challenges his professional responsibilities and capabilities as they should be challenged it must be a role which, first of all, recognizes the importance and rightful place of the other professionals and, secondly, accepts a fair share of professional responsibility for market control and protection of the investor.

It seems apparent from the statements of financial analysts quoted in this chapter that typical financial statements do not, in themselves, provide adequate information for investment decisions.

---

[49] Fred S. King, "Is There a Field for Accountants in the Future of Labor Negotiations?", *The Journal of Accountancy*, July, 1947, pp. 10-12. Mr. King was then the vice-president of Musing-Wear, Inc.

These experts whose specialty is to research business data for the purpose of reaching conclusions about investment decisions require and use additional financial information. It appears that auditors would do well to co-operate with them in expanding our concepts of financial reporting and devote some serious attention to the application of auditing techniques to the nonfinancial statement data which investment analysts find useful.

An additional thought should be advanced here. As a profession, auditing has duties to all those who rely upon its work. As a profession it cannot wait until it is forced by such pressures as the market can bring to bear to expand its understanding and practice with respect to adequacy of disclosure. Without prompting from the market, there should be continuing effort by auditing to improve and extend its services, to keep up to date with the realities of the environment in which it operates. As a profession, auditing has significant social responsibilities; unless it accepts these social responsibilities it will not long merit the status of a profession.

Among these responsibilities may well be included that of keeping abreast of the disclosure necessary to satisfy the needs of the investment market. Along with this responsibility for recognizing the interests of others in disclosure and for leading the way in the development of realistic disclosure standards goes a further responsibility to develop ways of making disclosure effective. Unless the information disclosed is subjected to verification, that is review by an independent expert, it cannot be considered completely satisfactory for its purposes. As the only factor in the financial market concerned with the performance of verification work, auditing must accept the responsibility for developing methods and procedures of verification of the additional disclosures required by financial analysts and others in the investment market.

This leads us to a somewhat new concept of adequate disclosure. First, it is one which all interests in enterprise financial data have a voice in establishing. Second, it is concerned not only with insuring that those who use such information are not misled, but that the investors who ultimately rely on the advice of those who analyze such data directly are protected. "Protected disclosure" requires adequate verified information. It has been emphasized earlier in this work that there is no necessary conflict of interest between the auditor and the management of the enterprise under audit. It should also be emphasized that there is a limit to the mutuality of interest of the two. Certainly an audit serves management, but it also serves other and equally important interests, and some of these interests are in a much more vulnerable position than management. In the final analysis, those who rely on enterprise data to the extent that they commit their funds accordingly are the ones most in need of the services of independent auditors. And the independent auditor has not provided them the service to which they are entitled unless he has (1) assured himself that sufficient information for investment decisions under current market conditions has been made available, (2) indicated his ability and willingness as an expert to subject that information to review and thereafter to express his professional opinion as to its reliability, and (3) adopted throughout an attitude of protecting the interests of investors to the best of his professional abilities.

Informative Disclosures as a Part of Public Policy. To those who would protest that such a concept of adequate disclosure places too great a burden on auditing we must reply, first, that it is more in the nature of an opportunity than a burden; second, that new developments in the financial market make such a concept inevitable if auditing is to hold its present enviable position and fulfill its professional responsibilities; and third, that effective in the American economy today are tendencies which may well heap even greater opportunities and responsibilities on the shoulders of the independent auditor if he will but respond to the challenges of the times.

Different periods in the development of civilization have been described with words that tended to epitomize or characterize the time in question. Thus we have the bronze age, the iron age, the age of reason, and others. Ours might well be called the "age of information." With a populace whose relative level of education, formal and informal, is far beyond that ever before encountered in this country or elsewhere, there appears more and more the tendency to exercise control by making pertinent information available. Few indeed are those who now operate in any important capacity in this country in an aura of complete secrecy.

A multitude of interests ranging from the public press to Senate investigating committees devote themselves to informing the general public of facts that at one time would have been considered confidential. The Securities and Exchange Commission, for example, operates on the theory that its greatest service is in the provision of information to those who wish to invest funds. It in no way attempts to usurp the judgment function of the private investor; rather it permits him to function in an informed and intelligent manner if he will.

Recent and continuing investigations of prices in the oil and pharmaceutical industries have succeeded in supplying to the public a great deal of information about prices, costs, and marketing practices in these industries. Any major strike calls forth extended presentations of costs and profits by both parties to the controversy. As the general public becomes more and more able to understand facts and figures, government, industry, and labor alike combine to provide more information, each one trying through disclosure to help or influence the public.

For example, the purpose of the Welfare and Pension Plan Disclosure Act proposed by the administration in 1957 was described in these words:

> The public has been aware for some time of financial irregularities in the administration of welfare and pension plans. We are proposing action on a recommendation which the President has made repeatedly since 1954 to protect the equity which millions of workers have in these plans. Our proposal would require registration, reporting, and public disclosure of all health, welfare, and pension plans—whether they are union financed and operated, employer financed and operated, or jointly financed and operated.[50]

Note the emphasis on public disclosure. Apparently it is felt that disclosure of itself is enough to limit improprieties, probably on the theory that an informed public will demand legislation leading to the prevention of exploitation. Along the same line but in quite a different area we find pressure developing for the dis-

---

[50] Secretary of Labor James P. Mitchell, in an address before the Second Constitutional Convention of the American Federation of Labor and Congress of Industrial Organization in Atlantic City on December 7, 1957, published in *Monthly Labor Review*, January, 1958, pp. 45-47, at 45.

closure of information with respect to the pricing practices of big business in general. The introduction to a study entitled *Pricing in Big Business* includes the following comment:

> This monograph deals with price policy and pricing practices, a phase of the activities of large corporations that awakens in the public the most lively interest.[51]

Later in the same work, the authors state:

> Economists, legislators, and the public generally would like to see pricing decisions by big companies analyzed in logical fashion, with historical comparisons of competitors' prices, cost factors, and profit margins given consistent and quantitative weight in detailed memoranda of officials involved.[52]

More and more the mood in this country is one calling for as few secrets as possible. "He who has nothing to hide will freely disclose; he who refuses to disclose must have something to hide" seems to be the prevailing attitude. The current trend in favor of obtaining and maintaining equity through legislation aimed at preventing exploitation requires accurate, objective, and reliable information in order to provide a basis for the implementation of suitable control measures. Pertinent to any institution vested with a public interest is certain information likewise vested with a public interest. If such information is susceptible to manipulation, exploitation is less controllable. It is not only information that is required; it is reliable information.

As any good accountant knows, there is information and information. Only as efforts have been made to review and verify information can it be considered reliable. The general public is coming to a similar realization. This is why new laws requiring financial disclosures also call for audited reports. Accompanying the demands for more information will be demands for more reliable information. Thus we can expect a continuation and even an increasing emphasis on the provision of verified information as an important part of public policy in this country. When our age of information becomes an age of *reliable* information, then its goals can be more effectively accomplished.

---

[51] A. D. Kaplan, Joel B. Dirlam, and Robert F. Lanzillotti, *Pricing in Big Business* (Washington, D.C.: The Brookings Institution, 1958), p. 3.

[52] *Ibid.*, p. 5.

At the present time the members of only one profession concern themselves with the validation of published information. A number of other groups in one way or another give attention to the verification of asserted facts. Public weighers will attest to weights; various laboratories will make chemical and other analyses; engineers will test concrete and other building materials. But no group has anything like the position enjoyed by auditing with respect to the verification of asserted facts. The important question, then, is just how far is auditing willing to extend its verification services. With its theory of evidence, its techniques of verification, its experience in both verification and reporting, auditing is in a unique and enviable position. As the public requires more and more verified information, much of it well beyond that currently found in financial statements, will auditing see and seize the opportunity to extend its range of service? If it does, there are literally no bounds to its future. If on the other hand, it either deliberately or unconsciously limits itself to but a small fraction of the total of verifiable information, its position of eminence may be lost to those who do seize the larger opportunity.

Auditing has long performed an important function in facilitating the flow of credit in the money market; if it wishes to continue to perform this important function it must look well beyond the present horizons of its service function and see itself as the potential reviewer of any published information on which important control decisions are based; it must see itself as an essential part of the mechanism for accomplishing public policy.

Audit Obligation

We have discussed at some length the auditor's responsibility for accounting propriety and adequacy of disclosure in financial statements he examines. The auditor's responsibility for disclosure and for fair presentation does not end, however, with the client's statements. The auditor also presents a report of his own work; and brief though it may be, he has responsibilities of fair presentation in connection with his own report just as he does for the reports of those companies under examination. Although this part of the concept of fair presentation is as important as the parts already discussed in this chapter, it can be dealt with more briefly, first because a portion of the preceding discussion is also pertinent here, but more importantly, because the literature of the profession already contains the essence of this concept. Thus we need to do little more than draw attention to that which has already been well worked out.

The fourth standard of reporting in the 1954 revised edition of *Generally Accepted Auditing Standards* includes the following statement:

> In all cases where an auditor's name is associated with financial statements the report should contain a clear-cut indication of the character of the auditor's examination, if any, and the degree of responsibility he is taking.[53]

This standard is later described as applying only to financial statements which present financial position and results of operations, but Statement on Auditing Procedure Number 28 extends the basic idea to reports in general:

> The fourth standard of reporting requires that the report shall contain either an expression of opinion, or an assertion to the effect that an opinion cannot be expressed and the reasons therefor. This standard also requires that the report should contain a clear-cut indication of the character of the auditor's examination, if any, and the degree of responsibility he is taking. At the time this standard was adopted the major concern was with statements purporting to show financial position or results of operations. The requirements of this auditing standard, however, are, in the committee's opinion, applicable to special reports.[54]

These statements, plus the general tenor of Statements on Auditing Procedure No. 27 and 28 and the requirements of the Rules of Professional Conduct of the American Institute of Certified Public Accountants, charge the auditor with a responsibility for disclosure of his own actions and judgments that seems thoroughly compatible with the responsibilities we think he must accept for disclosing information about the company under ex-

---

[53] "*Generally Accepted Auditing Standards,*" Special Report by the Committee on Auditing Procedure (New York: The American Institute of Accountants, 1954), p. 14.

[54] Committee on Auditing Procedures of the American Institute of Certified Public Accountants, Statements on Auditing Procedure, No. 28, October, 1957, p. 32.

amination. That is, he must take steps to protect those who read his report from being misled either on the extent of his examination or the nature of his opinion. At this point it might be pertinent and useful to trace in some detail the historical development of the standard short-form auditor's opinion and the emergence of the attitude expressed in reporting standard No. 4. However this has been adequately reported elsewhere, and since this monograph is already far exceeding our expectations of length we restrain ourselves with little difficulty.

We do feel obliged, however, to extend the essence of this concept of audit obligation to agree with the ideas previously expressed in this chapter. The scope of auditing must expand to serve not only the current needs of other professionals in the investment market but ultimately as a means of accomplishing public policy. Bulletins 27 and 28 have already come to grips with the problems of expressing in realistic terms the auditor's responsibility for data beyond those commonly included in the standard financial statements which present financial condition or results of operations. As auditors are called on to review and verify such financial presentations as budgets, plans for capital expenditures, advertising programs, and the like, the standard short-form of the auditor's opinion will become less and less useful. It will become more and more difficult to find acceptable phrases to describe the auditor's examination of such data and to express his judgment. Whatever words are used for these purposes, they should:

1. Recognize that even professional readers may have difficulty in distinguishing niceties of expression which the auditor relies on to absolve himself of certain legal responsibilities.
2. State clearly and unequivocally, and in a style befitting the profession, the nature of the examination performed to provide a basis for the auditor's judgment.
3. Express the auditor's judgment in straightforward terms.

We are particularly concerned with the first of these three requirements. Too often, we think independent auditors have permitted use of their names for little more than prestige purposes. What possible good can come from an independent auditor's permitting his name (by means of a letterhead, watermark, or signature) to be associated with financial statements or financial data of any kind if he has not performed an examination satisfactory to himself? Those who see his name and have respect for the profession are almost certain to feel that his name lends some credence to the statements. Just how much it actually lends is difficult for even another independent auditor to judge. How then can a reader, whether a professional analyst or not, determine the significance of an auditor's signature or name without a clear statement by the auditor?

The service which an auditor makes available to the business community is an examination as an independent expert; use of his name and position to lend unwarranted prestige lessens the usefulness of that important service. As indicated in the discussion of adequacy of disclosure, auditors should adopt a protective attitude toward readers of financial statements and audited reports. This idea must be extended to the auditor's part of the report also. We feel strongly that unless an auditor has performed an examination and is willing to express an opinion on the basis of it, he should not permit his name to be associated in any way with the financial data concerned. To do otherwise is to be unfair to those who may be misled by such use. To contend that he is not responsible for oral, as opposed to written, associations of his name with financial information may be valid under present conditions but need not and should not continue so. The independent auditor should make clear to all those who come to him for service that he will not tolerate irresponsible use of his name for prestige purposes. If this is done the auditor can bring strong pressure, if not legal action, to bear upon those who infringe on this right.

Part of the difficulty encountered by the profession in stating the extent of an examination of data other than that purporting to show financial position or results of operations lies in the fact that auditors have too long been willing to perform as little or as much examination as clients desired. In this they served more like public accountants than like auditors. For example, some clients ask for a brief review of the data required for the preparation of an income tax return. Others request their auditors to review ledger balances, scan bank reconciliations, and perhaps prepare or review financial statements for propriety without making an audit. These are useful services and we do not wish to suggest that they should not be available to clients who desire them. But there is real danger that both the client and those to whom the statements are distributed will mistake such work for an audit. To any but the most sophisticated, distinctions with respect to the extent of an auditor's examination are likely to be, if not meaningless, at least somewhat less informative than desirable. Even such traditional phrases as "in accordance with generally accepted auditing standards" and "in our opinion" have little informative value, and there is reason to question whether their protective value is as great as some anticipate.

At the present time we are reluctant to suggest anything so radical as abandonment of the present short-form report, but we feel that, as the basic concepts of auditing become more clearly expressed and more widely accepted, abandonment is the logical outcome. In time a statement such as this will be found not only sufficiently protective to the auditor but more in line with the responsibility accepted by the profession:

> We have examined with due audit care the data found in (name of statement or statements) and find that they present fairly (the purpose of the statement).

Chapter 8

Independence

The significance of independence in the work of the independent auditor is so well established that little justification is needed to establish this concept as one of the cornerstones in any structure of auditing theory. Nevertheless, it may be desirable to draw attention to the comments of some of those who have had occasion to discuss this subject. In Chapter 13 of *The CPA Handbook*, Mr. E. B. Wilcox writes:

> Independence is an essential auditing standard because the opinion of the independent accountant is furnished for the purpose of adding justified credibility to financial statements which are primarily the representations of management. If the accountant were not independent of the management of his clients, his opinion would add nothing. Those who rely on the credibility he furnishes are apt to be creditors or investors, or sometimes employees, customers, or governmental agencies. It is for their assurance that the independent expert opinions are provided, and the accountant incurs a profoundly professional obligation to this unseen audience even though he does not know who they are. He must fulfill this obligation even when it means opposing and denying the wishes of those who have employed him, and who, he knows, may cease to do so. It is a requirement unparalleled in any other field. It places such demands on the integrity of the accountant that there are those who doubt that it is or can be achieved, yet the very prestige of the accounting profession today is evidence that it is achieved. The continued prestige and usefulness of accounting depends in large measure on its continued achievement.[1]

Mr. Carman Blough adds another useful thought in the following:

> Since one's usefulness as an auditor is impaired by any feeling on the part of third parties that he is likely to lack independence, he has the responsibility of not only maintaining independence in fact but of avoiding any appearance of lacking independence.[2]

Together, these writers not only emphasize the importance of independence to auditing but point out that independence must

[1]*CPA Handbook*, Edited by Robert L. Kane, Jr. (New York: The American Institute of Accountants, 1952), Chapter 13, p. 8.

[2]Carman G. Blough, "Responsibility to Third Parties," *The Journal of Accountancy*, May, 1960, p. 58, at 60.

be evident as well as real. This is to say that real independence is of little value if those who read an auditor's report refuse to acknowledge that independence does exist. Thus there are two aspects of independence requiring attention if a useful concept is to be developed; these are, first, the real independence of the individual practitioner in the performance of his work and, second, the apparent independence of auditors as a professional group. For the purposes of this chapter we will refer to these as "practitioner-independence" and "profession-independence" respectively.

The meaning of practitioner-independence seems clear. It has to do with the ability of the individual practitioner to maintain the proper attitude in the planning of his audit program, the performance of his verification work, and the preparation of his report. Profession-independence has to do with the image of auditors as a group brought to mind when the term "auditor" or CPA is used. How does the public think of auditors; as thoroughly independent professional men or as hired employees like bookkeepers and payroll clerks? It is not enough to claim that the image of the profession is made up of the real-life actions of its practitioners. To many people who have never had direct acquaintance with independent auditors, the term still has meaning, a meaning which they have gained from what they have read, from the impression various forms of mass communication media have made upon them, and from the ideas passed on to them by various opinion leaders. There are many people who, although they know an individual auditor and think highly of him, may well have quite another impression of the profession. When the time comes for them to rely on the work of unknown auditors, it is their general impression that will govern. Thus we feel that serious consideration of the subject of profession-independence is in order.

Practitioner-Independence. The subject of practitioner-independence has been given substantial attention in recent years. Mr. John L. Carey notes two meanings of independence: first, the self-reliance of any professional person and, second, the special significance the term has with respect to the auditor's opinion on financial statements. He writes:

> Independence, in the sense of being self-reliant, not subordinate, is essential to the practice of all professions. It is a part of professional

integrity. No self-respecting physician, lawyer or certified public accountant will subordinate his professional judgment to that of the client or anyone else. It is a part of his professional duty to assume responsibility for the advice, the opinions, and the recommendations which he offers, and he cannot shift this responsibility. If his patients or clients do not like his advice, the practitioner may regret it; but no one would condone his changing his honest opinion in order to avoid offense or to secure his fee.

In all phases of his work—auditing, tax practice, and management services— the certified public accountant must be independent in this general sense of the word. If he subordinated his professional judgment to the views of clients, government agencies, bankers, or anyone else, he would soon come to be considered not worth his salt.

But independence has come to have a special meaning to certified public accountants in conjunction with auditing and expressing opinions on financial statements. Here independence has come to be almost a "term of art." The reason is that investors, credit grantors, prospective purchasers of businesses, regulatory agencies of government, and others may rely on a certified public accountant's opinion that financial statements fairly reflect the financial position and results of operations of the enterprise which he has audited. It is most important that the CPA not only shall refuse to subordinate his judgment to that of others but that he *be independent of any self-interest which might warp his judgment* even subconsciously in reporting whether or not the financial position and net income are fairly presented. Independence in this context means objectivity or lack of bias in forming delicate judgments.[3]

In another publication we have given extended consideration to the general subject of practitioner-independence.[4] We can agree with those who contend that independence is basically a state of mind. We can agree, also, with those who contend that an individual practitioner can maintain this "honest disinterestedness...in the formulation and expression of his opinion, which means unbiased judgment and objective consideration of facts as the determinants of that opinion."[5] To do this successfully, however, the individual practitioner must have a thor-

---

[3]John L. Carey, *Professional Ethics of Certified Public Accountants* (New York: The American Institute of Accountants), pp. 20-21.

[4]Hussein A. Sharaf and R. K. Mautz, "An Operational Concept of Independence," *The Journal of Accountancy*, April, 1960, pp. 49-54.

[5]*Generally Accepted Auditing Standards*, American Institute of Accountants, New York, 1954, p. 21.

ough understanding of the pressures and factors, some of which may be so subtle as to be scarcely recognizable, which may color or influence his disinterestedness. Thus we have advocated recognition of three dimensions of independence as follows:

> 1. Programming Independence: Freedom from control or undue influence in the selection of audit techniques and procedures and in the extent of their application. This requires that the auditor have freedom to develop his own program, both as to steps to be included and the amount of work to be performed, within the over-all bounds of the engagement.
>
> 2. Investigative Independence: Freedom from control or undue influence in the selection of areas, activities, personal relationships, and managerial policies to be examined. This requires that no legitimate source of information be closed to the auditor.
>
> 3. Reporting Independence: Freedom from control or undue influence in the statement of facts revealed by the examination or in the expression of recommendations or opinions as a result of the examination. The relationship of reporting to the examination has been neatly expressed in the following: You tell us what to do and we'll tell you what we can write in our report; you tell us what you want us to say in our report and we'll tell you what we have to do.[6]

Within the bounds of these three dimensions, a number of guides or clues indicating whether there has been any infringement on his independence can be developed for the guidance of the practitioner. The following are suggested:

Programming Independence

> 1. Freedom from managerial interference or friction intended to eliminate, specify, or modify any portion of the audit.
>
> 2. Freedom from interference with or an unco-operative attitude respecting the application of selected procedures.
>
> 3. Freedom from any outside attempts to subject the audit work to review other than that provided for in the audit process.

Investigative Independence

> 1. Direct and free access to all company books, records, officers and employees, and other sources of information with respect to business activities, obligations, and resources.

---

[6]Sharaf and Mautz, *loc. cit.*, p. 52.

2. Active co-operation from managerial personnel during the course of the auditor's examination.

3. Freedom from any managerial attempt to assign or specify the activities to be examined or to establish the acceptability of evidential matter.

4. Freedom from personal interests or relationships leading to exclusion from or limitation of the examination of any activity, record, or person that otherwise would have been included in the audit.

Reporting Independence

1. Freedom from any feeling of loyalty or obligation to modify the impact of reported facts on any party.

2. Avoidance of the practice of excluding significant matters from the formal report in favor of their inclusion in an informal report of any kind.

3. Avoidance of intentional or unintentional use of ambiguous language in the statement of facts, opinions, and recommendations, and in their interpretation.

4. Freedom from any attempt to overrule the auditor's judgment as to appropriate content of the audit report, either factual matter or his opinion.[7]

Guides such as these should have usefulness to those who find it necessary to evaluate the degree of independence actually enjoyed by a given practitioner under specific conditions. They should be even more useful to practitioners themselves. With such a set of guides available to him, the individual practitioner can continually examine himself and his work and determine the extent to which he is actually maintaining the necessary degree of independence. He should recognize that control may be exerted and influences may be effective when neither he nor his client realizes this or desires it. Personal relationships may give rise to unrecognized prejudices; personal characteristics and desires may influence one's attitude substantially; the desire to be of service may get out of hand. Only when the auditor is fully aware of the dangers involved can he take the necessary precautions.

---

[7] *Ibid.*, p. 53.

These guides, or similar ones, will be helpful only to the extent that the practitioner develops an ability and a habit of introspection or self-review. If he is aware of the nature of independence and the guides to its evaluation, and if he can submit his own activities and situation to a critical study, a practitioner can evaluate his relative position within each of the dimensions of independence. He must ask himself some hard, straightforward questions to do this; and he must answer these questions objectively. Having done this, he is in a position to assess his own degree of independence and, if necessary, to take such remedial action as seems desirable.

Here as elsewhere in the field of auditing, a reasonable balance must be maintained between the ideal and the practical. Minor infringements of an auditor's complete independence are to be expected and may be quite irrelevant to the validity and usefulness of his opinion. On the other hand, minor matters sometimes develop into important considerations. Prudence requires this most treasured virtue be guarded jealously. This is assured only if we are constantly aware of all the possible hazards to which the auditor's independence is subjected.[8]

In the last analysis, except in extreme cases, the problem of maintaining independence must rest with the individual practitioner. Occasionally, of course, infringement will be so flagrant that it will come to the attention of those who use the auditor's report or of regulatory agencies or fellow practitioners, and steps will be taken to review the auditor's actions and relationship with the company in question. In a great many more cases, however, the greatest threat to his independence is a slow, gradual, almost casual erosion of his "honest disinterestedness." This possibility requires constant attention to the maintenance of independence by all concerned. Through advance instruction and in review, the auditor in charge must constantly remind his assistants of the importance and operational meaning of independence. Staff training and professional education should provide emphasis and opportunities for neophytes and experienced auditors alike to learn and be reminded frequently of their responsibilities in this area.

The Independence of the Profession. We agree with Mr. Blough that to be as useful as possible, a practitioner must avoid any ap-

---

[8]*Ibid.*

pearance of lacking independence. But we add to this that, like the individual practitioner, the profession as a whole must avoid any appearance of lacking independence. Unless the general public as well as the direct users of audit reports have confidence in the independence and integrity of the profession, the individual practitioner will not have maximum opportunities for service.

The importance of public acceptance of auditing is essential to any substantial expansion of auditing as a means of accomplishing public policy. This seems apparent. General acceptance is also necessary to effective performance of the present limited role of auditing as the verifier of financial data. We have seen that financial analysts and investment counselors already find it necessary to rely on unaudited data to a much larger extent than is commonly realized. If they do not have faith in the independence of auditors, it is likely that they will tend more and more to rely on unaudited data rather than to insist that data presently unaudited be included within the auditor's examination. If a tendency in this direction were to be accompanied by the as yet unforeseen development of some competing type of verification activity, the results for auditing could be disastrous.

That there are those who do question the independence of certified public accountants is indicated in the following:

> At the outset, I will mention a problem that has puzzled me considerably. The accountant has many functions. One of them is to set up systems of accounts. Another is to carry out audits. In the latter capacity, the accountant is usually referred to as the "independent accountant." He puts his certificate on the company's balance sheets and published reports; and investors and bankers, the SEC and the stock exchange, and others, rely heavily on the accountant's independent judgment. In performing this function, the accountant acts in a very real sense judicially. He must decide questions, and he must be wholly free to decide questions against his client's interest if his investigation and judgment lead him to that conclusion.
>
> My question is this, and it bothers me: Can this independent quasi-judicial function be properly performed by a person who also undertakes to act as advocate for the client? Suppose the accountant comes to the client and says: "I think I can get larger depreciation allowances for you." What then does he put into the company's published accounts to which he adds his signature? Does he put there what he thinks to be a sound depreciation allowance or what he

> thinks he can get the Treasury to allow? Many questions of this sort could be asked. The accountants have an important function in being independent examiners, and they have a long and honorable history in that work. Is this function really consistent with their acting as advocates for their clients before the Treasury? Perhaps they are able to rationalize this difficulty, but it seems to me that there is a problem here which requires some careful thinking.[9]

Here we find a distinguished leader in another profession questioning the ability of independent auditors to remain independent as auditors and at the same time engage in other activities which traditionally have been considered within their range of competence and appropriate activity. The point is not whether his question is justified or whether his objection can be met, as was skillfully done in an accompanying paper,[10] the point is that there are those who do have doubts about the independence of independent auditors. The profession has not yet created the image of disinterestedness that must be created if it is to serve effectively as a verifier of financial data to be relied upon by all interested parties.

Auditing, unfortunately, does not have any "built-in" characteristics that assure the skeptic of its integrity and independence. The structure of the judiciary, for example, in which judges are appointed by the state, may be cited in contrast. Judges are in no way dependent on "clients" for income or continuance in office and, except in their official capacity, have no connection with those whose cases come before them. This creates an impression of as nearly complete independence as can be obtained. In addition, we have a hierarchy of courts so that the decisions of lesser judges may be subjected to the scrutiny of those who, by dint of long service, have attained positions surrounded by an aura of such calm, clear justice that to question their independence seems almost sacrilegious. Nothing like this exists in auditing. Certainly the CPA designation is widely understood as a mark of competence; do we know that it is understood as anything more? So far as the layman is concerned, our claims to independence are claims

---

[9]Erwin N. Griswold, "The Tax Practice Problem I," *The Journal of Accountancy*, December, 1955, p. 31.

[10]Maurice H. Stans, "The Tax Practice Problem II," *The Journal of Accountancy*, December, 1955, p. 36.

only and have for visible support little more than our own protestations of good faith. It is true that certain agencies of the government, for example the S.E.C., apparently accept such claims, and the recognition of the independent status of CPAs by government is increasing, but this is more than offset in the eyes of many by the fact that examinations by the Internal Revenue Service and various regulatory audits are made not by independent CPAs but by employees of the government.

It may be desirable at this point to remind the reader that we are not ourselves questioning the independence of the CPA in these paragraphs. We are merely trying to "see ourselves as others see us." We are trying in honesty and candor to assess the view which others have of the CPA.

This lack of "built-in" assurances of independence is doubly unfortunate because auditing suffers from what may be described as "built-in anti-independence factors." Inherent in the nature of public accounting work as now performed are a number of features which, to the layman, are almost certain to cast the shadow of suspicion on the auditor's protests of complete independence. Some of these have been suggested previously but bear repeating at this time. We would include:

A. The close relationship which the profession of public accounting has with business.
    1. Apparent financial dependence.
    2. Existence of a confidential relationship.
    3. Strong emphasis on service to management.
B. The organization of the profession.
    1. Tendency toward emergence of a limited number of large firms.
    2. Lack of professional solidarity.
    3. Tendency to introduce "salesmanship."

In reading the following paragraphs it should be remembered that our primary interest is in profession-independence and not the independence of individual practitioners. We are here pointing out those characteristics of the practice of auditing, and of course public accounting, which tend to influence the lay public to question the independent nature of auditing as a profession.

It may well be that individual auditors are strong enough not to have their personal detachment or independence affected in the least by these characteristics. Yet, if those who need the services of members of the profession do not themselves believe in the independence of its practitioners, they may deny themselves the services of auditing. Thus it is important that we give serious consideration to the impression or the image the profession makes in the minds of laymen.

Close Relationship of Public Accounting and Business. Certainly public accounting, and with it auditing, is closely related to business. Accounting has had its greatest development in the field of business enterprise. Audits of business companies make up the bulk of the work of most public accounting firms, and other types of services to such clients compose the greater part of the remainder. It is a fact of life in public accounting that fees come from clients, and public accountants are directly dependent on business companies for the greater part of their revenues. Thus an intimate association with business is so obvious a characteristic of public accounting and auditing that we may fail to see its influence on the minds of laymen. To them, it may be difficult indeed to see auditing as sufficiently independent of business that its judgments carry the weight auditors feel they should.

When we couple this intimate financial association with the confidential relationship that exists between an auditor and the companies whose statements he examines, we find yet another reason why outsiders may have difficulty in appreciating the reality of the auditor's professed independence. During the course of an examination, an independent auditor acquires considerable information which could be used to the detriment of the company under examination. Rule 16 of the Rules of Professional Conduct of the American Institute of Certified Public Accountants expresses this relationship in the following words:

> A member shall not violate the confidential relationship between himself and his client.

Although there has not been general legal recognition of a privileged status for communications between auditors and their clients, maintenance of the confidential relationship is of great importance professionally and certainly has the support of the profession.

Now let us view this relationship from the standpoint of an outsider. Does it seem likely to one who does not understand the full nature of the auditor-client relationship that a confidant could also be completely independent of the one who reposes confidence in him? In the simplest terms, secrets imply a considerable degree of intimacy. To those of us who understand the necessity and importance of the confidential relationship rule, it poses no peculiar problems of independence. To those who are not aware of its necessity and of its restricted extent, it may raise serious questions as to the possible extent of independence of the parties to such a relationship particularly in view of the fact that it is not required by law but is accepted voluntarily by the parties concerned.

The third characteristic of public accounting stressing close association of auditors and business is the considerable emphasis on service to management. Our own literature is replete with references to accounting as "the tool of business." Many writers have emphasized the importance of making an audit more than "just an audit" by being alert to opportunities to make recommendations and give advice to management on a wide range of subjects. The relationship between auditors and clients is such that the management of the client company is the only interest with whom the auditor has any direct dealings. He discusses the proposed audit report with representatives of management; he appears at stockholders' meetings along with management to explain any questions raised about the report; he works closely with management in planning the annual report and in working out the necessary disclosure for regulatory agencies. He takes management's point of view in tax controversies; and the fact that management's view here is likely to be the same as that of stockholders and other interests does not alter the fact that he is closely associated with management and attempts to serve management's interests in as many legitimate ways as possible.

Again, let us point out that in this section we are not interested so much in whether this close association actually lessens the independence of an individual practitioner as we are in whether a profession with such characteristics can appear independent to outsiders. In a later section we will examine more fully the performance of management services by independent accountants and the effect of such performance on independence.

Neither do we wish to raise a question at this point as to whether independent CPAs should be as closely associated with business and with management as they appear actually to be. As has been pointed out by others, the appearance of independence is almost as important as independence itself. Unless auditing has the confidence and respect of those who use its services, such services will not long be in demand and certainly will not be expanded into the broader areas of public policy.

Organization of the Profession. To our knowledge, no other profession is organized quite like public accounting. In no other profession do huge national firms even exist, much less dominate practice to the extent that they do in public accounting. The substantial number of mergers in the decade of the fifties reduced significantly the number of medium-sized firms as one after another was merged into larger firms. It can hardly be denied that a substantial concentration of practice has taken place and that if the present trend continues, except for a few rare exceptions, medium-sized firms will disappear and the profession will consist of a small number of very large firms and a large number of very small firms with little in between these extremes.

Of course there are valid reasons for these developments, and some of these reasons are directly related to the maintenance rather than the impairment of independence. A small firm has neither the financial resources, the research facilities, nor the staff to perform an examination of a giant corporation such as those relatively common on the American scene today. And even if it did, the unfortunate possibility always exists that a single major client might compose such a significant proportion of its practice and contribute so substantially to its revenues as to raise embarrassing questions respecting an accounting firm's actual economic independence from such a client. Once a few extremely important clients begin to dominate the practice of a public accounting firm, the maintenance of real independence becomes a truly crucial problem. Hence, the development of large firms has been a natural one, required to keep pace with the development of large clients, clients found in large governmental enterprises as well as in business.

Although this has been a necessary and therefore a beneficial development, it is not without its problems. As a public accounting firm grows larger, its interest in small clients tends to decline. The several services rendered by the small practitioner to small clients tend to be missing from the big firm, big client relationship. As client and accounting firm both increase in size, more and more of the work of each is performed by employees. Hence direct knowledge of the details of the examination and the relations of his staff with the client's staff by the audit partner tends to decrease. However high the audit partner's personal standards of independence and professional dignity may be, maintenance of equally high standards throughout his staff presents a problem.

An interesting and not irrelevant question may be raised here. At what point does an employee of a public accounting firm become a professional man? Do college graduates become professional men the moment they are employed? Is possession of a CPA certificate an essential or even an important component of such standing? Is membership in professional organizations required? In short, what are the essentials of professional status? Few who understand the nature of public accounting would question the professional status of partners. Many might question whether assistants merit such a designation.

If a considerable portion of the work on an examination is performed by employees who might not be considered by outsiders to have professional stature, one wonders whether they appear independent. Do they add the prestige and stature the profession needs? Again, it might be noted, we are not challenging the propriety of the practice; we merely raise a question regarding the impression it makes on others.

Some writers point out that as a public accounting firm grows larger, its overhead increases as does its responsibility to hold together a substantial staff. These increased costs require a considerable volume of business if idle time is to be held to a reasonable minimum. Whether increased costs lead large firms to become more conscious of the need for additional engagements is, of course, debatable. That it forces them to be businesslike in operating policies, few would deny. And of course businesslike procedures are not in any way improper or unprofessional. However, they may well give the appearance of a business operation rather than a professional type of service to those who view us from positions of less advantage than our own.

One unfortunate manifestation of this tendency toward a business type of operation is found in the assertions of some practitioners in recent years that accountants must indulge in engagement-seeking on a basis similar to that of the tradesman or commercial business.

> But what we are suggesting is a basic doctrine known to every sales manager: *The salesman must make regular calls on customers.*
>
> This, then, is the substance of the third ingredient in developing a practice.
>
> 1. Know your product (the skills available in the profession).
> 2. Know your client—his needs, his temperament, his personnel.
> 3. Call on your clients regularly and show them how their needs can be satisfied by your skill (or product).
> 4. Ask for the order.[11]

This idea of a "regular sales program" to build up a practitioner's practice is quite at odds with the following selection from Mr. John L. Carey's *Professional Ethics of Certified Public Accountants:*

> Solicitation of professional engagements has always been regarded with disfavor by intelligent members of any profession. There is something inherently distasteful and humiliating in offering for sale one's own personal skill and integrity.... In addition, of course, solicitation contradicts the professional attitude. It is the equivalent of salesmanship in the commercial world. It leads to the impression that money-making, not service, is the primary motive.[12]

Whether the type of sales promotion activity recommended by Mr. La France results from the entry of public accountants

---

[11]John W. La France, "Salesmanship in Accounting Practice," *The Journal of Accountancy*, September, 1959, p. 51 at 55.

[12]Carey, *op. cit.*, pp. 70-71.

into the general area of management services or from the development of firms whose heavy overhead requires them to keep their staff men busy as much of the time as possible is unimportant. The implication seems clear. There are those who care less about the status of the profession than about the opportunity to render service. Here we must be fair. There are those who feel that the function of the profession is to be of service and that no opportunity to be of service should be omitted. Motivated by the highest ideals, they may feel that public accountants should make every effort to increase the extent of the services they render.

It should not be overlooked, however, that the professions have no monopoly on service. The trades and many other types of activity provide services also. A profession is marked by something more than the rendering of service; and if these distinguishing characteristics are lost, it is doubtful if auditing will long continue to be of substantial service to the economic community.

Professional Solidarity. A final aspect of the organization of the profession has to do with what, for lack of a better term, may be called "professional solidarity." This involves the support given an independent auditor by other members of the profession when a client indicates his desire to forsake his present auditor and seek the services of another.

In England, the relationship of an auditor to the companies he examines is such that it is rather difficult for the company to "discharge" its auditors. When a situation arises in which a company feels this is desirable, it is obligated to give the auditor a hearing at a stockholders' meeting. This is a development sufficiently unusual that the stockholders will expect an explanation from the company and want to hear the auditor's side of the story. Obviously, this right adds somewhat to the auditor's independence. Furthermore, the Institute of Chartered Accountants in 1937 passed a resolution making it a duty of a chartered accountant to communicate with the predecessor auditor before accepting an engagement in which he knew the company's financial statements had been previously subjected to examination. In the case of a partnership or individual, the same rule is held applicable, although then it is considered only a matter of professional courtesy. The 1951 edition of Dicksee's *Auditing* states:

...it is generally understood that where one auditor is about to give up an engagement, or has been deprived thereof, another auditor does not step in his place without first referring to his colleague and giving him an opportunity of making observations. In 1937 the Council of the Institute of Chartered Accountants passed the following resolution:

> Where a change of auditors of *a company* is proposed, it shall be the duty of any member of the Institute before accepting nomination for election to communicate with the existing auditors with a view to ascertaining the circumstances in which a change of auditors is proposed.

Some years later the Council passed a further resolution in the following terms:

> The appointment of an auditor by a *private individual* or partnership is a matter wholly at the discretion of such private individuals or the members of the partnership and in this respect differs from the nomination by a member of a company as such where the interest of other shareholders are concerned. Nevertheless it is the view of the Council that in all such cases a member requested to act should, *as a matter of professional courtesy*, communicate with his predecessor (even if he has resigned) before accepting the appointment.

This rule, obviously, does not operate so widely as to give an auditor a freehold in his appointment, but it creates a very desirable solidarity which is calculated to make clients think twice before persisting in an obstructive attitude.[13]

A statement pointed out as recently as 1951 that the purpose of such a communication was more than a mere courtesy to the outgoing auditor.

> Some members appear to have assumed that if the person proposed to be appointed believes himself to be aware of the circumstances in which the change is proposed, then he is relieved from the duty of communicating; the Council therefore wishes to make clear that the duty to communicate exists in every case. *It is essential* that the member who is proposed for appointment, whether as auditor or as professional accountant, shall have an opportunity of knowing all the reasons for the change and this requirement can only be fulfilled by direct communication with the holder of the existing appointment.

---

[13]Lawrence R. Dicksee, *Auditing* (Seventeenth Edition, London: Gee and Company, 27-28 Basinghall Street, E. C. 2, 1951), pp. 287-288, Emphasis added.

> Apart from any question of professional courtesy it is important that the legitimate interests of the public and the independence of the existing auditor or professional accountant should be safeguarded and that a communication should take place even though the change is a matter wholly within the discretion of the appointer. The duty to communicate is not confined to cases where the previous appointment was held by a member of the Institute....[14]

We have no such rule in this country, although it is a common practice among certain public accounting firms to communicate with one another when such an event as a change of auditors occurs. A number of reasons may be suggested for the lack of a special rule to foster solidarity within the profession in this country. Mergers of business companies into one another are relatively common, and in almost every case the dominant management will desire to retain its own auditors. This means that frequently an auditor loses an engagement in what might be considered an entirely normal fashion with no suggestion of complaint or criticism about his work. In such a case, a rule requiring communication between the new and retiring auditors appears unnecessary. Another reason that might be advanced is the relative youth of the profession in this country; such a rule has not yet been found necessary although it may become so in time.

Another reason for the lack of such a rule, and one we may not be inclined to stress, is competition among public accounting firms for clients. This is partly because the profession in this country is young and partly because Americans put a strong emphasis on the benefits of competition in all fields of endeavor. Many public accounting firms are young and their members are ambitious. With a desire to grow and a real faith in their own abilities, these members are anxious to make their services available to more and more clients. If a business corporation finds its present accountants unsatisfactory for almost any reason, a number of other firms are more than willing to accept the engagement if it is offered to them. Furthermore, a strong feeling exists that a company should have the right to obtain the best talent

---

[14]Quoted from: James Blakey, "The President's Address," to the Institute of Chartered Accountants, 21st Annual Meeting, Published in *The Accountant*, October 17, 1953, p. 439, at 443.

and the best service available. If its present auditors are not providing the kind of service the management desires, it should be free to seek elsewhere. By competing in a friendly, gentlemanly sort of fashion, each firm will be encouraged to do its best to provide better services.

When all this is put together, however, it seems clear that there are forces at work within the profession presenting some challenges to the image of profession-independence we would like to see impressed upon others. Public accounting appears to be intimately associated with business and to have certain business-like characteristics in its own structure and operation. There is little about public accounting that would encourage the uninformed person, whether he be a member of another profession or engaged in nonprofessional activities, to see auditors as possessing the ultimate in independence. And if we are completely honest with ourselves, we will see that some of these forces may have a deleterious effect on the real independence of some practitioners.

Certainly some practitioners are strong enough to resist any temptation and any pressure that may be brought to bear on their independence. And just as certainly other practitioners find real independence a little more than they can manage in the face of considerable pressure and under the conditions of professional practice.

As pointed out throughout this discussion, some of these characteristics which appear to cast a cloud over the independence of the profession are inevitable and indeed may work to the strengthening of independence. The existence of large firms, the close relationship with business, the desire to be of service to management, are unlikely to change. Others, such as the development of an attitude of salesmanship and the competition among firms for opportunities to be of service to clients could well be controlled by joint professional action. But perhaps even more than this is necessary: we should like to give attention to the compatibility of auditing and management services and the desirability of specialization within the general field of public accounting before reaching a final conclusion on the steps necessary to create and preserve the kind of profession-independence essential to development of the full potential for service inherent in independent auditing.

Compatibility of Auditing and Management Services

The case for the performance of management services by public accountants is a simple one and a strong one: it increases the opportunities for service. The desire to be of maximum service to clients is a natural one for any professional person. To the extent that his training, experience, and judgment can help his clients, he has a natural desire to make them available. This inclination probably accounts for the tremendous expansion into management services by public accountants in the last few years.

The case against the performance of managerial services by public accountants is neither so simple nor so strong. Yet it has points which merit consideration. They may be considered under two headings: (1) the difficulty of establishing professional standards for this type of work; and, (2) the influence of the performance of such work on the accountant's independence.

Professional Standards for Management Services. Although some study has been given to the problem, there has yet been no definitive statement of the appropriate limits of managerial services. No one knows just what can and cannot properly be done by an independent accountant in this area. If we can believe what we read in the literature of the profession, we get the impression that some practitioners go far afield from those activities we normally consider to be accounting. Certainly there is little in the rules of professional conduct to restrict offerings in this area.

Because management services have not been accurately defined, we have no basis for qualifying those who wish to perform them. At the present time, anyone who wishes to supply such services can proclaim himself an expert and proceed to offer services of a wide variety. Although some of these activities call for specialized training not normally comprehended in traditional education for accountancy, there is no requirement that the would-be specialist in management services possess such training. Neither is there any required level of performance to indicate when the practitioner has performed with professional competence.

> There are no existing, accepted standards of quality of work to guide the CPA in this area, such as the guides which have been developed for auditing....[15]

---

[15]Roger Wellington, "Management Services: A Challenge to the Profession," *The Journal of Accountancy*, October, 1957, pp. 54-58, at 56.

A special problem exists here because much of the work is foreign to accounting and can actually be performed at least as well by others.

> This work commonly requires abilities not typical of many CPAs; much work in this field is well suited to the abilities and training of engineers or other non-CPAs....[16]

In this connection it is interesting to note that many practitioners feel accountants can qualify themselves for this type of work by self-study and professional reading. Although they support the idea that professional training and a qualifying examination are necessary for a person to enter their own ranks as a CPA, they apparently support the somewhat contradictory position that without any further professional training or qualifying examinations they can expand the scope of their professional services in some rather unusual respects.

> In fact the suggestion that the average accountant take courses, read books and otherwise prepare himself to take on these "non-traditional" engagements smacks of the sort of professional preparation that lawyers, doctors, and even accountants have denied recognition to for years. The self-taught expert (the non-licensed public-bookkeeper-tax-expert in our profession) has been the bane of existence in all recognized professions for many years. This is the precise reason that a uniformly prepared examination impartial and as fair as conditions will permit must be taken before a candidate can practice in any recognized profession.[17]

The difficulty of establishing standards for the performance of management services is in no way an argument in favor of abandoning this type of work completely. Much of what has recently received increased attention under the heading of management services has long been a part of the public accountant's accepted scope of service. Certainly attempts have been made to include some work which is "non-traditional" in nature; other services are entirely traditional. As Professor Lawrence points out, however, there are dangers in pressing the boundaries of professional services too far.

> The fine line dividing activities properly a part of public accounting from those not a proper part will always be subject to review and

---

[16] *Ibid.*

[17] Charles Lawrence, "Management Services and the Accounting Profession," *The New York Certified Public Accountant*, October, 1957, p. 671 at 673.

question. However, it does not appear reasonable to consider the business boundaries of the public accounting profession to be limitless. By the very nature of a profession, it must have limits, else how can it be recognized?[18]

The following observations made many years ago appear pertinent to this point:

> A profession consists of a limited and clearly marked group of men who are trained by education and experience to perform certain functions better than their fellowmen.... In general the standards of any profession are menaced if the line of demarcation between it and other activities is not clear, or if its members may indulge in highly profitable ventures in easily accessible alternate activities.... Every man owes it to his profession to indicate clearly what his business is, otherwise he has no right to the benefits accruing to the members of that profession. On the other hand, any profession which fails to insist on the identity of its members must take the consequences; the offenses of its marginal and ambiguous members react unfavorably on the profession as a whole.[19]

It would be an error for anyone to assert that the entire area of managerial services should be barred to independent public accountants. At the same time, there is a grave danger in the wholesale and uncontrolled entry of public accountants into this field. Not only may the profession suffer from a loss of identity as its members begin to compete with the various types of management service firms already in the field, but this continued close association with management inevitably raises questions of independence.

Influence of Management Services on Independence. Proponents of the performance of management services by independent public accountants have taken the position that such performance need in no way affect the accountant's independence. They support this contention on the following grounds:

1. There is a real and substantial difference between giving advice to management and serving as management.
2. Because independence is a state of mind, the competent auditor can maintain his personal independence in auditing engagements irrespective of other relations with the client.

---

[18]*Ibid.*, p. 676.

[19]Carl F. Taeusch, *Professional and Business Ethics* (New York: Henry Holt and Company, 1926), pp. 13-14.

Management decisions are seldom made solely by an individual, or even a small group, after requesting, receiving, and reviewing the advice of a number of experts. In most cases management decisions are worked out by a group which includes the experts, whether they be members of the company's staff or are independent. This is the only feasible way to operate because even expert advice is flexible. In presenting an opinion, the expert cannot know all the alternative possibilities which may influence his judgment. Thus he must sit in on the final discussion to discover whether any assumptions are changed, what other experts recommend, and what influence a possible change in circumstances may have on his judgment. Those entrusted with the final decision want their advisers available so that all the various ramifications of advantages and disadvantages can be reviewed and evaluated. Although the final decision may rest in the hands of one man, he is almost certain to be guided by what amounts to a group consensus.

Management, of course, is at liberty to accept, modify, or reject a given piece of expert advice. But advice is requested on the premise that it will be given rational consideration. It is requested because management feels its own inability to know all the alternative solutions to the problem at issue and to evaluate them and choose from among them. Management wants the advice and intends to use it; advice is sought and paid for to be followed, not to be ignored. It seems folly indeed to separate advising and judgment making. This is true whether the advice is concerned with income tax, systems, or general business decisions.

The substantial increase in the growth of business consultants of all kinds in recent years reflects a development in business management which may not have received sufficient attention from accountants. A considerable number of companies now use independent consultants as an alternative to the development of large internal staffs. On the theory that the advice and services of consultants can be obtained whenever desired and without either long-run commitment or the expense of hiring staff experts, some managements find this approach entirely satisfactory. In such a situation, management would use such outside experts just as another company would use its staff advisers.

Management will pose the problem, give the consultants time to do the research they feel is required for judgment, and then meet with them to work out a solution in a common sort of effort.

The independent accountant serving in the capacity of a business consultant or management services expert is no exception. Although he does not have a formal place in the managerial hierarchy and does not cast a formal vote on the problem at issue, he nevertheless is, de facto, a participant in management decisions. This is particularly true when the same accountant is continually consulted. Many accountants have contended the CPA should provide the small and medium-sized company with the benefits which a large company obtains from its own controller and his staff. Involvement in business counseling to this extent would seem to have serious implications for the CPA's independence with respect to the client in question.

There tends to come a time in any arrangement for management services when the mutuality of interest of the consultant and the client becomes so significant that the accountant ceases to be independent in the sense that we feel he should be for auditing purposes. Management requests advice because it expects to use it; the consultant gives it to be used; the consultant knows that as a consultant he will be judged by the ultimate usefulness of his advice in bringing success to management's efforts. He has had a hand in shaping managerial decisions and will be judged by management on the same basis that the management itself will be judged. How then can he claim to be completely independent?

Accountants who offer management services often assert that it is their very independence which makes their advice valuable. Because they are not intimately connected with the enterprise, they can look upon it without emotion, and calmly and coolly make decisions based on an objective evaluation of the situation. This assertion may well be true, but the objectivity described is a part of the first type of independence mentioned by Mr. Carey, not audit independence. Once advice leading to business decisions is given, a mutuality of interest between the consultant and the company begins to develop. He now has an interest in that company, a financial interest based on his prestige as a successful adviser; and his interest differs not in kind but only in degree from that of the full-time employee.

If we grant that independence is a state of mind, we must also recognize influences on one's state of mind that are not always apparent. The requirements of practitioner-independence suggested earlier in this chapter require the independent auditor to be alert to a number of rather subtle influences including social and personal relationships as well as economic influences. As emphasized previously, there is a considerable range of individual abilities within the profession; some accountants are strong enough and alert enough to control themselves under the most adverse and perhaps even the most subtle influences; others are not so fortunate. If the profession is to have the standing it requires to perform its present function and to reach its potential for the future, consideration must be given to the needs and abilities of all members of the profession, not just to those above the average in ability and character.

Finally, we must consider the matter of profession-independence. Does anyone really believe that we can offer the managerial consulting type of advice to management on a fee basis and still appear completely independent to alert and intelligent outsiders? More and more, independent auditors will work in the harsh, cold light of public scrutiny; it will not be enough that we feel we are independent and can convince our clients of the same fact. More and more we will have to convince others. The difficulty that the S.E.C. has found in accepting the independence of public accountants in a number of cases is an indication of the difficulty other interests will continue to find in increasing measure if we fail to take the necessary steps to insure not only actual but apparent independence.

Managerial services of some kinds are certainly well within the province of the independent CPA; managerial services of other kinds are probably well outside his scope of education and competence. At the present time there is no basis for readily distinguishing these, nor are there standards for judging the performance of services which are appropriately supplied by independent accountants. Even in the narrowest sense, management services have become a significant part of the total services performed by the profession, and it is unlikely that they will ever be abandoned. Indeed, they should not be. Yet the performance of managerial services of almost any kind has important implications for profession-independence and even for practitioner-independence. Here lies the difficulty. It is because of this conflict that we find performance of managerial services and auditing for the same client by the same accountant a combination of incompatible services. This incompatibility leads to no other solution than the desirability and indeed the necessity for a separation of these two types of service. If auditing is to continue to enjoy the respect of those who rely on its services, it must be and must appear to be quite independent. If auditing is to take its place as part of the mechanism of social control, it must be accepted as thoroughly independent.

Specialization Within the Profession

An obvious but not necessarily satisfactory solution to the problem of maintaining the independence of auditors while still permitting independent public accountants to participate in the performance of management services is found in the possibility of specialization within the profession. If individual practitioners will restrict themselves to a part of the total possible services offered by the profession generally, it may be possible to limit the performance of incompatible functions by individual practitioners. Because this seems to present such an obvious solution to the problem, we have inquired into the nature, extent, and success of specialization in medicine and law and, to a more limited extent, in other professions. Our findings and our conclusions as to the usefulness of this possible solution to the problem in auditing follow.

There are two extremes which may be encountered in the introduction of specialization in any profession. One is a situation similar to the one we now find in public accounting in which no specialization is formally recognized although there are subdivisions of general practice within which individuals tend to specialize in an informal way. The disadvantages of this situation have already been discussed and consist primarily of the difficulties of establishing and maintaining any real standards whatever with respect to the competence and qualifications of those who specialize in such an informal fashion. If there are no formal specialists, anyone can be an informal fashion. If there are no formal specialists, anyone can be an informal specialist and within the bounds of the general rules of conduct of the profession he can make such claims about his abilities and services as he desires.

At the other extreme we find a situation in which a large number of well-defined fields of specialization have been formally established with stated requirements for qualification and a high degree of control over entry into practice within the special area. Medicine is perhaps the best example of a profession in which a substantial number of finely divided, well-established specialties have developed. There are those both within and outside the medical profession who feel that specialization has been carried too far. It is not our purpose to enter such an argument, but some of the criticisms of specialization by those who feel it has been abused may be of help to us.

Among the more important criticisms is that specialists may tend to give entirely too much attention to their narrow field of interest, to become inward-looking, and to lose the opportunity to become well-rounded and to grow in broad professional interests. They learn more and more about less and less; and as their interests and knowledge narrows, so does their attitude and professional outlook. Another criticism is that the development of numerous specialties leads to overlapping, competition, and contention. Membership in organizations of specialists becomes more important than membership in the profession as a whole. As a result, the profession becomes splintered, less effective as a group, and tends to lose prestige. Any contention between rival groups within the profession is of course unfortunate; divisive forces seldom if ever add strength.

On the other hand, there are some real advantages to specialization. One is the high degree of expertness that specialization permits and encourages. Another is that, through the establishment and recognition of specialties, it is possible to establish and maintain high standards both for entrance and for performance. Note, for example, the following requirements for a doctor who wishes to qualify as a specialist in anesthesiology:

A. Eligibility requirements for application:

1. Graduation from a recognized medical school and an internship period.

2. Possession of license to practice medicine.

3. Reputation for high ethical and professional standing.

4. Special training in anesthesiology—(see below).

5. Proof that he has restricted his practice to anesthesiology as a specialty for five years, of which at least two years have been in formal clinical training approved by the board, and statement to the effect that he intends to continue to limit his practice to anesthesiology in the future.

6. Membership in American Medical Association, local society, and American Society of Anesthesiologists.

B. Examinations testing competence to practice:

1. Written examinations covering anatomy, chemistry, physics, pharmacology, pathology, and physiology.

2. A survey examination conducted by one or more diplomates of the board who visit the applicant in his own locality to observe him in the practice of anesthesiology. The examiner may interview other individuals in the community to determine whether the candidate is of high ethical and professional standing.

3. An oral examination by directors of the board plus diplomates who assist as associate examiners. Oral examinations cover all phases of anesthesiology; however, emphasis is placed on chemical application.

4. At the discretion of the board, a practical examination may be added to include inspection of clinical reports, reports of departmental activities, library facilities, available apparatus and demonstration of the application of anesthetic agents, methods, and techniques.[20]

It is interesting and educational to compare these requirements with the complete absence of any requirements for the public accountant, or anyone else, who wishes to practice as a management services specialist in budgeting, systems work, or any other phase. Whatever the disadvantages of over-specialization, some specialization certainly provides an opportunity for the erection of standards of competence and performance.

---

[20]Approved Examining Boards in the Medical Specialties—Advisory Board for Medical Specialists, B. R. Kirkin, Secretary-Treasurer, *Journal of American Medical Association*, September 26, 1953, Vol. 153, No. 4, pp. 389-430.

A second advantage of specialization is that it provides a means of avoiding the performance of incompatible functions. Medicine requires that specialists restrict themselves to their specialty. This is done primarily on the theory that if the specialty is a justified one the practitioner's entire time and effort are required to keep him abreast of the field and acquainted with current developments. Thus restricting the specialist to his specialty is a matter of maintaining competence. Protecting the practitioner from indulging in incompatible functions likewise is a means of maintaining his competence; and we feel that specialization, if properly controlled, provides the most feasible solution to the incompatibility of management services and auditing.

The profession of law is one that has largely avoided the recognition of specialists and specialties. It is true that lawyers in certain geographical areas tend to find the bulk of their practice in a given division, such as maritime law in coastal areas and water and land rights in the semi-arid regions of the west. But such specialization is on an informal basis only with no restrictions or specialist organizations. In an interesting article published in 1955, Professor Charles W. Joiner of the Law Faculty, the University of Michigan, discusses the general problem of specialization in the legal profession.[21] After a thorough study of the subject he concludes that controlled specialization can be beneficial but uncontrolled specialization can do great harm. He notes the need for a limited number of specialists available on a referral basis to "general practitioners" of the law. If specialization is permitted to get out of hand, Professor Joiner sees great potential damage to the development and advancement of the legal profession. If it is properly controlled so that the general practitioner is never denied the privilege of practicing any field of law he chooses, it can be a great help.[22]

This is interesting to public accountants because it points out clearly that specialization is not an end in itself; it is merely a means to an end. It is the means of rendering greater service by

---

[21]Charles W. Joiner, "Specialization in the Law: Control It or It Will Destroy the Profession," *American Bar Association Journal*, Vol. 41, No. 12, December, 1955, pp. 1105-1108 and 1170-1172.

[22]*Ibid.*, p. 1107.

the profession and should be seen as such. Thus specialization must be adapted to the needs of the particular profession considering its use. Rampant specialization in a field where general practitioners are needed would be disastrous. Likewise, no specialization in a field where incompatible functions exist might likewise be disastrous.

Anyone with a little imagination and a fair knowledge of public accounting could easily develop a lengthy list of possible specialties. We might specialize by type of service such as tax work, management services, and auditing, as some now tend to do in an informal way. Or we might go further and break management services into systems work, budgeting, business counselling, and any number of other divisions. Again, we might specialize by type of industry and restrict practitioners to clients in the extractive industries, heavy manufacturing, light manufacturing, utilities, retail trade and merchandising, and the like, which, as a matter of fact, is actually now done to some extent, although only informally. But nothing in the practice of public accounting makes extensive specialization of this kind necessary or professionally desirable. Here a distinction made by Professor Joiner between "interest groups" and "proficiency groups" is useful.[23] An interest group is one in which a number of practitioners have a common interest and find ways to meet to discuss matters of such common interest. The individual may have either great or little proficiency in the area of interest, yet he is a welcome member of the interest group. A proficiency group is one which separates itself from all other practitioners on the basis of proficiency in some given area. Its members become interested in establishing standards and qualifications that distinguish them from other members of the profession, and they tend to become jealous of their abilities and area of service. Interest groups are useful and can be encouraged without danger to the profession. Proficiency groups likewise may be useful, but their encouragement leads to fractionalization of the profession and this potential must be recognized. These groups must be carefully controlled. Their development may be advantageous to the profession but must be regarded with care and handled with caution.

It seems apparent that we have a great many interest groups in public accounting. Indeed, any one of the many successful

[23] *Ibid.*, p. 1106.

"graduate study conferences" might qualify as an interest group. Some of the recurring tax conferences certainly represent such groups in action. Do we have any proficiency groups? It seems apparent that we do. Some of those who specialize in management services definitely have proficiencies that others do not. Likewise, some who specialize in auditing have proficiencies that many management services specialists or tax men, who have their own proficiencies, many not have. Thus we do have potential proficiency groups within public accounting. As Professor Joiner indicates, here lies a potential for danger to the profession.

We feel, however, that the best solution to the problem of independence in auditing is to recognize boldly and forcefully one of these proficiency groups. For the good of the profession, auditing must be recognized as a specialty separate from the remaining functions of public accountants. Accountants who serve as auditors should perform no other functions for their clients, and those who perform other functions should not engage in opinion audits. Our reason for so contending is the incompatibility of auditing with other services. We see auditing as something more than a skilled craft. Auditing is a quasi-judicial function and requires a type of independence entirely different from that required for the performance of any other public accounting type of service. Auditing, like any judicial work, calls for a detachment best described in the following words of Justice Learned Hand:

> One ingredient (of wisdom) I think I do know; the wise man is the detached man. By that I mean more than detached from his grosser interest—his advancement and his gain. Many of us can be that—I dare to believe that most judges can be, and are. I am thinking of something far more subtly interfused.
>
> Our convictions, our outlook, the whole make-up of our thinking, which we cannot help bringing to the decision of every question, is the creature of our past; and into our past have been woven all sorts of frustrated ambitions with their envies and of hopes of preferment with their corruptions, which, long since forgotten, still determine our conclusions.
>
> A wise man is one exempt from the handicap of such a past; he is a runner stripped for the race; he can weigh the conflicting factors of his problems without always finding himself in one scale or the other.[24]

---

[24]From an article by Justice Learned Hand, entitled "Mr. Justice Cardozo," *The Yale Law Journal*, Vol. 48, January, 1939, pp. 361-363 at 362-3.

Whether we can attain the wisdom described by Justice Learned Hand may be questionable. But certainly the function of independent verification, whether of the fairness of financial statements or of any other information, requires that we be as free as possible not only from our "grosser interests" but from any prejudices and commitments. And even more than this, if auditors as a profession are to hold the respect of all people, they must take steps to build into their professional structure safeguards that not only assure the individual practitioner of conditions protective of his personal independence but which assure to any who may be concerned that independent auditing is truly independent. This requires something more than the mere protests of those engaged in this work.

We are not prepared at this time to comment on the establishment of other specialties. As a matter of fact, we do not think of this separation of auditing from other services as establishing specialties in the real sense at all. This recommendation merely recognizes two important features of the practice of public accounting: first, that independence, actual and apparent, is essential in the practice of auditing; second, that independence, either actual or apparent, is unlikely if auditing is combined with those services in which the immediate interests of the accountant and the client are identical.

Implementation of This Recommendation. Lest anyone feel that this recommendation is made casually and without due regard for its implications in practice we add the following observations.

Any attempt to restrict the practice of public accounting firms to auditing or to other services, whether by rules of conduct or voluntary action, would work considerable hardship on client companies as well as on the accountants concerned. Clients are accustomed to receiving a variety of service from the same firm, often made available through the one partner with whom they have frequent contact. Suddenly to disrupt such carefully developed relations would do business and the profession great damage. This might well be the remedy that would kill rather than cure. We do not recommend it.

As suggested earlier, there is already considerable informal specialization within firms. Many men serve only on the audit staff;

others are tax men; still others consider themselves management services specialists. We recommend that the division between auditors and others be made more definite. At all levels below that of partner, we recommend that staff members be declared auditors or not auditors and thereafter be restricted to whichever type of work they select. This does not mean that a man could never change his mind; it does mean that such a choice is a serious commitment and an indication that he intends to work in that area and in that area only for the foreseeable future.

Obviously, this division does not give the full measure of independence to auditing which we feel is needed. It is a useful step in that direction. A second step, to be taken more leisurely, will separate partners into audit partners and others. This also may require little change in many cases and would certainly be an important move in attaining independence for the audit function.

Once these steps have been achieved, profession-wide consideration should be given to the feasibility of dividing each of the large public accounting firms into two parts, the audit staff and the non-audit staff. Actually dividing the firm into two firms would be one possibility, of course; another would be to operate two independent divisions under one executive body. Profession-wide consideration would be necessary to determine which of these provides the more suitable alternative. We feel that by the time the first two steps have been taken, development of the profession and the attitude of an even more informed general public will make the choice less difficult than it now appears. Taken together, these measures will give a degree of independence structurally and actually not now present.

What then of the small firm which does not have a similar opportunity for specialization? It would seem there are three possibilities:

1. Forbid the small firm to perform auditing services on the theory that it cannot appropriately perform both and that auditing is much less likely to be a major source of revenue to the small firm.
2. Require each small firm to choose which of the two fields of specialization it will adopt.
3. Permit the small firm to carry on as it now does, performing a variety of services for its clients.

At this time, we tend to prefer the third course of action. Our reason is not that we need "general practitioners" in public accounting, although this may be a sufficient reason for some. Our preference recognizes the fact that very few small firms make what may be called a public audit. When audits are made by small firms they are of a restricted usefulness, generally performed at the request of a bank. Such audits seldom carry any implications of general public interest. Local banks tend to know local accounting practitioners and to know which ones they can rely on. We feel that to restrict in any way small accounting firms from performing audits would only make it more difficult to service their clients and others with no substantial offsetting benefits resulting from such restriction. However, as soon as a given client becomes of sufficient size that there is a substantial public interest in its audited financial statements, we feel a strict separation of auditing and other services should be effected, if not by division within the accounting firm, then by employment of separate accountants for the two types of services.

Conclusion

Three phases of independence are important in independent auditing. First is the independence of approach and attitude which any professional man should have if he is engaged in truly professional work. This is a combination of self-reliance, freedom from client control, expert skill and ability, and considered judgment based on training and experience not available to those who are not members of the profession. Without this kind of independence, one is merely a skilled craftsman, not a member of a profession. All practitioners of public accounting must have this degree of independence whether they perform in the area of tax practice, systems work, business counselling, or auditing.

The second phase of independence is that required by an auditor if he is to perform his function of review and verification in a satisfactory manner. Independence here consists of freedom from bias and prejudice, whether recognized or not. To obtain this kind of independence, the practitioner must be aware of the various pressures, some obvious and some subtle, which tend to influence his attitude and thereby to erode slowly but surely his independence. To maintain independence under the many pressures of practice, an auditor must be constantly alert to any deleterious influences on his planning, investigative, or reporting independence. Unless he is alert and continuously concerned, it is possible that his independence will be weakened, and it may be impaired to such an extent that his usefulness as an auditor is lost.

The third phase of independence recognizes the fact that public recognition and acceptance of the auditor's status is significant to the successful accomplishment of his purpose. It recognizes also that within the broad range of public accounting services, important differences exist between auditing and other services. These differences are such that performance of these services by the same individual is incompatible with the idea of independence. Non-auditing services result in an identification of the interests of auditors and their clients that is not found in auditing engagements. In the latter, we find only the absence of any conflict of interests, not an identification of interests. If auditing is to be really and apparently independent, steps must be taken to separate the two divisions of public accounting, first to protect practitioners against unrecognized pressures and influences, secondly, to build into the structure of the profession some solid assurances of independence that will bring trust and acceptance from outsiders. Only as these assurances are built in can auditing hope to develop in others the trust and confidence it must have to reach its full potential for social service.

Chapter 9

Ethical Conduct

In the development of the concepts already discussed in this book, we have given considerable attention to some of the various responsibilities of the independent auditor. In addition to these, he has another kind of responsibility which flows directly from his professional status. As a professional man, he has obligations that do not rest upon the non-professional. These obligations may be stated as a series of specific rules of conduct or, in more general terms, may be described as an attitude or set of ideals. It is the purpose of this chapter to explore the ideas of ethics and ethical conduct and their applicability to auditing with a view toward expressing as succinctly as possible the essence of a concept of ethical conduct.

The theory of ethics has been a subject of interest to philosophers since the beginning of recorded thought. Because philosophers are concerned with the good of all mankind, their discussions have been concerned with what we may call general ethics rather than with the ethics of small groups such as the members of a given profession. We cannot look, therefore, to their philosophical theories for direct solutions to our special problems. Nevertheless, their work with general ethics is of primary importance to the development of an appropriate concept in any special field. Ethical behavior in auditing or in any other activity is no more than a special application of the general notion of ethical conduct devised by philosophers for men generally. Ethical conduct in auditing draws its justification and basic nature from the general theory of ethics. Thus we are well advised to give some attention to the ideas and reasoning of some of the great philosophers on this subject.

Bases for General Theories of Ethics. At various times and by various philosophers a number of different bases for a theory of ethics have been advanced. A review of the writings of some of the great philosophers will provide guidance in understanding the rationale behind ethics and ethical conduct. Obviously, we can do little more than gain a brief glimpse of the entire field, but even this will be helpful.

Socrates was among the first to try to construct a rational basis for right conduct. He based his theory of ethics on "knowledge," and emphasized the role it plays in providing a practical guide to the ethical conduct of man. The following excerpt from *A History of Philosophy* gives insight into Socrates' thinking on ethics:

> Socrates' faith in knowledge, in clear and reasoned thinking, is strong—so strong that he sees in it the cure of all our ills. He applies his method to all human problems, particularly to the problems of morality, and seeks to find a rational basis for conduct.... The central thesis of the Socratic ethics is contained in the formula: "Knowledge is virtue." Right thinking is essential for right action.... Knowing what virtue is, he (man) will be virtuous. Knowledge is both the necessary and sufficient condition of virtue: Without knowledge virtue is impossible, and its possession insures virtuous action. "No man is voluntarily bad or involuntarily good." No man voluntarily pursues evil or that which he thinks to be evil.... Since virtue is knowledge it follows also that virtue is one: Knowledge is a unity, an organized system of truth and hence the several virtues are merely so many different forms of virtue as such.[1]

Hume took quite another approach. He was an empiricist and relied upon this approach in all his philosophical work. First, he aimed at explaining ethics in terms of empirically verifiable observations and relationships, what is done rather than what should be done.

> Thus Hume introduced into his ethical theory the empiricism we have found in his metaphysics and theory of knowledge. He did not ask, "What ought men do?" or "Why ought they do it?" He asked, "What do they mean when they use such terms as 'ought,' 'virtue,' 'moral?'" ...If we can show that all the activities which are approved fall into certain classes, we shall have explained moral approbation, in exactly the same way as we explain heat by ascertaining the phenomena with which it is constantly conjoined....[2]

It is likely that there are those in public accounting practice today who interpret ethical conduct in much the same terms. They are interested primarily in what is being done; and they feel that if their own conduct meets the current standards of actual

---

[1]Frank Thilly and Ledger Wood, *A History of Philosophy*, Third Edition (New York: Henry Holt & Co., 1957), pp. 69-70.

[2]W. T. Jones, *A History of Western Philosophy* (New York: Harcourt, Brace, and Co., 1952), p. 794.

practice little more can be asked of them. The obvious weakness in this approach, however, is first, that "general acceptance" may not, at times, provide a reliable guide to ethical conduct or sound practice, and second, if this is stipulated as a basic guide, there will be no way to raise the level of actual conduct or practice should it once slip.

Second, Hume attacked the idea that ethical conduct could be accounted for on a basis of reason. He contended that good stems from some human sentiment, an internal taste or feeling, which makes virtue an end, desirable on its own account and for the immediate satisfaction that it conveys.

> ...the ultimate ends of human action can never, in any case, be accounted for by *reason*, but recommend themselves entirely on the sentiments and affections of mankind without any dependence on the intellectual faculties. Ask a man *why he uses exercise;* he will answer, *because he desires to keep his health.* If you then inquire *why he desires health,* he will readily reply, *because sickness is painful.* If you push your inquiries further and desire a reason *why he hates pain,* it is impossible he can ever give any. This is an ultimate end and is never referred to any other object.
>
> —
>
> Something must be desirable of its own account, and because of its immediate accord or agreement with human sentiment and affection.[3]

Besides, Hume maintained that the "personal merit" of an individual consists in the possession of qualities of character and personality useful or agreeable to the person himself or to others. He felt this was such an obvious principle as to warrant little discussion, yet he does elaborate on it somewhat and classifies "personal merit" into:[4]

1. Qualities useful to others,
2. Qualities useful to the person himself,
3. Qualities immediately agreeable to others,
4. Qualities immediately agreeable to the person himself.

In view of the fact that an auditor must deal with many other people, his professional colleagues, the staff of his firm, employ-

---

[3] *An Inquiry Concerning the Principles of Morals*, David Hume, Edited by Charles W. Hendel (Liberal Arts Press, New York, 1957), Appendix I, p. 111.

[4] *Ibid.*, Section IX, pp. 90-91.

ees of his clients, and the general public, the importance of "personal merit" seems obvious.

John Locke developed a different theory. He reasoned that truth, ethical conduct, and moral principles are not innate. They can only be acquired through perception and conception. And although Locke recognized the role that conscience, the still small voice, plays, he argued that it was not the sole source of moral knowledge:

> Conscience is no proof of any innate moral rule. To which I answer, that I doubt not but, without being written on their hearts, many men may, be the same way that they come to the knowledge of other things, come to assent to several moral rules, and be convinced of their obligation. Others also may come to the same mind, from their education, company, and customs to their country; which persuasion, however got, will serve to set conscience on work, which is nothing else but our opinion or judgment of the moral rectitude or pravity of our own actions. An if conscience be a proof of innate principles, contraries may be innate principles; since some men, with the same bent of conscience prosecute what others avoid.[5]

His attack on the theory that there are innate moral truths, which need no proof, is based on this logical analysis.

> Moral rules need a proof; ergo, not innate—Another reason that makes me doubt of any innate principles, is that I think there cannot any one moral rule be proposed whereof a man may not justly demand a reason; which would be perfectly ridiculous and absurd, if they were innate, or so much as self-evident; ...Should that most unshaken rule of morality, and foundation of all social virtue, "That one should do as he would be done unto," be proposed to one who never heard it before, but yet is a capacity to understand its meaning; might be not without any absurdity ask a reason why? and were not he that proposed it bound to make out the truth and reasonableness of it to him? ...So that the truth of all these moral rules plainly depends upon some other antecedent to them, and from which they must be deduced, which could not be if either they were innate, or so much as self-evident.[6]

Locke then propounds the basis on which he felt that ethical conduct could be judged. In his view, "law" is the criterion of

---

[5] *An Essay Concerning Human Understanding*, by John Locke (edited and published by "George Routledge and Sons Ltd." New York: E. P. Dutton & Co., No date), Book I, Chapter 3, Section 8, p. 30.

[6] *Ibid.*, p. 28.

judging whether any action is morally good or bad. In his words, "Moral good or evil is only the conformity of or disagreement of our voluntary actions to some law." In this respect, Locke recognizes three types of laws: the divine law, the civil law, and the law of opinion and reputation:

> Good and evil...are nothing but pleasure or pain, or that which occasions or procures pleasure or pain to us. Moral good and evil, then, is only the conformity or disagreement of our voluntary actions to some law, whereby good and evil is drawn on us from the will and power of the law-maker; which good and evil, pleasure or pain, attending our observance or breach of the law, by the decree of the law-maker is what we call "rewards" and "punishment."
>
> Moral rules—Of these moral rules or laws, to which men generally refer, and by which they judge of the rectitude or pravity of their actions, there seems to be three sorts, with their different enforcements, or rewards, and punishments....
>
> (1) The divine law.
>
> (2) The civil law.
>
> (3) The law of opinion or reputation, if I may so call it.
>
> By the relation they bear to the first of these, men judge whether their actions are sins or duties; by the second, whether they be criminal or innocent; and by the third, whether they be virtues or vices.[7]

Careful analysis of the Rules of Professional Conduct would indicate that these three types of laws interjoin to provide a well-integrated foundation of such rules.[8]

Kant looks at ethical conduct from a somewhat different point of view. To him, self-imposed action conforming with one's sense of duty is the supreme source of morality. He believes that moral acts should be done, not to make the individual merely successful or happy, but because it is the individual's duty so to act. It is duty for duty's sake that ranks above all other types of motive. Duty, he conceives of as acting from respect of law. However, this is not the type of respect that arises from fear of retribution or punishment. Nor is it the type of law that is impressed from the outside. Kant uses the expression "law" as a universal guide

[7] *Ibid.*, pp. 279-280.

[8] We refer with approval to H. T. Scovill, "The Accountant and His Conscience," *The Illinois Certified Public Accountant*, March, 1952, pp. 28-32.

to action which the individual accepts as binding upon himself as well as on others:

> Duty is the necessity of acting from respect for law, i.e., from a principle accepted as binding on oneself and on all others, an all occasions in which it is relevant.[9]

Thus, to Kant, once one imposes the law on himself, he needs no pressure from outside. His own will becomes an autonomous, supreme source of good. Of course the will needs some discipline and control. For this, Kant provides two rules:

(1) Act only on maxims which you can at the same time wish that they would become universal laws, and (2) So act, as to treat humanity, whether in your own person or that of another, in every case as an end, never as a means only.

These rules require the individual to treat others as he would wish to be treated and thus to put aside selfish motives.

It is difficult to synthesize out of these diverse theories any single theory of ethical conduct and it may be that this is not necessary. Perhaps it is enough that for the moment we recognize some of the basic connotations of ethical conduct with which philosophers have been concerned.

The Nature of a Profession. Writing in 1915, Abraham Flexner offered six criteria which he proposed as the identifying marks of a profession. These are: (1) intellectual operations coupled with large individual responsibilities, (2) raw materials drawn from science and learning, (3) practical application, (4) an educationally communicable technique, (5) tendency toward self-organization, and (6) increasingly altruistic motivation.[10] Independent auditing, as we have conceived of it in this monograph, certainly meets these requirements. The ethical responsibilities of the professional man are found in the first, fifth, and sixth requirement in Flexner's list. Some brief attention to these responsibilities may be in order.

We customarily discuss the responsibilities of a professional man under three headings: (1) responsibility to his client, (2) responsibility to society, (3) responsibility to other members of his

---

[9]Sir David Ross, *Kant's Ethical Theory* (Oxford: Oxford University Press, Amen House, London, E. C. 4, 1954), p. 93.

[10]Abraham Flexner, "Is Social Work a Profession?", *School and Society*, Vol. I, No. 26, June 26, 1915, pp. 901-911, at 904.

profession. To these should be added (4) responsibility to himself. If he neglects any one of these or permits any one to get out of balance with the others he is failing in the appropriate discharge of his professional responsibilities. We feel these four separately stated responsibilities can be expressed as one fundamental requirement: *to facilitate the continuation of the profession and the service it renders.*

Professional ethics are but a special application of general ethics. General ethics emphasize that there are certain guides by means of which an individual can govern his conduct. Knowledge of the ultimate outcome of his actions on himself and others, awareness of the requirements of the society in which he lives, respect for divine law, acceptance of duty, obligation to act toward others as one would want all men to act at all times, and recognition of the norms of ethical conduct in the society in which one operates all aid the individual to attain a high degree of ethical conduct. These apply to the group or the profession as well. Putting these together we obtain a concept which, in the field of ethical conduct, is similar to the concept of due audit care in the performance of an engagement.

The individual practitioner, because he claims the status of a professional man, has responsibilities beyond those of the ordinary craftsman. He has an obligation to understand the ideals and functions of his profession (we would like to think this monograph is a fair presentation of the ideals and functions of independent auditing); he has an obligation to consider the possible outcome of any proposed action; he has an obligation to refrain from those activities which detract from the healthy survival of the profession. In this it is assumed that he has the intelligence, knowledge, and experience to understand the impact which his activities may have on the profession. The practitioner who pleads ignorance of these, except in unusual cases, has largely disqualified himself from a professional status. The practitioner who ignores them in deciding on a given course of action may commit negligence sufficiently gross to make fraudulent his claim of a professional status.

At this point it is instructive to turn to a fellow profession for its experience. Frequently we learn a great deal and may even spare ourselves real difficulties if we will take the time and have the courage to learn from the experiences of others. Some of the experience of the legal profession is particularly useful to us in this respect.

The canons of legal ethics, in their present form, date back to the last quarter of the nineteenth century. The necessity for their development at that time was an unfortunate trend in legal practice which some described as the "movement toward the commercialization of law." The following passage by Mr. Richard Hofstadter describers the situation:

> Around the turn of the century, the professional talents of courtroom advocacy and brief-making were referred to again and again as "lost arts," as the occupation of the successful lawyer centered more and more upon counseling clients and offering business advice. General and versatile talent, less needed than in the old days, was replaced by specialized practice and the division of labor within law firms. The firms themselves grew larger; the process of concentration and combination in business, which limited profitable counseling to fewer and larger firms, engendered a like concentration in the law. Metropolitan law firms, as they grew larger and more profitable, moved into closer relationships with and became "house counsel" of large investment houses, banks, or industrial firms, that provided them with most of their business. But the relation that was the source of profit brought with it a loss of independence to the great practitioners. The smaller independent practitioner was affected in another, still more serious way: much of his work was taken from him by real-estate, trust, and insurance companies, collection agencies, and banks, which took upon themselves larger and larger amounts of what had once been entirely legal business....[11]

This trend led some of the leaders of the legal profession to take firm measures to control the drift away from appropriate professional activities:

> About 1875 the leaders of the Bar, realizing the deplorable condition into which their profession was falling, as well as the imperative necessity of taking a firm stand against the rising tide of commercialism and the growing influence of those who would turn the profession from a "branch of the administration of justice" into a "mere money-getting-trade" began the movement for the re-establishment at the Bar of standards of character, education, and training, and also for the organization of bar associations all over the country.[12]

---

[11]Richard Hofstadter, *The Age of Reform* (New York: Vintage Books, Inc., 1960), pp. 158-159.

[12]Henry S. Drinker, "Legal Ethics," *The Annals of the American Academy of Political Sciences*, Vol. 297, January, 1955, pp. 37-45, at 38.

This statement emphasizes the importance of a high standard of ethical conduct for the profession and a concept that looks to protection of the service potential of the profession above all else.

We have no intention of implying that independent auditing has approached anything like the unsatisfactory state which the law had apparently reached at the time described in these quotations. The Rules of Professional Conduct of the American Institute of Certified Public Accountants, together with the strengthening force of rulings by the Securities and Exchange Commission and the stock exchanges, have done much to protect the practice of auditing. Nor do we wish to suggest that such rules be abandoned in favor of more general statements such as those we have advanced here. Such specific statements provide useful guides in day-by-day activities. It is our suggestion that a general statement such as the one mentioned here should be adopted by those who draft specific rules of conduct. It could serve as the basic guide by which such rules are tested and as the best possible guide to all practitioners in their daily pursuits when specific rules have not yet been promulgated on a given issue.

If we feel that auditing performs a useful service and that this service should be continued, we have an obligation to protect the professional institutions that make this service available to the public. We may modify or alter the nature and variety of such service if we will, but with this privilege goes an important responsibility to do so only if it is unquestionably in the best long range interests of society. A profession exists, not to compensate its members more or less handsomely, but to serve society. Dean Roscoe Pound has defined a profession as:

> A group of men pursuing a learned art as a common calling in the spirit of public service—no less a public service because it may incidentally be a means of livelihood.[13]

As Mr. Carey points out, it is the emphasis on public service that largely distinguishes a profession from business:

> This is the concept which largely distinguishes a profession from business—that professional men assume an obligation to place public service ahead of reward.[14]

---

[13]Roscoe Pound, *The Lawyer From Antiquity to Modern Times* (St. Paul, Minnesota: West Publishing Company, 1953), p. 5.

[14]Carey, *op. cit.*, p. 50.

Here we have the clue to the solution of the value problems pointed out in Chapter 2, particularly those on the profession level. Such problems must always be solved with the best interests of all at heart if we are to preserve the profession of independent auditing for the future good of society. And if we customarily solve such problems on any other basis we have at once renounced our right to hold professional status and sealed the ultimate doom of the profession as such.

Chapter 10

Auditing in Perspective

In recent years considerable interest in philosophical studies of various special fields of knowledge has been evident. Individuals working within special fields have become curious about the nature of their subject matter, its relationship to other fields of knowledge, especially the basic disciplines, and the extent of progress it has made in developing a sound theory structure. Writing on "The Order and Integration of Knowledge," William O. Martin states:

> There is evidence that specialists in various fields of knowledge are becoming increasingly concerned with the nature of the kind of knowledge with which they identify themselves professionally. The interest is not new, but the urgency of the concern is....
>
> If the problem were merely verbal, a question of correct naming of kinds of knowledge, the matter would be relatively trivial. In fact it is a very serious one having to do with the nature and order of various kinds of knowledge. For if a person who is professionally identified with a subject does not know clearly its nature, which includes not only what it is but what it is not, then how can he know when he is practitioner of his subject and when he is not? How can he know whether a question is relevant to his subject or not? How can he know what evidence is and is not relevant to a problem? What kind of evidence is relevant in the demonstration of the truth of what kind of propositions and what kind of knowledge? If all this is not clear, a person may wander far afield from the subject he knows under the delusion that in some manner or other his special subject "proves" something in a subject about which he may know very little.[1]

We can have an acquaintance with a field of knowledge at any one of several levels. We may have only a very superficial notion of the field, a recognition that it exists and a hazy idea of its subject matter, or we may actually work in the field and be competent to handle its methodology and subject matter. Finally, we may have a real insight into the kind of knowledge in the field, the nature, strength, and weaknesses of its methodology, and the problem areas which still pose difficulties. There is as

---

[1]William Oliver Martin, *The Order and Integration of Knowledge* (Ann Arbor: The University of Michigan Press, 1957), pp. 3-4.

much difference between the second and third types of acquaintance mentioned here as between the first and second. Professor Martin was concerned with the deep insight described in the third type of familiarity; without real insight, one can easily be led far astray.

In this study we have been concerned with attaining that type of insight into the subject matter of auditing. We have attempted to uncover its basic assumptions and to describe its own peculiar methodology. Using these as a basis, we have then attempted to develop some of its central concepts which in turn led us to proposed solutions to some of the practical problems of professional auditing. It now remains to take a brief over-view of auditing as a field of knowledge, as an intellectual discipline, and as a field of professional practice.

Historical Development. Space does not permit anything like a comprehensive review of the historical development of auditing here, and such a work is better left to others in any case. But it is desirable to note even briefly the development of auditing over the years both to see important changes and the more constant characteristics.

Richard Brown points out the early appearance of auditing in these words:

> The origin of auditing goes back to times scarcely less remote than that of accounting.... Whenever the advance of civilization brought about the necessity of one man being entrusted to some extent with the property of another the advisability of some kind of check upon the fidelity of the former would become apparent.[2]

Among the earliest audits of which we have written records are manorial audits of the period between the thirteenth and sixteenth centuries in Great Britain. In the manorial household, the auditor was a person of considerable importance. Some of his authority came from the parties by whom he was appointed, the nobleman he served; and additional authority came from statutes. Probably the earliest statute of this kind was one passed by Edward I in 1285 which read:

> Concerning servants, bailiffs, Chamberlains, and all manners of Receivers, which are bound to yield Accompt, ...when the Masters

---

[2]Richard Brown, *op. cit.*, p. 74.

> of such Servants do assign Auditors to take their accompt, and they be found in arrerages upon the Accompt, all Things allowed which ought to be allowed, their Bodies shall be arrested, and by the Testimony of the Auditors of the same Accompt, shall be sent or delivered unto the next Gaol in those Parts....[3]

About the same time the practice of submitting trusted servants to an audit was extended to certain public officials, particularly tax collectors.

These early audits were intended to provide an independent review of the accounting records and reports and of the work of those subjected to audit. The method was little more than a careful comparison of reported facts with actual amounts on hand, documents, and any other available evidence. The audits were detailed, no reliance being placed on sampling at that early date. The audit was performed either by an individual auditor for the nobleman, or by a committee, in the case of a public official. Thus the report could be delivered directly and there was little problem of communication. Auditors, of course, had no professional status although they were expected to discharge their duties honestly, skillfully, and with due regard for their employer's interests. Independence was obtained through appointment by the nobleman and prevention of any private contact between the auditor and the auditee. There was no third party interest at that early date.

Later, the practice of auditing was extended to trustees' and bankrupts' accounts. The auditing of a trustee's accounts added the technical problem of distinguishing between capital and income, a problem not evident in the early manorial audit. The audit of the accounts of bankrupts added an element of extreme skepticism not normally found in the master-servant relationship. In those early days bankrupts were looked upon with disfavor and as probable speculators or criminals rather than as the unfortunate victims of adverse business conditions. In both trustee and bankruptcy audits, courts usually had an interest. This added still another element to the relationship, as the court was in effect a third party interested not only in the representations made by the reporting party but also in the administration of the affairs of the person subjected to audit.

---

[3]Quoted from Brown, *op. cit.*, p. 76.

Thus we see auditing expanding in scope and extent of responsibility to meet the needs of changing conditions.

Out of these early examinations came creditorship audits and in time the corporate audits with which we are familiar today. There seems no need to recount the unfortunate history of some of the early joint stock companies in England, the wave of speculation and even fraud that almost stopped their formation, and the consequent intervention of Parliament by the passage of the various Companies Acts which, among other things, provided for independent audits, a pattern of financial statements, and the rights and duties of the auditors.

Auditing in this country developed somewhat differently, but again there is no need to review the various steps which have brought us to the present stage of auditing development.

If we compare present audits with the earlier examinations of accounts, we find considerable change in the methodology, but relatively little change in purpose or point of view. Substantial progress has been made in the adoption of sampling methods, and even now we seem at the threshold of further progress as statistical sampling principles receive more and more attention. New techniques such as confirmation and examination of documentary evidence have become possible because of the development of business practices generally, and we have had a general recognition of the difference between techniques and standards. But the purpose of an audit still seems to be to provide certain interested parties with an attestation of the reliability of certain information supplied by those entrusted with the property of others.

As a group, independent auditors have made progress not only in obtaining general recognition as a profession with high standards of ethical conduct, but also in imposing such standards on most members of the profession.

Recently, however, there have been indications that auditing and auditors are not accepting as much responsibility or providing quite the kinds of service desired by some members of our society. At the same time, new opportunities for service in a number of directions have made their appearance, and a realistic appraisal of the situation suggests that some of these opportunities entail responsibilities incompatible with others.

Auditing has thus changed with the times in the past, and there are indications that it should be prepared to change with the times now and in the future. In changing, however, it is important that auditing leadership recognize the limitations and potential of the profession and the field of knowledge with which it is concerned. No profession can afford to spread itself over a number of widely divergent and even conflicting types of activity without careful consideration of the hazards involved.

Auditing as a Field of Knowledge. Both in practice and in its academic environment, auditing has appeared as a branch or subdivision of accounting. We have neither a profession of auditing nor departments of auditing in universities; instead we have certified public accountants and departments of accountancy. But as others have pointed out, this is the way new fields commonly appear.[4] By a process similar to that of cell division, in which one cell divides into two, an established field of study finds that some phase or portion of its activities becomes sufficiently well developed to stand alone and sufficiently distinguished from other activities to merit separate identity. This is the case with auditing. Although it first appeared as a division of accounting, it is fast reaching the status of a separate discipline. Indeed, its future development depends to a considerable extent on according it the independent status and study it deserves.

But the process of cell division is not as accurate an analogy as we need to describe the development of auditing and its separation from accounting. For auditing is not as closely related to accounting as the figure of speech implies. It takes much from other fields too, perhaps more than from accounting. For the purposes of explaining this relationship and the nature of auditing as a field of study, we find Robinson's classification of sciences particularly helpful. He proposes a five-fold classification: (1) abstract and formal sciences, (2) general descriptive sciences, (3) special derivative sciences, (4) synoptic sciences, and (5) applied sciences. In the first class are the most basic types of organized knowledge, metaphysics, logic, and mathematics. To a considerable extent, all other fields rely more or less directly on these

---

[4]Kenneth E. Boulding, *The Image* (Ann Arbor: The University of Michigan Press, 1959), Chapter 10, particularly pp. 160-61.

basic disciplines. The second group includes those which are based on observation and description of actual phenomena; chemistry, biology, and sociology are illustrations. From these are derived the narrower and more specialized fields in the third class such as mineralogy, botany, and ethnology. Next, In Robinson's own words:

> A special group of the derivative special sciences is known as the *synoptic sciences*. These are really combinations of parts of other sciences. That is to say, they use the methods and many of the principles of other sciences, but develop such a unique interpretation of the subject matter as to entitle them to separate rank. Geology, for instance, focuses attention upon the earth, but it combines parts of physics, chemistry and paleontology. Geography and anthropology are other examples. Even astronomy, one of the most ancient and sublime of all sciences, is really a mixture of mechanics, thermodynamics, optics and chemistry, with special reference to the constitution and movements of sun, moon, planets, stars, and other celestial phenomena.
>
> Finally we have to speak of *applied sciences*. They are either separate departments of the various special sciences, or combinations of principles taken from several of these with special reference to their bearing on practical life, particularly the arts and crafts. Examples are engineering, agricultural science, medicine, educational psychology and aeronautics. The very new science of vocational psychology is an applied science within the field of theoretical psychology.[5]

Auditing partakes of the nature of a synoptic science in that it borrows much from other fields and does not fit neatly as a department of any one larger field. Thus, even at the risk of repetition, we can illustrate this by pointing out that the nature of evidence and the formation of audit opinions are dependent on the theory of knowledge; reliance on tests and samples is based on probability theory and mathematics; fair presentation draws upon accounting principles, financial analysis , and communication theory; due audit care recognizes ethical and legal relationships. At the same time, auditing is an applied field, making its ultimate contribution at the practice level. Thus it has an organized body of theory supporting a professional type of applica-

---

[5]Robinson, *op. cit.*, pp. 222-224.

tion. On the theory side it must have regard for the nature of its theoretical structure; on the practice side it must respect the requirements of professional status and ethical conduct.

In quoting Robinson we have raised the unfortunate question of whether auditing can appropriately be described as a "science" at all. Although this is not a question with which we are much concerned, brief attention to it will be helpful in understanding further the nature of auditing. Much depends on the meaning of the term "science." If we conceive of science as an organized body of knowledge, then auditing can lay some claim to meeting the requirements. If science is interpreted to mean the application of a method requiring the rigorous weighing of evidence and the application of a systematic method to a variety of situations, again auditing may be considered to qualify. But if we accept as sciences only those fields which have the power to explain, predict, and control given phenomena, then auditing falls well short. Together with accounting, auditing does have some powers of explanation. However, at its present stage of development it has almost no predictive power, although it is conceivable that in time it will attain such ability. Again in connection with accounting, it plays a part in the control of investment decisions by reporting the results of income calculations and thus helping to direct the flow of capital funds. And of course it has a control function in the reduction of irregularities. Finally, the designation "science" is sometimes reserved for those systems in which all propositions are logically and mathematically connected by laws or principles. By this test, neither auditing nor any of the social sciences, as they currently stand, would qualify. Indeed this is a goal rather than a test, and even some of the natural sciences are still struggling toward its achievement.

Thus the status of auditing as a science depends more upon the meaning of the term "science" than on anything else. But it is not important whether auditing is a science. What is important is that we see it for what it is, a rigorous field of study able to make a substantial contribution to our economic life and one requiring considerable attention not only to the development of a systematic and satisfactory theory but to the application of such a theory to its practical problems.

To obtain a comprehensive view of auditing, one should see it as a five-level structure. At the base lies its philosophical foundation which in turn rests on the most fundamental disciplines, in Robinson's terms, the abstract sciences. Out of this philosophical foundation can be drawn the postulates which in turn provide a groundwork for the development of essential concepts. Next appears its conceptual structure, the elemental generalizations around which the bulk of its theory is organized. Out of these concepts and deriving their strength from them appear certain more or less obvious directives for the guidance of the practitioner; we feel these may properly be described as precepts. Finally there is the superstructure of practical applications in which the precepts are applied to actual situations. Thus levels one, two, and three, the basic philosophy, postulates, and conceptual structure, produce the precepts which guide practice. Practice is concerned directly with the precepts only, but as the precepts are based on the other levels of the structure, if practice follows the precepts and if the precepts are properly developed, practice also rests on a strong foundation of theory.

In this work we have given no attention to precepts, chiefly because of limitations of time. Obviously we would prefer to present a completed scheme of auditing knowledge. But we recognize the advantages in proceeding at a more cautions pace. Until the concepts and postulates proposed in this monograph have been subjected to critical examination and refinement through discussion and experience, they are not yet ready to serve as origins for the extraction of precepts. Auditing needs precepts badly, but even more it needs attention to the necessary underlying theory.

This scheme of auditing knowledge might be pictured in the form of a pie-shaped chart. The entire chart represents knowledge, all knowledge. At the center is a hard core of the most fundamental types of knowledge, metaphysics, logic, and mathematics. Touching this core and drawing strength from it is the groundwork level of auditing knowledge, its philosophical foundation. Included in this level of knowledge is definition of purpose of the field and the fundamental nature of its knowledge and methodology. Its postulates, the basis for inferring concepts, must relate to and be harmonious with this purpose and recognize the possibilities and limi-

FIGURE V
DIAGRAM SHOWING STRUCTURE OF AUDITING AS A FIELD OF KNOWLEDGE

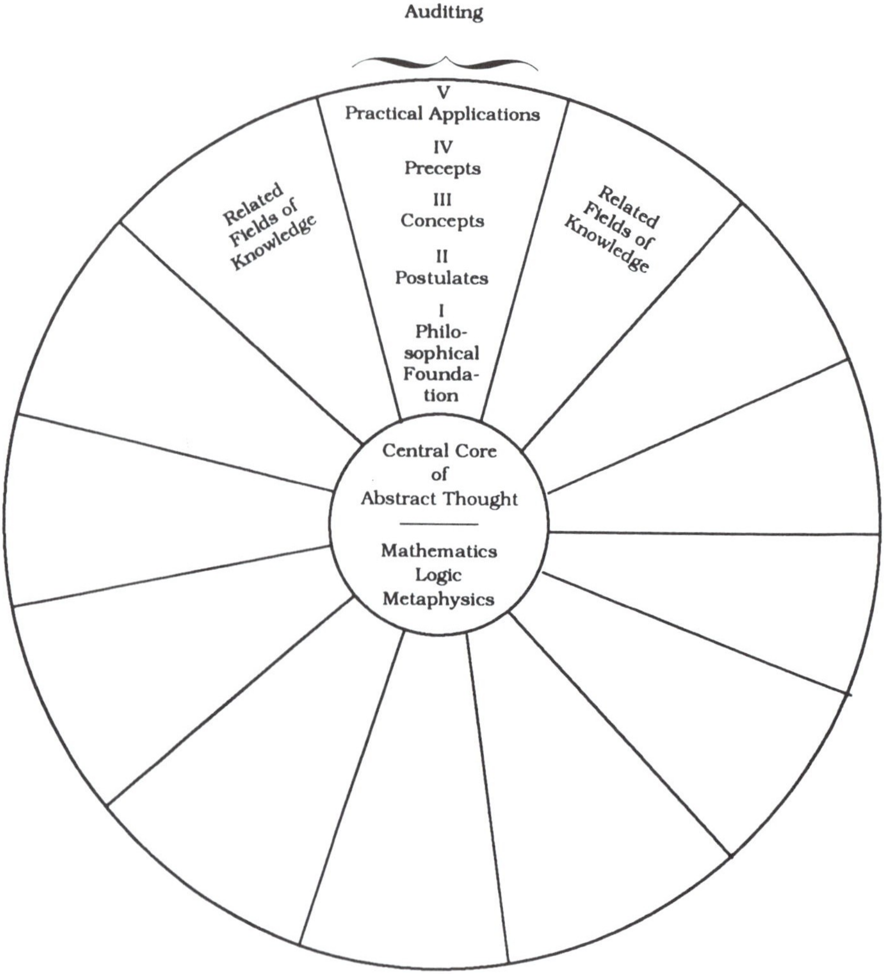

tations of its methodology. Every field must have just such a foundation and it must never permit itself to become separated from the elemental disciplines from which it draws its strength. There is a particular danger in this for the applied fields which may become so concerned with the problems of practice that they neglect their relationship to knowledge generally. To do this is to lose touch, not only with theory, but also with the reality of the given field. The practical man who has no use for theory is inadvertently choosing the most difficult of paths; he is abandoning those essential guides to truth which mankind has developed so laboriously and carefully and which alone can give the practitioner assurance of consistency and propriety in his daily work.

As the field of auditing grows outward from its philosophical foundation, it enters the area of conceptual structure. Here we find the concepts developed in this monograph and many more. We have had time to deal only with a small number of the major concepts. There may be many others to be developed before this structure is completed. Then come the precepts and the area of practice.

An advantage of the circular chart is that it permits the showing of adjacent fields of knowledge from which auditing draws some of its ideas. These would include accounting, law, ethics, management, communications, and others. But a two-dimensional chart has definite limitations. Actually, we need a sphere to depict knowledge: auditing in the shape of a cone would rest on the core of basic knowledge and widen as it develops outward to the surface. Then, touching auditing and influencing it are a great number of other cones of knowledge.

Of course, any analogy, any figure, has limitations and imperfections and we do not wish to press this one beyond the point of usefulness. It is our intention to suggest only the interrelationship of the levels of auditing knowledge and the equally important interrelationship of auditing with other disciplines.

In the past, auditing has been conceived only as a practical subject with little need for or possibility of any underlying theory. Thus attention has been given to its practical applications to the almost complete exclusion of theoretical considerations. We hope we have indicated the close connection between the theory and practice of auditing, for we are convinced that the only sure solution to practical problems is through the development and use of theory. Auditing stands at the threshold of service opportunities we can as yet scarcely foresee, even in dim outline. With a well-developed theory it will not only be prepared to take advantage of such opportunities but will be able to escape confusion and misplaced effort in its desire for real service.

